Unspoken Politics

Implicit Attitudes and Political Thinking

This book explains why people acquire implicit attitudes, how they affect political thinking, and where in the mass public they have its strongest – and weakest – influences. A theoretically ambitious book, *Unspoken Politics* establishes that implicit attitudes exist outside the tightly controlled confines of the laboratory, showing that they emerge in a public opinion survey setting, which underlines their real-world impact. It also lays bare, in painstaking detail, the mechanics of a leading measure of implicit attitudes, the implicit association test (IAT). Accordingly, it outlines the strengths and limitations of this measure, while providing an illustration of how to develop an IAT for one's own purposes. By explaining how to analyze and interpret the data produced by the IAT, Efrén Pérez leads to a better understanding of people's unspoken cognitions and the impacts these have on the politics that individuals openly profess.

Efrén O. Pérez is an associate professor at the Department of Political Science of Vanderbilt University. His research uses psychological insights to investigate the political attitudes and behaviors of US racial and ethnic groups. Substantively, he studies implicit political cognition, group identity, and language and political thinking. Methodologically, he designs and implements experiments, especially in the realm of racial and ethnic politics. He has published articles on these topics in the *American Journal of Political Science*, *Political Analysis*, and *Political Behavior*. His research on implicit cognition received the Lucius Barker Award for the best paper on race/ethnicity and politics at the annual meeting of the Midwest Political Science Association.

Cambridge Studies in Public Opinion and Political Psychology

Cambridge Studies in Public Opinion and Political Psychology publishes innovative research from a variety of theoretical and methodological perspectives on the mass public foundations of politics and society. Research in the series focuses on the origins and influence of mass opinion, the dynamics of information and deliberation, and the emotional, normative, and instrumental bases of political choice. In addition to examining psychological processes, the series explores the organization of groups, the association between individual and collective preferences, and the impact of institutions on beliefs and behavior.

Cambridge Studies in Public Opinion and Political Psychology is dedicated to furthering theoretical and empirical research on the relationship between the political system and the attitudes and actions of citizens.

Books in the series are listed on the page following the Index.

Unspoken Politics

Implicit Attitudes and Political Thinking

EFRÉN O. PÉREZ
Vanderbilt University, Nashville, Tennessee

CAMBRIDGE
UNIVERSITY PRESS

University Printing House, Cambridge CB2 8BS, United Kingdom

One Liberty Plaza, 20th Floor, New York, NY 10006, USA

477 Williamstown Road, Port Melbourne, VIC 3207, Australia

314-321, 3rd Floor, Plot 3, Splendor Forum, Jasola District Centre, New Delhi-110025, India

79 Anson Road, #06-04/06, Singapore 079906

Cambridge University Press is part of the University of Cambridge.

It furthers the University's mission by disseminating knowledge in the pursuit of education, learning and research at the highest international levels of excellence.

www.cambridge.org
Information on this title: www.cambridge.org/9781107591219

First published 2016

A catalogue record for this publication is available from the British Library

Library of Congress Cataloging in Publication data
Pirez, Efrin Osvaldo, 1977– author.
Unspoken politics : implicit attitudes and political thinking / Efrén O. Pérez.
New York, NY : Cambridge University Press, 2016.
Cambridge studies in public opinion and political psychology
Includes bibliographical references.
LCCN 2015029112 ISBN 9781107133730 (hardback)
ISBN 9781107591219 (paperback)
LCSH: Political psychology. Public opinion – Political aspects.
LCC JA74.5.P47 2016 DDC 320.01/9–dc23
LC record available at http://lccn.loc.gov/2015029112

ISBN 978-1-107-13373-0 Hardback
ISBN 978-1-107-59121-9 Paperback

Contents

List of Tables and Figures *page* vii
Acknowledgments xi

1 Implicit Thoughts, Explicit Decisions 1
2 Two Ways of Thinking, Two Types of Attitudes 24
3 Implicit Expectations and Explicit Political Reasoning 43
4 Ghost in the Associative Machine 54
5 Unstated: The Measurement of Implicit Attitudes 77
6 Incognito: The Subconscious Nature of Implicit Expectations 111
7 In Deliberation's Shadow: Education, (Un)awareness, and Implicit Attitudes 129
8 In Black and White: Race, Group Position, and Implicit Attitudes in Politics 148
9 Conclusion: Implicit Attitudes and Explicit Politics 169

Note on the Studies 187
References 189
Index 211

List of Tables and Figures

Tables

4.1 Validation of Measures for Illegal Immigration News Coverage (Newspapers) *page* 68
4.2 Validation of Measures for Legal Immigration News Coverage (Newspapers) 68
A4.1 Validation of Measures for Illegal and Legal Immigration News Coverage (Television) 76
5.1 Hypothetical Flower–Insect IAT 82
5.2 Illustration of IAT Sequence: Latino versus White Immigrants 88
5.3 The Relationship between Implicit Attitude toward Latinos and Social and Political Predispositions 94
5.4 Negative Feelings toward Immigrants by Implicit Attitude toward Latinos 98
5.5 The Influence of Implicit Attitudes on Explicit Opposition to Illegal Immigration 104
5.6 The Influence of Implicit Attitudes on Explicit Opposition to Legal Immigration 107
A5.1 Negative Feelings toward Immigrants by Implicit Attitude (full results) 109
A5.2 Confirmatory Factor Analysis – Illegal and Legal Immigration Policy 110
6.1 Support for Deportation as a Function of Implicit Attitude toward Latinos 118
6.2 Opposition to Legal Immigration as a Function of Implicit Attitude toward Latinos 124

6.3 Opposition to Legal Immigration as a Function of Implicit Attitude toward Latinos (Collapsed Latino Condition) 126
A7.1 Opposition to Legal Immigration by Explicit Attitude, Implicit Attitude, and Levels of Education – Pairwise Interactive Model 146
A7.2 Opposition to Legal Immigration by Explicit Attitude, Implicit Attitude, Education, and Experimental Condition – Fully Interactive Model 147
8.1 Negative Feelings toward Immigrants by Implicit Attitude and Race 160
A8.1 Negative Feelings toward Immigrants by Implicit Attitude and Race (full results) 167
A8.2 The Influence of Implicit Attitude Conditioned by Immigrant Cues and Race – Interactive Model 168

Figures

4.1 Percentage of European, Asian, and Latin American immigrants obtaining legal permanent residence (LPR) by decade: 1930–2010 57
4.2 Annual number of unauthorized immigrants arrested, 1960–2010 61
4.3 Proportion of Latin American, Asian, and European immigrants of total immigration, 1990–2004 62
4.4 Illegal immigration stories on Latinos by major newspapers: 1990–2010 66
4.5 Legal immigration news stories on Latinos by major newspapers, 1990–2010 67
4.6 Estimated number of illegal and legal immigration stories focused on Latinos (newspapers), 1990–2010 69
4.7 Estimated number of illegal and legal immigration stories focused on Latinos (television), 1990–2010 70
4.8 Estimated number of stories on illegal Latino immigration versus stories on other political issues (television) 71
4.9 Estimated percentage of illegal and legal immigrants among Latino foreign-born, 2000–2010 73
4.10 Estimated percentage of news on illegal Latinos compared with estimated percentage of actual illegal Latinos, 2000–2010 73
4.11 Estimated percentage of news on legal Latinos compared with estimated percentage of actual legal Latinos, 2000–2010 74
5.1 (a) Hypothetical IAT classification scheme: Insects negatively evaluated and flowers positively evaluated.

	(b) Hypothetical IAT classification scheme: Flowers negatively evaluated and insects positively evaluated	81
5.2	Average response times by key block in IAT	90
5.3	(a) Distribution of explicit attitude (immigrants) – national study. (b) Distribution of explicit attitude (Latinos) – national study. (c) Distribution of implicit attitude (Latinos) – national study	92
5.4	Proportions of strongly negative explicit and implicit attitudes – national study	93
5.5	IAT effect by IAT version (95% confidence intervals)	99
5.6	Explicit and implicit attitude by education	101
6.1	The deportation experiment	115
6.2	Marginal effect of implicit attitude by experimental condition (90% confidence intervals)	119
6.3	The Legal Immigration Experiment	122
6.4	Marginal effect of implicit attitude by experimental condition (90% confidence intervals)	125
6.5	Marginal effect of implicit attitude by experimental condition (90% confidence intervals)	126
7.1	(a) Hypothetical effect of explicit attitude (Latinos) on opposition to immigration when non-Latinos are cued. (b) Hypothetical effect of implicit attitude (Latinos) on opposition to immigration when non-Latinos are cued. (c) Hypothetical effect of implicit attitude (Latinos) on opposition to immigration when non-Latinos are cued	137
7.2	Explicit attitude and opposition to legal immigration by level of education (90% confidence intervals)	140
7.3	Implicit attitude and opposition to legal immigration by level of education (90% confidence intervals)	141
7.4	Explicit attitude and opposition to legal immigration by level of education – Latino condition (90% confidence intervals)	142
7.5	Explicit attitude and opposition to legal immigration by level of education – Chinese condition (90% confidence intervals)	143
7.6	Implicit attitude and opposition to legal immigration by level of education – Latino condition (90% confidence intervals)	143
7.7	Implicit attitude and opposition to legal immigration by level of education – Chinese condition (90% confidence intervals)	144
8.1	Explicit attitude toward immigrants by race	156
8.2	Explicit attitude toward Latinos by race	157
8.3	Mean reaction time differences in IAT by race	158

8.4 Marginal effect of implicit attitude on negative feelings toward Latino immigrants by race 161
8.5 Marginal effect of implicit attitude on negative feelings toward white immigrants by race 161
8.6 Marginal effect of black implicit attitude on opposition to immigration 164
8.7 Marginal effect of white implicit attitude on opposition to immigration 165

Acknowledgments

I am a second-generation Mexican American. People like me are not usually expected to write books. The fact that I have is less a manifestation of personal ability and more a testament to numerous individuals who have bothered enough to invest in me and my manuscript. This is public acknowledgment of those debts.

The book in your hands is the borne fruit of a kernel of an idea that was my dissertation at Duke University. During that time, I was fortunate enough to fall under the steady hand of Paula McClain, my thesis advisor. To this day, I still do not know why Paula deemed me or my ideas worthy of her time. But she did. And she furnished me with the intellectual space and self-confidence that I needed to complete my work. Complementing Paula's efforts were those of John Aldrich, Kerry Haynie, and Vince Hutchings, who also served on my dissertation committee. John played a vital role, enabling me to test my ideas by funding subject payment for the experiment that formed my project's core. Kerry helped me to lay the theoretical groundwork for my project by leading a directed readings course early in my graduate career. And Vince, he furnished me with candid and constructive feedback that allowed me to eventually build on my dissertation once I started my first job. I am deeply grateful for each of these acts of kindness.

Beyond the official channels of Duke political science, the people who carried me the most so that I could finish the first messy versions of this project were Niambi Carter, Victoria DeFrancesco-Soto, Alisa Kessel, Monique Lyle, Ben Mauk, and Shayla Nunnally. Besides providing me with feedback and camaraderie, they carved out a home away from home for my wife and me. Truthfully, I don't think I could have finished graduate school or my dissertation without their friendship. I also wish to thank Jorge Bravo and Jie Lu, who with patience and encouragement, taught me how to tie my statistical shoes during my first semesters in graduate school.

If Duke University allowed me to plant the seeds of this book, Vanderbilt University provided me with the hardware and know-how to reap as high a yield as possible. These assets also came in the form of people. John Geer, Marc Hetherington, Cindy Kam, and Liz Zechmeister have done more than I deserve to help me fashion my ideas into projects, projects into chapters, and chapters into a book. Within this group, John and Cindy deserve special recognition, if only to illustrate what powerful mentorship looks like. Throughout my time at Vanderbilt, John has been a tireless advocate, helping to ensure that I had the resources, setting, and encouragement to do the research that led to this book. His efforts canceled much of the head noise that can keep a young scholar from finishing a book. In turn, Cindy made it a priority to socialize me into the profession, its norms, and its standards. She taught me how to view my work from the vantage point of critics and how to genuinely engage and incorporate their feedback. If there is any merit to this book, it is due in large part to her wisdom, candor, and unflagging support.

Vanderbilt political science has increasingly gained a reputation for having a collegial and vibrant department culture, of which this book is a prime beneficiary. This reputation is a function of the department's people, individuals who ask penetrating questions, encourage novel thinking, and hold their colleagues to a higher standard. During the time I was writing this book, those specific people were Larry Bartels, Joshua Clinton, Dave Lewis, Kristin Michelitch, Cecilia Mo, Emily Nacol, Bruce Oppenheimer, Zeynep Somer-Topcu, and Alan Wiseman. My book has profited an incalculable amount from the intellectual examples these individuals have set for me.

As a first-time author, the path from esoteric dissertation to audience-friendly book has been, at times, quite rough and bumpy. For helping me get through some of this turbulence, I thank Jane Junn, Don Kinder, Taeku Lee, and Nick Valentino, who generously gave of their time and expertise as participants in a book colloquium that Vanderbilt hosted on my behalf. Besides raising trenchant objections about some of the book's argument and evidence, they also provided guidance and injected nuance into my thinking about the book's main ideas. It is up to them to judge how well I integrated their feedback. But I can say with certainty that the book before you is orders better than it would have been without their help. I also thank my editors at Cambridge University Press – Lew Bateman, Dennis Chong, and Jim Kuklinski – for giving my book a shot and for pushing me to improve its content with each round of revisions.

Outside the halls of academia, I have also had the fortune of having good people to provide me with solace when the writing took an unexpected turn, and to help me celebrate when it actually went as hoped for. My wife, Tammy, and my sons, Efrén III and Emiliano, have done the most here. Writing a book while raising two boys and nurturing a marriage is no easy feat. But without their presence in my life, I don't know that this book would have as much meaning for me. So I thank each of them for being a part of my life and for filling me with joy each day. I also thank Samuel, Nancy, Isabel, and Samantha

Nieves – all friends who have treated my family like their own. Living in the South has not been easy for us Californians, but the Nieves family has taught me to let slide some of those challenges, while appreciating some of the benefits about being here, including the opportunity to write a book. I also thank Amada Armenta and Natalie Masuoka for being such generous colleagues and wonderful friends to Tammy.

I am also grateful for my sisters, Jennifer and Gabriela Pérez, and my cousins, Carlos Covarrubias and Gustavo Pérez. The former two have been, since my youth, unfaltering cheerleaders of any and all of my endeavors. They have also taught me what it means to have unconditional love for someone. I often thought of them during the lowest points in writing this book. As for the latter two, they have been my best of friends, regularly checking up on me and this project from afar. More importantly, they always made sure that when I was back home in L.A., I created enough distance from the book so that I could better appreciate what it was really all about. When frustration with the book would set in, I often fell back on the great times we shared.

My deepest thanks, however, I reserve for my parents, Efrén and Maricela Pérez. My folks were children of the earth, both from families who lived from what they could sow in lands near El Grullo, Jalisco, México. Theirs was a typical but precarious existence. They grew up poor and without any expectation that they would live more comfortably than those before them. But my mom and dad took the risk to change things for themselves by immigrating to the United States. It is never lost on me that my parents' kind of life could have easily been mine, too: back-breaking work, minimal education, and only the bare minimum to eat. But for reasons that I still don't understand, they chose to break that cycle by sheltering my sisters and me from hard labor, sending us to Catholic school and expecting nothing less than a college education from each of us. And most of this, I hasten to add, against the criticisms of many of their peers, who thought that finishing high school was more than enough for children like us; that a teenage son should focus more on paid work, rather than his studies; and that going to college was something that only wealthy Americans do.

I am the product of my parent's courage. This book would have been impossible without their inspiration. Indeed, there were many days when I would have rather quit this undertaking, but their memory helped me not to. I hope they are as proud of this book as I am proud of them. I also wish to say that I regret very much not living as close to them as I would have liked these last few years – similar to them, work has taken me far from those I love. But despite this distance, they should know that I take comfort each day in three lessons they taught me as good immigrants: that there is dignity in a hard day's work; that one should never forget where one comes from; and that sometimes a good job is not where home is. For these and so many other reasons, I dedicate this book to both of them.

1

Implicit Thoughts, Explicit Decisions

The mind is like an iceberg, it floats with one-seventh of its bulk above water.
– Sigmund Freud

December 18, 2008, South Texas. US immigration officers remove handcuffs and shackles from José Thomas and order him to cross into the border city of Reynosa, Mexico, effectively deporting this unauthorized immigrant back to his native homeland.

The ordeal culminating in José's deportation had begun much earlier in August of that same year, when he was arrested for a misdemeanor and sentenced to one hundred days at Neuse Correctional Institution in Goldsboro, North Carolina. Not unlike other state and local law enforcement agencies, North Carolina's prison system had agreed to cooperate with US Immigration and Customs Enforcement (ICE) by identifying inmates who were suspected of being undocumented immigrants. José appeared to fit this bill. Besides his name, many other personal details seemed consistent with the charge that he was in the United States illegally. He was brown skinned; born in Mexico; and, perhaps most revealingly, used the alias "Mark D. Lyttle."

It was therefore hardly a surprise when, on December 9, 2008, Judge William A. Cassidy sentenced José and twenty-nine other alleged illegal immigrants to deportation. The real surprise, however, came *after* José's expulsion from the United States. Details soon emerged that the man who had been deported to Mexico in late 2008 was not really José, but Mark – as in Mark D. Lyttle. Mr. Lyttle, it turns out, had been born in Rowan County, North Carolina thirty-one years earlier. At the age of seven, he had been adopted by Thomas and Jeanne Lyttle. Diagnosed as bipolar, Mark had spent many years in and out of psychiatric institutions, group homes, and jails. Clearly, immigration authorities had made a grave error. Misjudged as foreign-born, Spanish-speaking, and Mexican, Mark Lyttle was anything but – he was native-born, spoke only English, and had lived in the United States his entire life.[1]

So how is an American citizen mistakenly deported? Through a series of unspoken assumptions, it seems. At every point of contact between Mark Lyttle and law enforcement agencies, relevant authorities clung to the notion that this mentally disabled man was an immigrant. For example, Mr. Lyttle's brown complexion automatically raised the suspicions of the intake clerk at Neuse prison who, after probing Mark for further information, decided that his name was an alias for José: an undocumented Latino immigrant. These details formed part of Neuse's records, which were later consulted by an ICE agent who further interrogated Mark. Not only had "Mark" been born in Mexico, the ICE officer concluded; he had also entered the United States illegally at the age of three.

The relevant authorities in the Mark Lyttle case did not intend to deport an American citizen. But their unquestioned assumptions about Mark led them to see someone who was not really there. The intake clerk at Neuse and the ICE deportation officer were both interested in filtering out possible illegal immigrants from a larger pool of criminals. When they encountered Mark, they spontaneously sensed he was more a José. Only later would it emerge that a simple background check could have verified Mark's US citizenship status, which would have quickly ended the train of presumptions about his identity. But the initial suspicions about Mark Lyttle proved too strong, deeply coloring what officials saw in this man. All pieces of the puzzle seemed to suggest strongly that he was an illegal immigrant, not an American citizen.

The Mark Lyttle episode vividly highlights a tragic error in individual judgment. But cognitive lapses such as these are not aberrations. They occur more often and more widely than is commonly assumed. And although they are rarely this serious, they might nonetheless be distressing to those who have unyielding faith in the power of judicious thinking to discipline and guide the conclusions that people draw from the information they encounter. That is because the interplay between spontaneous, involuntary thoughts and more intentional and controlled forms of thinking creates a powerful dynamic that structures human judgment across various social realms. In the shadow of one's deliberations runs a stream of decision making that is *implicit* – rapid, nonverbalized, and capable of shaping people's thoughts and actions without their control (cf. Bargh 1994; Fazio et al. 1986; Forgas and Tan 2011; Greenwald and Banaji 1995; Haidt 2012; Kahneman 2011; Krueger 2012; Leander and Chartrand 2011; Payne et al. 2005).

This book is about these implicit processes and how they can color people's politics about immigration. This might strike you as an odd choice. Political

[1] For further and richer details on this case, see Stevens (2009) and Finnegan (2013).

inquiry and commentary seem strongly wedded to the "conviction that convictions are driving political behavior" (Nosek et al. 2010: 549), leaving seemingly little room for deep impulses to affect our most reasoned political views. Indeed, if the authorities in the Mark Lyttle case drew their conclusions about him in the heat of the moment, then members of the mass public arguably respond to politics within more relaxed time constraints and with access to less ambiguous information. So what, really, can implicit mental processes reveal about how people judge immigration politics?

A great deal, actually. If, as Freud once suggested, the mind is like an iceberg, then much of what political scientists know about decision making on political issues such as immigration revolves around thinking that occurs above the waters of people's consciousness (e.g., Lodge and Taber 2013; Taber and Young 2013). These are the political opinions that people verbalize, that they actively control and edit – the stuff of standard public opinion polls. Yet beneath what people report to researchers is a vast array of cognitions that are often ignored yet just as capable of structuring people's political views, even when they don't intend them to. This book aims to explain these attitudes, document their prevalence, and demonstrate their relevance for how one understands political decision making in the American mass public as it relates to immigration policy – one of the more potent and durable lines of conflict in US politics (King 2000; Ngai 2004; Tichenor 2002).

Political Man and His Thinking: Deliberative and Controlled

Many political scientists – although certainly not all (e.g., see Gruszczynski et al. 2013; Ksiazkiewicz and Hedrick 2013; Lodge and Taber 2013; Mendelberg 2001; Mo 2014; Smith et al. 2011; Valentino et al. 2002; Winter 2008) – see *homo politicus* as fully privy to the contents of his mind (e.g., Sniderman et al. 1991; Tourangeau et al. 2000; Zaller 1992). He is, by these influential accounts, aware of the political thoughts that dance in his head and how these affect his views of public figures and public policies (cf. Zaller and Feldman 1992). Yet this portrait is partly a function of how political scientists measure political attitudes. For more than five decades, self-reported attitudes have been the mainstay of US public opinion research. When political scientists wish to know what Americans think about politics, they typically engage in the "age-old practice of finding things out by asking people questions" (Tourangeau et al. 2000: 1).

To be sure, researchers disagree over the depth and coherence of Americans' attitudes toward politics (Achen 1975; Converse 1964; Zaller 1992). Yet their collective faith in citizens' ability to explicitly *voice* their opinions is unshakable. Citizens might not pay much attention to politics, it is acknowledged (Delli Carpini and Keeter 1996). But when asked to register their political attitudes, citizens will report an opinion, even if it means constructing one on the spot (Zaller 1992; Zaller and Feldman 1992). Indeed, even when people do not have complete knowledge of their political opinions, they at least know how to draw on basic "rules of thumb" to reveal these preferences to themselves and the researchers who inquire about them (i.e., heuristics; Brady and Sniderman 1985; Lupia 1994; Lupia and McCubbins 2000; Ottati 1990; Simon 1985; Sniderman et al. 1991).

These basic assumptions guide how political scientists generally study the formation and expression of American public opinion today. Without direct access to people's attitudes, we typically rely on what people are *able* and *willing* to tell us, including whether they voted (e.g., Silver et al. 1986); what they believe about racial minorities (e.g., Schuman et al. 1997); and how much political news they consume (e.g., Prior 2009). Yet a growing cavalcade of research from social psychology indicates that introspection provides very limited access to the full content of people's minds (e.g., Nisbett and Wilson 1977; Banaji et al. 1995; Greenwald and Banaji 1995; Fazio et al. 1995; Greenwald et al. 1998; Leander and Chartrand 2011; see also Lodge and Taber 2013; Lodge et al. 1989, 1995). Beyond people's self-reported attitudes is a trove of unspoken thoughts that nonetheless leave an imprint on the opinions and evaluations one verbally expresses (e.g., Ashburn-Nardo et al. 2003; Greenwald et al. 2009; Nosek et al. 2002; Wiers et al. 2002).

Can these implicit thoughts affect what people think about immigration? I will claim that they do. More specifically, I will argue that implicit attitudes are a crucial component of citizens' political psyche. Although political man is a reasoning creature, some of this thinking occurs without his knowledge. People, we are increasingly learning, acquire and use attitudes by way of cognitive processes that require little direction and effort (Bargh 1994; Fazio et al. 1986, 1995; Forgas and Tan 2011; Kahneman 2011; Krueger 2012; McConnell and Leibold 2001; Payne et al. 2005). In politics, these processes lead citizens to develop implicit attitudes toward the groups and personas that figure in political debates around them. These implicit attitudes, unlike their self-reported counterparts, operate beyond people's immediate awareness. More precisely, they shape one's deliberative thoughts without the person knowing how this influence actually occurs or that it has even taken place (e.g., Gawronski et al. 2006). Hence, when a political topic such as immigration is broached, relevant implicit attitudes are spontaneously activated and made mentally accessible to people. Akin to the authorities in the Mark Lyttle case, these implicit attitudes can affect not only the political opinions citizens express but also the very interpretation of the information they use to arrive at those opinions (cf. Fazio and Dunton 1997; Forgas and Tan 2011; Gawronski et al. 2003; Hugenberg and Bodenhausen 2003; Leander and Chartrand 2011).

The Unspoken Thoughts People Have

That people's thinking about immigration can occur outside of awareness is a tantalizing possibility. But is it an accurate portrayal of how individuals politically judge this issue? Surely, any spontaneous and nonverbalized thoughts that individuals have are nothing more than flotsam, the opening and inconsequential act to one's more effortful deliberations about immigration policy proposals. There is no denying, of course, that our conscious thoughts and feelings do in fact play a key role in the formation of our opinions and judgments. Yet this view is incompatible with what social psychologists have been learning about how the human mind collects and makes sense of information in its everyday functioning (e.g., Deutsch and Strack 2010; Giner-Sorolla 2012; Kahneman 2011; Krueger 2012; Leander and Chartrand 2011; Rydell and McConnell 2010; Sloman 1996; Smith and DeCoster 2000; Sritharan and Gawronski 2010).

For more than two decades now, social psychologists have increasingly shown that the human mind is quite limited in the amount of information it can consciously pay attention to and process at any one time (e.g., Posner and Snyder 1975; Shiffrin and Schneider 1977). Much of people's thinking thus occurs implicitly. That is, it shapes decisions without one's full awareness or control (for comprehensive overviews, see Bargh 2007; Gawronski and Payne 2010; Petty, Fazio, and Briñol 2009; Wittenbrink and Schwarz 2007). The grip of implicit cognition on people's judgments and behaviors is as much a powerful as it is a subtle one. For example, several social psychologists have conducted carefully controlled experiments to illuminate how these spontaneous cognitive forces can bias police officers' decision to shoot African American suspects. In one set of these lab studies (Correll et al. 2002), white subjects played a videogame in which they had to "shoot" or "not shoot" targets who (1) were either black or white and (2) holding a gun or some other object. These investigators found that subjects were quicker to shoot an armed target when he was black and quicker to decide against shooting an unarmed target when he was white. Consistent with these findings, another research team (Payne et al. 2002) showed that experimentally priming subjects with black (versus white) faces caused them to misidentify objects as guns. Such misidentifications occurred even when subjects were directly encouraged to avoid letting race affect their judgments of inanimate objects as weapons.

As these and other studies indicate, people have well-formed yet unexpressed ideas about social objects, such as racial groups (Greenwald et al. 1998; Kramer et al. 2011; Leander and Chartrand 2011; Nosek et al. 2002). These ideas, moreover, can be evoked spontaneously by stimuli in one's surroundings, such as encountering a member of a racial group on the street (Bargh and Pietromonaco 1982; Fazio et al. 1986; Forgas and Tan 2011; Hassin et al. 2007). And, once stimulated, these ideas often assume a life of their own, sometimes at odds with who people seem, or wish, to be (Bargh et al. 1992; Devos and Banaji 2005; Fazio et al. 1995; Payne 2006).

Still sound too good to be true? You would not be alone in thinking so. The view that unspoken thoughts can shape what we consciously say and do is in the minority within political science (e.g., Albertson 2011; Lodge and Taber 2013;

Mendelberg 2001; Mo 2014; see also Gruszczynski et al. 2013; Smith et al. 2011), which more often stresses citizens' use of reason – however bounded – to make political decisions (e.g., Lupia et al. 2000; Simon 1985; Sniderman et al. 1991). But to appreciate how implicit processes *might* affect political thought, it is perhaps useful to see how these same processes can influence even the most mundane of human tasks. For that, we will travel back to the mid-1990s and visit the experimental lab of John Bargh, one of social psychology's pioneering researchers on implicit cognition.

Young People Acting "Old"

Bargh and his colleagues were interested in determining whether implicit processes could influence overt behaviors (Bargh et al. 1996). To this end, they devised an experiment in which they randomly assigned undergraduate students to a control group or a priming condition. The priming condition was designed to activate an *elderly* stereotype among study participants, a feat accomplished indirectly through a "scrambled sentence test" (Srull and Wyer 1979), in which subjects were asked to make grammatical sentences out of strings of jumbled words. Peppered in these strings were words consistent with an *elderly* stereotype, including *old*, *lonely*, *Florida*, and *bingo*. In the control group, subjects completed the same sentence test, except the stimuli were replaced with words unrelated to the *elderly* stereotype.

On completing their scrambled sentence test, subjects were individually walked to a hallway outside of the lab and directed to the elevator at the end of it. Near the elevator sat a research assistant in a chair, under the cover of waiting for an appointment with a professor at a nearby office. As each subject arrived at the elevator, the assistant recorded the time it took for him or her to walk the entire length of the hallway – 9.75 meters to be exact.

Now keep in mind that the subjects in the study were undergraduate college students, decades away from embodying any stereotypical elderly traits themselves. Nevertheless, Bargh and his team discovered that those in the elderly priming condition "acted old" by walking significantly more slowly than their counterparts in the control condition – about a second more slowly, in fact. In other words, just insinuating the notion of being elderly led individuals to act elderly.

Implicit Attitudes and Two Forms of Political Reasoning

Bargh's study and others like it contradict the view that people's thinking is driven entirely by cognitive processes that one actively and fully directs (Bargh and Pietromonaco 1982; Bargh et al. 1992; Correll et al. 2002; Fazio et al. 1986; Forgas and Tan 2011; Kahneman 2011; Kramer et al. 2011; Krueger 2012; Payne et al. 2002, 2005). People, it appears, hold ideas that affect their behavior without their control. My main objective in this book is to explain and illustrate how these implicit attitudes color Americans' political opposition to immigration policy proposals.

To this end, I will draw extensively on social psychological research like John Bargh's to make a simple but often underappreciated point: the political mind is characterized not by one, but by two forms of reasoning (Deutsch and Strack 2010; Gawronski and Bodenhausen 2011; Kahneman 2011; Krueger 2012; Rydell and McConnell 2006; Sloman 1996; Smith and DeCoster 2000). The first of these reasoning systems – which I label explicit cognition – is generally characterized by individual control, effort, and awareness (Posner and Snyder 1975; Shiffrin and Schneider 1977). People actively direct this form of reasoning (Kahneman 2011; Smith and DeCoster 2000). They decide how much mental effort to invest in it (Fazio and Towles-Schwen 1999; Olson and Fazio 2009). And, they are cognizant of its actual unfolding (Strack and Deutsch 2004). Of course, not all individuals display these characteristics to the same degree (see Eagly and Chaiken 1993: Chapter 7). But in relative terms, these hallmarks generally characterize explicit cognition as a form of thinking.

For political scientists, explicit cognition is perhaps most easily recognized in the dynamics involving survey response. When asked about a political topic, individual respondents control how much effort they invest in thinking about their views, how much they mull over considerations to form an opinion (Zaller 1992). Individuals also command the degree to which they actually reveal their opinion to researchers. As they see fit, survey respondents can alter their attitudes before reporting them to pollsters (Davis 1997; Hatchett and Schuman 1975–1976; Tourangeau et al. 2000).

In contrast, the second form of reasoning – implicit cognition – is characterized by automaticity (Bargh 1994). Whereas explicit cognition emerges at the discretion of individuals, implicit cognition unfolds spontaneously and involuntarily. In the presence of fitting stimuli, a host of unspoken thoughts, feelings, and beliefs are quickly called forth to mind before one's more effortful reasoning is initiated (e.g., Gawronski and Bodenhausen 2011; Haidt 2012; Kahneman 2011; Leander and Chartrand 2011; Lodge and Taber 2013; Olson and Fazio 2009). In this way, implicit cognition unfolds *prior* to explicit cognition. Thus, it can structure the very deliberations one undertakes. This sequence is encouraged by two characteristics displayed by implicit processes. First, these processes are cognitively efficient: they require minimal mental resources on the part of individuals (e.g., Bargh 1994; Bargh et al. 1996; Fazio et al. 1986). Second, these processes are generally characterized by a lack of awareness: they proceed without people knowing how their workings affect them (e.g., Gawronski et al. 2003, 2006).

My primary claim is that implicit cognition can, under many conditions, influence one's political views by affecting one's more effortful and controlled deliberations (cf. Lodge and Taber 2013). This activity is facilitated by public discourse on policy issues, which, I argue, provides people with strong cues about who the main protagonists are and how they should be judged. Such cues enable individuals to develop implicit associations about political objects (e.g., groups, candidates). These unspoken associations are inherently subjective. They are steeped in recurring patterns in the discourse that surrounds policy issues, without these regularities necessarily reflecting empirical reality. Yet however subjective these implicit associations might be, they are nonetheless evaluative and consequential. That is, they are nonverbalized judgments about political objects that can shape political decisions. As later chapters show, many Americans evaluate political information in a manner that is consistent with their implicit associations. For these reasons, implicit associations merit the label *attitude*, as they serve as dispositions that guide "an individual's response to all objects and situations with which it is related" (Allport 1935: 810; Nosek and Hansen 2008).

Implicit Attitudes and Immigration Politics

I aim to study the link between implicit attitudes toward Latino immigrants and public opposition to immigration. In doing so, I hope to clarify how and to what extent attitudes toward a specific class of immigrants affect public support for exclusionary immigration policies (e.g., Hainmueller and Hopkins 2014a, 2014b; Wright et al. 2014). In earlier times, the influence of group-based attitudes on immigration politics was unmistakable. Consider the formal exclusion of Asian immigrants that began with the 1882 Chinese Exclusion Act, which prohibited "coolies" from entering the United States. This was followed by the 1907 Gentlemen's Agreement, which used diplomatic channels to limit Japanese immigration to the United States. Then, in 1917, Congress passed an act decreeing, among other things, a "barred Asiatic zone" that excluded immigrants from most Asian countries in an area extending from Afghanistan to the Pacific Ocean (Ngai 2004).[2] As these examples attest, negative attitudes toward Asian immigrants helped to underwrite political support for exclusionary immigration policies.

But the current immigration era feels different, or so it is sometimes suggested. If many Americans hold foreigners in low regard today, it is claimed, it is not because of who the immigrants *are*, but because of what certain immigrants *do*. As an example, consider the 2014 surge of unaccompanied minors from countries such as El Salvador, Guatemala, and Honduras seeking to enter the United States without documentation. This unexpected swell in young unauthorized migrants caught US immigration authorities unprepared to house these youths during their formal processing. Hence, a solution: transport the

[2] These were most, but not all Asian nations. For example, the "barred Asiatic zone" did not include the Philippines, which was then a U.S. territory (Ngai 2004: 37).

undocumented minors to temporary shelters in communities throughout the nation until their status is resolved.

One of these cities was Murrieta, California, where protestors blocked the arrival of three busloads of these immigrants and pressured federal authorities to house them elsewhere. For some people, the protest seemed fueled by nothing more than negative attitude toward Latino immigrants: "If these children were from Canada," remarked one such person, "we would not be having this" (Martinez and Yan 2014). But as the mayor of Murrieta explained about the demonstration: "It's not against the immigrants … What we're protesting is the product of a broken system that finally reached the doorstep of our community" (Martinez and Yan 2014).

The mayor's reasoning about what drove opposition to these specific immigrants is emblematic of the type of principled stances that many individuals express during flashpoints in other US immigration debates – that public opposition to immigration has little, if anything, to do with how one feels about specific immigrants. But it is also the kind of position that sounds like the right thing to say publicly, especially if one acknowledges that the expression of negative attitudes toward racial and ethnic minorities is now socially censured (Mendelberg 2001; Valentino et al. 2002). Moreover, even if one sincerely professes to harbor no ill feelings toward a specific class of immigrants, the literature on implicit cognition suggests that such attitudes might affect people's political thinking without them being aware of this influence (for an overview, see Pérez 2013). Thus, a serious rethinking is needed about how people's feelings toward one group of foreigners can shape what they think about immigration policies that affect more than just this group.

Group-Centrism and Implicit Attitudes toward Latino Immigrants

To begin explaining why implicit attitudes toward Latino immigrants might shape public opposition to immigration, I draw on the notion of group-centrism. Historically, the immigration issue has regularly claimed space on the nation's political agenda, with political elites vigorously debating who is worthy of admission to the nation and on what grounds (cf. Higham 1981; King 2000; Ngai 2004; Tichenor 2002). Public discourse on this policy issue is multifaceted, with advocates and detractors disputing, among other things, the economic and cultural costs and benefits of immigration (cf. Chavez 2001; Simon and Alexander 1993). Yet notwithstanding the rich exchange of ideas, immigration discourse has often displayed a group-centric character, where specific immigrant groups serve as the axis along which arguments are made.

As such, group-centrism provides a lens through which the larger immigration issue is understood (Brader, Valentino, and Suhay 2008; more generally, see Kinder 1998; Nelson and Kinder 1996). A case in point is the political debate during the early 1900s over whether immigrants had the aptitude to meet the duties and responsibilities of US citizenship. Southern and Eastern Europeans featured prominently in these debates, which were capped by the 1924 National Origins Act that set quotas severely limiting the entry of these "undesirable" immigrants (Gerstle 2001; King 2000; Tichenor 2002). At this and other similar junctures, the public spotlight has been cast on some immigrants more than others.

Such group-centrism manifests itself today. Across nearly five decades, Latin American immigrants have emerged as the salient group in the stream of foreigners reaching our shores. In fact, as of 2010, slightly more than half (53 percent) of the nearly 40 million foreign-born individuals living in the United States trace their origins to Latin America (Passel and Cohn 2012). Not surprisingly, perhaps, public debate on immigration has increasingly centered on Latino immigrants. Valentino, Brader, and Jardina (2013), for example, show that in the last twenty years, Latinos have often been the focus of news stories on immigration – more often than Asians, Africans, and Muslims, who contribute substantially to current immigration flows.

This group-centrism has direct consequences for contemporary public opinion on immigration. In particular, chronic attention to Latinos in immigration discourse has made attitudes toward this group a key component of individual opposition to immigration. For instance, Valentino, Brader, and Jardina (2013) find that attitudes toward Latinos outperform attitudes toward other groups (e.g., Asians) in boosting opposition to immigration – a pattern that emerges after 1992, when Latinos became increasingly salient in immigration news (see also Branton et al. 2011; Burns and Gimpel 2000; Hartman, Newman, and Bell 2014). Indeed, in experimental work, Brader, Valentino, and Suhay (2008) demonstrate that centering public attention on Latinos elicits more exclusionary attitudes toward immigration than when non-Latino groups are the focus.

This general pattern between group-specific attitudes and immigration policy evaluations is consistent, robust, and independently reproduced by different research teams (e.g., Branton et al. 2011; Burns and Gimpel 2000; Hartman, Newman, and Bell 2014; Valentino, Brader, Jardina 2013). Invariably, however, the quantity of interest in this scholarship – attitude toward Latinos – is self-reported. Its influence on public opposition to immigration is unmistakable, to be sure. Yet this attitude reflects what people are able and willing to share with researchers; it is a predisposition that people can control, manipulate, and revise as they see fit. This matters especially in the realm of racial attitudes, where people are sometimes prone to misrepresent their opinions in an effort to give socially desirable responses (e.g., Kuklinski et al. 1997).

This book seizes on this established dynamic between attitudes toward Latinos, information about immigrants, and opposition to immigration (e.g., Brader et al. 2008; Branton et al. 2011; Burns and Gimpel 2000; Hartman et al. 2014; Valentino et al. 2013). Accordingly, I take a step back and investigate whether and how implicit attitudes toward the same group can automatically structure political decision making on immigration. Nascent research on the automaticity of emotional reactions to immigrant-related cues suggests this is a productive research avenue to pursue.

For example, Newman, Hartman, and Taber (2014) find that people who encounter cultural transaction costs related to immigration (e.g., exposure to the Spanish version of a public website) impulsively experience a heightened sense of anger, which sharpens the perception of immigrants as culturally threatening and increases support for exclusionary immigration policies (see also Newman, Hartman, and Taber 2012). These results are highly consistent with the pioneering work of George Marcus and colleagues, which shows that spontaneous emotional reactions to political stimuli can subtly, but powerfully, structure citizens' political ruminations and behavior (e.g., Brader 2006; Marcus 2003; Marcus, Neuman, and MacKuen 2000; for an overview, see Brader and Marcus 2013).

Seizing on this notion of automaticity, and exploring its direct relationship to citizens' implicit attitudes, I uncover several lessons about people's political position on immigration. But one in particular dominates my investigation: When asked about their opinions concerning immigration, many Americans automatically assume they are talking about Latino immigrants. As a result, their implicit attitude toward this group is spontaneously activated, rapidly giving individuals a deeply affective but unspoken sense of what they think about immigration policy proposals.

Implicit Attitudes and Prior Political Science Scholarship

Every idea has an intellectual heritage. In the case at hand, the influence of social psychology is easy to see. But my claim that implicit attitudes lurk in immigration politics also descends from the pioneering work of two Stony Brook University political scientists, Milton Lodge and Charles Taber. This pair of researchers has drawn on many of the same ideas as I do to develop a comprehensive model of implicit political cognition, which they report in their ground-breaking book, *The Rationalizing Voter* (Lodge and Taber 2013). Based on research spanning two decades, these authors lay out, in painstaking detail, how unconscious information processing colors political decision making. As such, this important contribution sets a solid theoretical foundation on which to build my own explanation for how implicit attitudes shape people's political thinking on immigration.

Lodge and Taber's (2013) model, dubbed *John Q. Public* (JQP), construes political cognition as running from an automatic/uncontrollable/implicit pole to a more effortful/controllable/explicit one. As citizens' thinking unfolds across this continuum, JQP stipulates that what transpires initially in this process has implications for the character of one's political judgments and evaluations further "downstream." This sequence begins the moment someone encounters a political stimulus (e.g., a campaign ad) and relevant political concepts are activated in their mind. Per JQP, people's political concepts are organized in long-term memory (LTM) in a lattice-like structure in which numerous concepts are linked to each other, to varied degrees, in an associative fashion. This architecture implies that activation of one concept will call forth related ones via spreading activation (Collins and Loftus 1975). This last point is crucial, as it helps to explain how people recruit considerations from their LTM into their working memory (WM) (i.e., "top of their head") to report an opinion or form a political judgment (Zaller 1992).

According to JQP, all political concepts are affectively tagged – that is, they are stored in LTM with a positive or negative charge. As a result, all political thinking is "hot," as stimulating a political concept will also call forth its evaluative tag. This implies that one's thinking is infused with affect from the start, thus setting the stage for the character and direction of one's subsequent information processing. Two key points follow. Affect is primary and its influence is automatic. The former means that initial feelings, however rudimentary and unarticulated, drive more effortful thought rather than the other way around. The latter entails that affect's effect on information processing and deliberation often occurs below one's level of full awareness and control – and often within the first few milliseconds after encountering a political stimulus.

Affect's immediacy and primacy are significant because, as JQP explains, they shape one's more controlled and effortful thinking through two key mechanisms. The first of these is *affect transfer*, in which the initial feelings induced by a political stimulus can directly influence a person's political judgment. For example, incidental exposure to the US flag might heighten positive emotions, thus producing more favorable evaluations of, say, the president. Similarly, deliberate exposure to religious symbols through, for example, a political ad, might stimulate positive feelings, which then yield a favorable evaluation of the sponsoring candidate (Lodge and Taber 2013: 20). Yet irrespective of whether the aroused affect is extrinsic or intrinsic to a political object, *affect transfer* suggests that people will freight their spontaneous feelings onto their explicit political judgments.

JQP's second mechanism is *affect contagion*. Because a person's information processing stream runs from automatic/uncontrollable to more effortful/controlled, the spontaneous feelings initially aroused by a mobilized political concept lead people to retrieve considerations that are congruent with this initial affective reaction, which biases people's more deliberative thoughts in the direction of this affective response. In other words, rather than even-handedly dredging considerations from LTM into WM to form an explicit judgment or thought, the initial affect sparked by a stimulated political concept encourages people to undertake a skewed dragnet of political considerations.

Distilled to its quintessential implication, these mechanisms suggest that most, if not all, political reasoning is motivated, such that citizens find it really hard to evaluate political information in a balanced and dispassionate way. In terms of immigration politics, this insight indicates that people might find it difficult to evaluate immigration policies in an impartial manner because of their implicit attitude toward Latino immigrants.

In the pages that follow, I seize on some of JQP's insights to inform and strengthen my own work. But from where I stand, I see some signs of potential trouble on the horizons of research on implicit political cognition. Some of these are challenges that Lodge and Taber (2013) anticipated, but did not completely address. Some of these were issues that both authors overlooked. Each of these concerns, however, stands to influence how receptive political science will be to implicit cognition research – very much including my own. It is to these areas, then, that I directly contribute to in an effort to strengthen and deepen fledgling research on implicit political cognition.

Beyond the Lab and Into "the Wild" of Politics

Notwithstanding its sophistication and precision, JQP is a model whose psychological mechanisms have been tested primarily through meticulously designed laboratory experiments on college undergraduates. The evidence supporting JQP's mechanisms is therefore remarkably strong on internal validity: the degree to which one can be confident that observed changes in judgments or behaviors are caused by an experimental manipulation(s) (McDermott 2011; Shadish et al. 2002). What is noticeably weaker about JQP, however, is its external validity. That is, the degree to which such evidence is reproduced in diverse populations and research settings, and with varied methods and measures (McDermott 2011; Shadish et al. 2002).

On the surface, this might seem an esoteric point, until one realizes that political science normatively privileges external over internal validity. As Rose McDermott (2011: 27) laments, political science's "concerns with external validity often border on the monomaniacal, leading to the neglect, if not the complete dismissal, of attention to the important issues involved in internal validity." From this perspective, then, Lodge and Taber's (2013) emphasis on internal validity is easy to appreciate and understand. Lab experiments provide researchers unrivaled leverage and control over the manipulation of stimuli and the assessment of outcomes, thus positioning researchers to infer more confidently that an experimental treatment "worked," while ruling out possible extraneous mediating forces in the evaluation of such effects. As Lodge and Taber (2013: 65) explain: "[i]n our studies, we opt to maximize internal validity, because if the internal validity of a survey or experiment is compromised, questioning the external validity would be moot."

True enough, but a major challenge in implicit cognition research, both in social psychology and political science, is that evidence in favor of this phenomenon is inordinately strong on internal validity, remarkably weaker on external validity, and very rarely powerful on both fronts simultaneously. Yet evidence that tackles both of these considerations, in tandem, is what is most likely to convince skeptical political scientists that implicit cognition is something that matters "out there" in the rough-and-tumble world of politics.

So, although I draw on Lodge and Taber's (2013) insights to develop my own story about the link between implicit attitudes toward Latinos and explicit immigration policy judgments, I corroborate my framework with evidence from experiments embedded in a national survey of US adults. By retaining the inferential power of experimentation within a setting less controlled than a lab, my survey experiments illuminate some of the psychological mechanisms animating the influence of implicit attitudes (e.g., affect transfer), while establishing their operation in a key population – US adults, rather than "college sophomores" (Sears 1986; see also Henrich et al. 2010). Moreover, setting aside these experiments, observational analyses of these survey data reveal that immigration policy judgments are strongly associated with implicit attitudes, independently of standard self-reported predictors of public opinion (e.g., partisanship, education). And, because I utilize a measure of implicit attitude – the Implicit Association Test (IAT) – that is distinct from the ones used by Lodge and Taber (2013), my evidence suggests the political influence of implicit attitudes is not a function of how they are assessed by researchers. In these ways, my parallel emphasis on internal and external validity helps to advance scholarship on implicit political cognition a few key positions forward from the vital foothold secured by Lodge and Taber (2013).

Whence, Implicit Attitudes?

In Lodge and Taber (2013), implicit attitudes are an LTM component that can be galvanized in at least two ways. One route is for a person to form an implicit attitude "on the spot" from the LTM considerations that are spontaneously activated by political stimuli. A second avenue is for one's preformed implicit attitude (stored in LTM) to be roused into action by a political stimulus. Lodge and Taber (2013) demonstrate that either process can be set into motion by stimuli that are expressly political or nonpolitical, as well as consciously seen or unseen. But with the exception of a few lines in one paragraph (Lodge and Taber 2013: 31), these authors say little about where these implicit attitudes – or the considerations from which they are constructed – come from.

I summon an answer to this question by tracing the development of implicit attitudes to one key wellspring: political discourse transmitted via news media. I argue that political discourse informs people about how policy disagreements should be understood, who the protagonists in these policy disputes are, and how these policies and their protagonists should be evaluated. Dominant patterns in this discourse win out, as their dissemination and repetition encourage people to develop implicit attitudes toward political objects through a process of evaluative conditioning, where "repeated pairings of potential attitude objects . . . with positively and negatively valenced stimuli" lead people to form an attitude toward the object in the prevailing direction of these pairings (Olson and Fazio 2001: 413).[3]

[3] In the few lines where Lodge and Taber (2013: 31) discuss the origins of implicit attitudes, their remarks center on the notion of evaluative conditioning, which I examine in depth in Chapter 4.

I support this claim by showing how immigration news coverage across the last two decades centers overwhelmingly on its illegal component and its ties to one group, i.e., Latinos – despite the fact that many Latino immigrants are here legally. I reason that the negative valence of these imbalanced information flows encourages many individuals to form an automatic and unfavorable evaluation of Latino immigrants, an assertion I support with survey data revealing a high mean and low variance of implicit attitudes toward this group among US adults. Equally important, and in contrast to Lodge and Taber (2013), I focus greater attention on individual differences in these implicit attitudes. For instance, I demonstrate that individual differences in these implicit attitudes correspond quite strongly with individual differences in people's political views on immigration. Moreover, I illustrate how individual differences in implicit attitudes condition citizens' processing of explicit cues concerning specific immigrants and immigration policy proposals. Thus, by focusing greater attention on the media origins of some implicit attitudes, I suggest that the psychology of implicit attitudes is deeply embedded in a key structural feature of US politics.

Race and the Psychology of Implicit Attitudes

John Q. Public is an elegant model with the highest of ambitions: to explain the influence of implicit cognition on *citizens'* political thinking. To meet this high standard, Lodge and Taber (2013) cast their theory at a very broad level. Accordingly, their unit of analysis is the individual voter – or, more precisely, the rationalizing voter. But voters are a heterogeneous lot, varying widely in terms of ability, motivation, and – often less appreciated – social position. Lodge and Taber (2013) recognize the importance of the first two (i.e., ability and motivation) – hence their insight that many of implicit cognition's effects are pronounced among the more sophisticated elements of our citizenry. But the thread that is lost in JQP is the one involving the influence of social position. This omission matters because it elides a deeper understanding of the functional underpinnings of implicit attitudes: the notion that the expression of implicit attitudes might be rooted, at least in part, in the specific function(s) that these evaluations perform for people (e.g., value expression, ego defense) (e.g., Eagly and Chaiken 1993; Katz 1960; Sarnoff 1960; Sidanius et al. 1997; Stenner 2005).

In an effort to recover this thread and establish its relevance to political decision making, I examine the interface between race and implicit attitudes. Specifically, I center attention on America's racial hierarchy to test whether one's position in it modulates the political expression of implicit attitudes. For all of the racial progress our nation has witnessed across the last fifty years, racial groups are still arrayed in a widely recognized order of descending status, with

In evaluative conditioning, the attitude object is technically known as the conditioned stimulus (CS), as it is conditioned to evoke a spontaneous response via repeated pairings with valenced stimuli, which are technically known as unconditioned stimuli (US) because they already automatically stir a response in people (e.g., the smell of food makes one salivate).

whites in the most privileged position and African Americans occupying the lowest station (Fang et al. 1998; Ho et al. 2011; Kim 2000; Masuoka and Junn 2013; see also Hagendoorn 1995; Hagendoorn et al. 1998). For example, Kahn et al. (2009: 591) report that whites and non-whites display "strong agreement that Whites occupy the top position, followed by Asians, followed by Latinos and African-Americans at the bottom of their society." To be sure, acknowledging these differences does not necessarily entail endorsing them. But research by Jim Sidanius and his associates suggests that people's attitudes and behaviors often reflect their group's position in the racial order (Dowley and Silver 2000; Sidanius and Petrocik 2001; Sidanius et al. 1997; Sinclair et al. 1998; Staerklé et al. 2010; see also Doosje et al. 2002; Tajfel and Turner 1979). And one crucial manifestation of this is hostility toward an outgroup(s).

To understand why this occurs, we have to recognize that within social hierarchies, dominant groups are more powerful. That is, they possess more influence over the opportunities and outcomes of their subordinates (e.g., Fiske 1993; Goodwin et al. 2000; Richeson and Ambady 2003; Rodríguez-Bailón et al. 2000). Given this asymmetry in power, dominant group members have a weak incentive to distinguish between subordinate group members, as the prospects of the former depend weakly, if at all, on the latter. This facilitates the reification of an outgroup, thus setting it up as a possible target for the dominant group's hostility. In fact, the latter will occur to the extent that the outgroup is deemed threatening to the dominant group's position in the hierarchy (cf. Blumer 1958; Brewer 1999; Horowitz 1985; Tajfel and Turner 1979). In short, negative attitudes toward an outgroup *function* to preserve the higher rank of the dominant ingroup.

But racial hierarchy? In politics? Really? Although the link between hierarchy, implicit attitudes, and political views is an unknown I investigate in this book, it is becoming clearer that America's racial order plays a crucial but underappreciated role in shaping people's political judgments (cf. Dawson 2000; Kim 2000; Masuoka and Junn 2013; Philpot and White 2010). Indeed, one of the emerging insights from this line of inquiry is that failure to take racial hierarchy into account risks masking a remarkable degree of heterogeneity in how people engage and process political information. Hence, to avoid this situation, I theorize about the role of race in implicit political cognition. I argue that the influence of implicit attitudes toward Latino immigrants on preferences for stricter immigration policy should be stronger among whites, rather than blacks, because members of the former group are (1) in a more powerful position vis-à-vis Latinos and (2) political and media elites often frame Latinos as a cultural and economic threat to native-born Americans (cf. Brader et al. 2008; Chavez 2001; Huntington 2004). My analysis will yield evidence that is consistent with my claim that the political influence of implicit attitudes depends, in part, on whether these automatic evaluations satisfy deeper motivational needs for individuals, such as the preservation of one's privileged station in a racial order. In doing so, my results align with previous research on the relationship between racial hierarchy and social life (Dowley and Silver 2000; Sidanius and Petrocik 2001; Sidanius et al. 1997; Sinclair et al. 1998; Staerklé et al. 2010).[4]

Fortifying and Extending the Beachhead

Given the precedent set by Lodge and Taber (2013) and a voluminous psychological literature on automaticity (Gawronski and Payne 2010; Briñol et al. 2009; Bargh 2007), one would think that the notion of implicit attitudes would be widely welcomed by political scientists. But one would be wrong. Although political science scholarship using the concepts and tools of implicit cognition has been published (e.g., Mo 2014; Albertson 2011; Pérez 2010; Pasek et al. 2009; Craemer 2008; Arcuri et al. 2008; Kam 2007; Burdein et al. 2006), these research threads have not produced a tapestry of findings like the ones characterizing other areas of political science, which draw heavily on social psychological insights (e.g., emotions, personality). As Huddy and Feldman (2009: 437) lament: "[T]here are relatively few published studies that report the political effects of implicit attitudes, making it difficult to assess their current payoff for political scientists."

Political science's reception to implicit attitudes has been tepid (Pérez 2013). In fact, given that social psychology and political science have long enjoyed an "intellectual affair" (McGuire 1993: 9), one might say the two are oddly estranged over this concept. Not only are there relatively few published studies. Some of these have provoked efforts to invalidate their results, rather than inspire theoretical advancements or alternate research designs (Pasek et al. 2009; Kalmoe and Piston 2013).[5]

This state of affairs is somewhat understandable, for it can arise when new concepts are introduced. Take early skepticisms about symbolic racism (Banaji et al. 2004; Sears 2004). This research program claims that a new and subtle

[4] My work is also indirectly influenced by studies on implicit *communications* from political elites, which are theorized to elicit racial attitudes (Mendelberg 2001; Valentino et al. 2002). In those studies, racial attitudes are explicit (i.e., self-reported), but their activation occurs via implicit cues in elite discourse. In contrast, my research focuses on a different independent variable, implicit racial *attitude*, which is not self-reported. Despite differences in focus, both research programs collectively draw on the notion that some political thinking occurs implicitly.

[5] For instance, using a nationally representative survey of adults (i.e., ANES), Ditonto et al. (2013) find that after controlling for explicit racial and political attitudes, a weak and inconsistent association emerges between individual scores on an implicit attitude measure (i.e., Affect Misattribution Procedure) and several race-related dependent variables. This might seem like clear evidence against the political relevance of implicit attitudes. Yet at least two theoretical alternatives are untested: (1) explicit attitudes mediate the influence of implicit attitudes (cf. Payne et al. 2010; Pérez 2010); and (2) implicit attitudes shape the processing of information leading to explicit political decisions. Whereas the former can be tested via a correlational approach (Baron and Kenny 1986), the latter demands a more exacting research design to observe implicit attitude effects under varied conditions. In Chapters 6 and 7, I use experiments to reveal the imprint of implicit attitudes on political evaluations (see also Lodge and Taber 2013).

form of anti-black prejudice is afoot in the post–Civil Rights era (Kinder and Sanders 1996; Kinder and Sears 1981; McConahay and Hough 1976; Sears 1988). Unlike prior forms of racism, which stress the biological inferiority of African Americans, symbolic racism is said to be steeped in a blend of anti-black affect and conservative moral values (e.g., self-reliance). Opposition to this new concept was initially fierce, with critics alleging, for example, that measures of symbolic racism captured political conservatism instead of prejudice, which explained the strong association between symbolic racism and racial policy preferences (Sniderman and Tetlock 1986; Tetlock 1994). But fresh theorizing and manifold empirical tests gradually revealed that these speculations rest on shaky empirical ground. Measures of symbolic racism do appear to tap their target construct and scores on these measures do predict racial policy preferences net of political conservatism (Sears et al. 1997; Tarman and Sears 2005).

The larger lesson in this scholarly fracas is clear. Deep misgivings about new ideas can advance scientific knowledge when they are met with evidence rather than speculation. Hence, one overarching aim in this book is to articulate some of the major doubts political scientists might have about implicit attitudes, give these misgivings their due consideration, and rigorously test them against the alternative account I propose in this book – that implicit attitudes matter deeply for how we understand citizens' political thinking on an important issue such as immigration.

Plan of the Book

The road from claiming that implicit attitudes exist and that they matter for explicit political decision making on the issue of immigration is long and arduous. Several objectives must be met before we can even begin evaluating evidence for this claim. First among these is the need for a deeper conceptual understanding of implicit attitudes. What are implicit attitudes? Where and how do they emerge? And, most importantly, how do they operate? More detailed answers to these questions, and others, should make us more comfortable that at a theoretical level, at least, implicit attitudes really are different from explicit attitudes. Thus, Chapter 2 revisits and elaborates on the differences between implicit and explicit systems of reasoning. It does so in an effort to clear the conceptual underbrush and help build a sturdier theoretical framework to guide my empirical inquiries in later chapters. Accordingly, I explain in depth the varied cognitive principles by which these two mental systems operate in terms of information processing and attitude formation. This discussion will reveal that whereas explicit cognition relies on higher-order, verbalized reasoning, implicit cognition operates on the basis of lower-order, associational principles (Giner-Sorolla 2012; Kahneman 2011; Rydell and McConnell 2006; Smith and DeCoster 2000). Whereas the former produces self-reported attitudes, the latter generates implicit attitudes, which people form on the basis of dominant and recurring patterns of information about objects (e.g., groups, candidates).

Chapter 3 explains that implicit attitudes have two characteristics marking them off from their more familiar self-reported counterparts. First, implicit attitudes are spontaneously activated. When people encounter a political object or stimulus related to that object, one's implicit attitude toward the political target is automatically evoked (e.g., Bargh et al. 1992; Fazio et al. 1986). Second, implicit attitudes are deeply affective (e.g., Lodge and Taber 2013; Ranganath et al. 2008; Smith and Nosek 2011). As such, they provide a strong, quick, and nonverbalized sense of how one feels toward a political object (e.g., Murphy and Zajonc 1993; Zajonc 1980). Together, these attributes enable implicit attitudes to structure the nature of one's more explicit thinking about political issues by delivering early but strong input into one's deliberations (Lodge and Taber 2013). In particular, implicit attitudes toward Latino immigrants lead people to judge immigration policies in a way that is consistent with the unspoken expectations that implicit attitudes raise.

Chapter 4 addresses the connection between political discourse and the associational processes by which implicit attitudes are thought to form. Scholarship strongly suggests that implicit attitudes are formed on the basis of recurring patterns in information about objects (e.g., Gregg et al. 2006; Olson and Fazio 2002; see also Giner-Sorolla 2012). Moreover, people do not seem to have control over their formation of implicit attitudes (Gawronski et al. 2014a), nor explicit memories for the information that stimulates these evaluations (Olson and Fazio 2001). One plausible and systematic source of these information patterns is political discourse on policy issues. And, to the extent these regularities emerge here, they can help discipline expectations regarding the direction and intensity of implicit attitudes at the mass level.

Accordingly, I examine discourse on immigration politics as reflected in news coverage of this issue across the last twenty years (see also Merolla, Ramakrishnan, and Haynes 2013). Prior work (Valentino, Brader, and Jardina 2013) finds that print media more often focus on Latino immigrants than other foreigners when reporting on immigration. This visibility in immigration discourse helps explain why Latinos might serve as a target of implicit attitudes. Yet salience does not explain the direction or intensity that implicit attitudes toward this group might take. Hence, I extend the trend uncovered by Valentino et al. (2013) by showing that although Latinos are often the focus of immigration news stories in print and television, this attention is often imbalanced in its emphasis. Seizing on the distinction between illegal and legal immigration, I reveal that while the estimated proportion of foreign-born Latinos in the United States who are unauthorized is about 50 percent, roughly 85 percent of news stories on Latino immigrants focus on their illegal origins. In sharp contrast, although 50 percent of Latino immigrants living in the United States enjoy legal status, only about 15 percent of news stories focus on this group's legal origins.

Of course, one could argue that most news coverage *should* focus on Latino illegal immigrants. After all, news outlets are for-profit businesses, with stories focused on novel, sensational, or exceptional topics being more likely to increase audience shares (Gilens 1999). But even this coverage seems imbalanced. For example, in 2010, 76 percent of the estimated 11 million unauthorized immigrants in the United States were, in descending order, from Mexico, El Salvador, Guatemala, Honduras, and Ecuador (Hoefer et al. 2011). In that year, the three major news networks – ABC, CBS, and NBC – aired about eleven stories on unauthorized Latino immigrants. In contrast, about 9 percent and 3 percent of unauthorized immigrants in the United States during 2010 were from Asia or Europe (Hoefer et al. 2011). Yet the same networks did not air a single story on either group, a pattern characterizing most of the 1990–2010 era. Again, it may be unrealistic to expect news outlets to cover immigration in a way that more faithfully reflects empirical reality. But these distortions, I argue later, help to promote the development of implicit attitudes toward Latino immigrants.

Chapter 5 undertakes the delicate task of measuring attitudes that are spontaneous, hard to control, and nonverbalized – in a word, implicit (cf. Forgas et al. 2011; Gawronski and Payne 2010; Giner-Sorolla 2012; Kramer et al. 2011; Krueger 2012; Petty et al. 2009). To this end, I propose and defend the use of one such measure: the Implicit Association Test (IAT). Unlike measures of self-reported attitudes, which invite people to say what is on their minds, the IAT relies not on what people say, but on what they do and how fast they do it. Specifically, the IAT times how fast – on the order of milliseconds – people can sort exemplars of different targets (e.g., *Latino immigrants*) and attributes (e.g., *bad* or *good*) while using two different classification schemes. I will use these differences in sorting times to draw conclusions about whether, and to what extent, people have an implicit attitude toward Latinos that is distinct from their self-reported one.

I admit that such a measurement strategy is unorthodox. But the IAT is a measure that has been – and continues to be – extensively validated, in part because it is unconventional. Using nationally representative opinion data, Chapter 5 shows the IAT captures an implicit attitude toward Latinos that is different from what is obtained via self-reports. Consistent with Chapter 4's news content analysis, these implicit attitudes are both prevalent and remarkably negative. Chapter 5 also demonstrates the IAT taps an attitude that is not only hard to control, but also specifically directed at Latinos. Most importantly, Chapter 5 establishes that the IAT measures an attitude that substantively shapes people's political thinking about illegal and legal immigration, and that it does so independently from self-reported attitude toward Latinos, partisanship, education, authoritarianism, and other individual-level factors expected to affect opinions in this policy realm.

Having raised confidence in the IAT as a measure of implicit attitude, Chapter 6 turns to documenting the subconscious nature of this construct – that is, one of the key features that presumably makes implicit attitudes implicit.

I reason that if these attitudes are truly subconscious, they should be resistant to the conscious information one attends to. At first, this may seem inconsistent with my claim that immigration news coverage helps to promote the development of implicit attitudes toward Latinos, since news *is* information. But remember, I claim that people form implicit attitudes via associational reasoning, on the basis of long-term information patterns such as those in immigration news reports. This acquisition of implicit attitudes happens without a person's control (Gawronski et al. 2014a) or recollection of the information promoting these evaluations (Olson and Fazio 2001), which suggests that people are implicitly processing explicit information patterns. In contrast, when I say that implicit attitudes should be unaffected by conscious information, I mean to say short-term information that people knowingly focus on and process.

In the context of immigration politics, this suggests implicit attitudes toward Latino immigrants should influence immigration policy judgments even when people are induced to consciously think about non-Latino groups or individuals. This is a stringent test. By training individuals' attention on non-Latinos, one is in effect raising people's awareness that the focus of one's pending judgment is a non-Latino target. In other words, individuals are given an opportunity to suppress their implicit attitude toward Latino immigrants. Hence, if implicit attitude toward Latino immigrants has meaningful effects when non-Latino groups are cued, we can be more confident that such effects are due to its operation without people's awareness. Had they been aware, they should have stifled their implicit attitude. I test this proposition with two experiments embedded within a national opinion survey that vary the legal status and national origin of immigrants. The lesson emerging from each experiment is clear: negative implicit attitude toward Latinos increases support for exclusionary immigration policies, even if we direct individuals' conscious attention toward non-Latino groups or individuals.

In Chapter 7, I begin exploring heterogeneity in the interplay between implicit and explicit cognition by investigating how individual differences in education and the presence of unambiguous political information affect this dynamic. By one account, people who are more educated are believed to engage in more effortful and deliberative thinking. They have more consistent opinions across issues (Stimson 1975). Their storehouse of attitudes is often larger, more developed, and better organized in memory (Zaller and Feldman 1992). And they are more adept at drawing connections between their relevant attitudes to the demands of a particular judgment (Federico 2004; Sniderman et al. 1991). Moreover, highly educated individuals are more sensitive to the expression of racial bias in political decision-making (McClosky and Zaller 1984; Sniderman and Piazza 1993). These types of individuals should thus be able to minimize the role of implicit attitudes in their thinking by following through on their inclination toward more effortful thought.

By another account, however, education can strengthen the influence of implicit attitudes. Studies show that individuals are often motivated to defend relevant attitudes by, inter alia, discounting information that contradicts, and accepting information that affirms, their attitudes (Ditto and Lopez 1992; Kunda 1990). In politics, such motivated reasoning is more prevalent among people with greater cognitive sophistication (i.e., political knowledge) because, as Taber and Lodge (2006: 757) explain, these individuals "possess greater ammunition with which to counterargue incongruent facts" (cf. Lodge and Taber 2013). If implicit attitude operates without one's awareness, then this suggests, somewhat paradoxically, that the link between implicit attitude and explicit decision-making will be stronger among educated individuals, as they are more predisposed to bolster their implicit attitudes.

To these ends, I show that the effects of implicit attitude on immigration policy judgments do become stronger – not weaker – with higher education levels. Indeed, this occurs even when individuals' attention is consciously directed toward non-Latino immigrants. I also demonstrate that while highly educated individuals cannot suppress their implicit attitude, they *can* control their self-reported attitude toward Latinos when cued with information about non-Latinos, which further suggests the link between implicit attitude and explicit decision making occurs without awareness.

While the previous two chapters bore down on the individual psychology behind implicit attitudes, Chapter 8 demonstrates how this psychology is itself shaped by larger social forces by illustrating how implicit attitudes are modulated by race – or rather, the position of one's racial group within America's racial hierarchy (cf. Bobo and Hutchings 1996; Dawson 2000; Kim 2000; Peña and Sidanius 2002; Sidanius et al. 1997). As I explained earlier, I argue that the location of one's group within this racial order conditions the intensity and relevance of implicit attitudes. Specifically, I claim that members of privileged groups within this hierarchy face greater incentives to express implicit attitudes toward outgroups as a way to buttress their own social position.

Accordingly, I study the degree to which implicit attitudes vary among US blacks and whites.[6] I uncover two key pieces of evidence to support my claims about the interface between racial hierarchy and implicit attitudes. First, given blacks' lower position in America's racial order (Fang et al. 1998; Kahn et al. 2009; Kim 2001), I find that African Americans display weaker levels of implicit attitude toward Latinos than their white counterparts, which suggests that blacks are less likely to spontaneously hold Latinos in low regard. Second, in contrast to many whites, African American judgments of immigration are minimally affected by implicit attitude toward Latinos. In particular, blacks with higher levels of implicit bias are no more likely to support exclusionary immigration policy than blacks with lower levels of this attitude. Taken as a

[6] One might wonder why I do not also study implicit attitudes toward Latinos among Latinos themselves. I refrain from doing so because I consider the basis of Latinos' implicit attitudes to be different than for whites and blacks. Whereas implicit attitudes among blacks and whites reflect evaluations of Latinos as an *outgroup*, Latinos' implicit attitudes reflect their evaluations of Latinos as an *ingroup* (e.g., see Ashburn-Nardo et al. 2003; Dasgupta 2004: 160–162).

whole, these insights illuminate how larger social forces – in this case, racial hierarchy – shape the psychology behind people's use of implicit attitude in the political sphere.

Chapter 9 reviews and integrates the major empirical findings of the book. Specifically, I discuss their implications for citizen decision-making in immigration politics and beyond, paying special attention to how the presence and influence of implicit attitudes both complicates and deepens our understanding of reason and deliberation in the political realm. Finally, throughout my discussion here, I emphasize the normative implications raised by the presence of political attitudes whose influence is involuntary and unintended.

Alas, nine full chapters is a tall order. Let's begin our journey by turning to Chapter 2, where we will learn more about the organization of the mind and its reasoning faculties.

2

Two Ways of Thinking, Two Types of Attitudes

There is a certain novelty to implicit attitudes. The notion that people possess unspoken thoughts that can shape their judgments without their control is patently at odds with conventional wisdom about the deliberative and intentional nature of human reasoning (e.g., Bargh 2007: 1; Greenwald and Banaji 1995: 4; Taber 2003: 462). But novelty is not enough to carry a concept forward in political science. Without a detailed understanding about what implicit attitudes are, why they emerge, and what characteristics they display, the idea of implicit attitudes can easily become vacuous. Heavy conceptual lifting is therefore required before we even begin assembling a theoretical framework to explain the influence of implicit attitudes in the realm of immigration politics. Such is the goal of this chapter.

To this end, I begin by discussing and explaining social psychologists' (and a few political psychologists') changing views about human memory and reasoning. Here, researchers are increasingly learning that human thinking is organized into two systems, or forms, of reasoning that vary in terms of how they process and utilize information (e.g., Deutsch and Strack 2010; Gawronski and Bodenhausen 2011; Giner-Sorolla 2012; Haidt 2012; Kahneman 2011; Leander and Chartrand 2011; Lodge and Taber 2013; Rydell and McConnell 2006; Sloman 1996; Smith and DeCoster 2000). Each of these two systems operates under different rationales and by way of distinct cognitive principles. Whereas one system of reasoning is more conducive to the deliberative and controlled type of thinking that many political scientists are familiar with, the other form of reasoning facilitates more spontaneous and impulsive forms of thought. And, although many political scientists often think of deliberative thinking as primary (if not singular), research suggests people's impulsive reasoning often precedes their more deliberative cognitive efforts (e.g., Gawronski and Bodenhausen 2011; Lodge and Taber 2013; Olson and Fazio 2009).

Building on this difference between forms of thinking, I then explain the types of attitudes produced by each cognitive system, namely, explicit and implicit attitudes. Because explicit and implicit attitudes emanate from distinct reasoning systems, each type of attitude differs in its underlying substance and mode of operation (e.g., Rydell and McConnell 2006; Smith and DeCoster 2000; Wilson et al. 2000). Thus, for example, explicit attitudes reflect one's more considered thoughts; they enter one's judgments at the discretion of individuals (e.g., Gawronski and Bodenhausen 2006; Strack and Deutsch 2004). In contrast, implicit attitudes are deeply affective and spontaneously activated; they operate without people's full control (e.g., Fazio et al. 1995; Gawronski and Bodenhausen 2011; Payne et al. 2005; Smith and Nosek 2011).

In the third and last part of this chapter, I interrogate the qualitative differences between explicit and implicit attitudes by addressing some potential misgivings about the latter construct (e.g., Arkes and Tetlock 2004; Fazio and Olson 2003). To preview one of them: if implicit attitudes are hard to control and manipulate, does this mean they are beyond people's consciousness (e.g., Gawronski et al. 2006)? In wrestling with this and other skepticisms, my objective is not to settle these controversies. Instead, my more modest goal is to inject greater clarity and precision into my conceptualization and use of implicit attitudes. By doing so, I intend to lay a firmer foundation for the next chapter, which builds a theoretical framework around implicit attitudes to explain their origins and influence in US immigration politics.

But lest we get too ahead of ourselves, let's begin by examining the distinct forms of reasoning operating within people's minds.

Mental Structure: Two Systems of Reasoning

More and more, cognitive research is teaching us that human thinking can be thought of as being organized into two systems, or forms, of reasoning. These mental systems process information by way of distinct cognitive principles. As such, each system produces attitudes that vary in their underlying substance and nature, and in terms of how these varied attitudes operate in the service of decision making. The exact labels and specific criteria delimiting these cognitive systems can, and sometimes do, vary among teams of scholars (e.g., Deutsch and Strack 2010; Gawronski and Bodenhausen 2011; Kahneman 2011; Olson and Fazio 2009).[1] Yet the basic operating principles underlying these systems are widely acknowledged by researchers. Thus, I heuristically refer to these two forms of thinking as explicit and implicit cognition, a practice I adhere to in this chapter and the remainder of this book.

[1] For example, what I call implicit and explicit forms of reasoning are sometimes referred to as (respectively) system 1 and system 2 (Kahneman 2011), associative and propositional thinking (Gawronski and Bodenhausen 2011), impulsive and reflexive processes (Deutsch and Strack 2010), and spontaneous and deliberative processing (Olson and Fazio 2009).

Explicit Cognition: Making Meaning through Deliberation

Explicit cognition is theorized to operate on the basis of higher-order mental processes. More precisely, it enables people to use logic, language, and/or abstract representations to arrive at judgments and evaluations (e.g., Deutsch and Strack 2010; Fazio and Towles-Schwen 1999; Gawronski and Bodenhausen 2006; Kahneman 2011). As such, explicit cognition is a rule-based form of reasoning that allows individuals to interpret and validate information methodically (e.g., Smith and DeCoster 2000). To illustrate, consider the proposition 24 × 12. On the basis of explicit reasoning, one can assess this proposal by systematically employing a learned set of computational rules to arrive at the answer, which is 288. Similar cognitive principles underlie the survey response, a case more immediately familiar to many political scientists. From this view, a survey question is a proposition that is validated by individual respondents with an answer, an exercise resembling a rule-based process. For example, when confronted with a survey question, a respondent first actively works to interpret the query – what it actually means, and what it is asking for, precisely (Tourangeau et al. 2000). Based on this interpretation, the respondent then organizes and reports an answer by drawing on the considerations most immediately accessible to his mind (i.e., "at the top of the head") and matching this response to the available answer categories (Tourangeau et al. 2000; Zaller 1992; Zaller and Feldman 1992).

As these examples attest, explicit reasoning is a deliberative exercise involving nontrivial amounts of mental energy and focus. Indeed, Gailliot et al. (2007) have demonstrated that directing one's thoughts and attention actually reduces blood glucose levels, thus underlining the effortful character of explicit thought. Explicit cognition also entails self-awareness. As Rydell and McConnell (2006: 996) explain, "[j]udgments and behaviors rendered by this system are based on processes requiring at least some degree of conscious control." In the preceding examples, for instance, the novice mathematician has knowledge of the unfolding computation and the answer it produces, while the survey respondent is mindful of the opinion that she is verbally reporting. Thus, to describe explicit cognition as involving awareness is to say that people are cognizant of their deliberations (i.e., process), as well as the judgments and evaluations that it produces (i.e., outcomes) (Sloman 1996). In turn, the relatively effortful and conscious unfolding of explicit reasoning suggests it involves intentionality on the part of individuals. In other words, it takes place only if individuals voluntarily engage it, and it unfolds under their personal direction (e.g., Smith and DeCoster 2000).

As an effortful, controllable, and intentional form of reasoning, explicit cognition is a flexible form of thinking. Imagine, for example, an individual who, on the basis of explicit reasoning, is asked to make sense of the anagram UERSOIPPV. As Sloman (1996) explains, this person's first initial attempt to make a word out of the jumbled letters will likely be unsuccessful. But, with intention and effort, the person is likely to employ a different set of rules – perhaps by methodically rearranging the letters into plausible words – until deciphering the jumble as PURPOSIVE. In this way, explicit reasoning is pliable enough to allow people to adapt and respond systematically to the demands of information placed before them. Indeed, to return to the example of survey response, the pliability of explicit reasoning is what enables some individuals to construct an opinion on the spot, even if they have thought very little – if at all – about the topic being broached (e.g., Tourangeau et al. 2000; Zaller 1992).

Notwithstanding its strengths, however, explicit reasoning can also be grossly inefficient. Although explicit cognition enables humans to interpret and process information methodically, as the previous examples attest, its capacity to accomplish this end is inherently limited. For example, people's working memory – that part of the mind that is the focus of our conscious attention at any one time – is acutely circumscribed. Specifically, individuals can hold no more than 7 ± 2 chunks of information at any one time (Miller 1957). People's conscious attention to information, moreover, is serial in nature. For new information to enter our ken of awareness, extant information must be supplanted (e.g., Payne 1982; Shiffrin and Schneider 1977).

Thus, although flexible and adaptive, explicit reasoning is also limited in its capacity to ingest and process information. In light of these constraints, how is it that people avoid being completely overwhelmed by the complexity of information and decisions that they must regularly face in everyday life? Part of the answer, researchers are discovering, is that people's reasoning about pending decisions, judgments, and evaluations starts *before* they begin thinking explicitly, a feat accomplished by their capacity to reason implicitly.

Implicit Cognition: Making Meaning through Associations

In contrast to explicit cognition, implicit reasoning operates on the basis of lower-order, associational principles (e.g., Gawronski and Bodenhausen 2011; Giner-Sorolla 2012; Kahneman 2011; Rydell and McConnell 2006). As such, implicit reasoning is a nonverbalized form of thinking that enables individuals to form broad, but stable representations of what is *typical* in one's environment. This emphasis on typicality means implicit reasoning encodes and processes regularities that chronically emerge in one's surroundings. That is, it uncovers, learns, and stores recurring patterns in information we encounter. "This is important," Smith and DeCoster (2000: 109) explain, "so that general expectancies and long-term stable knowledge can be based on the average, typical properties of the environment." In this way, implicit reasoning facilitates one's explicit thinking by quickly providing working knowledge about previous decisions, judgments, or evaluations that resemble the current context demanding one's more effortful thoughts.

Implicit reasoning unfolds automatically. In this regard, Bargh (1994) reminds us that automatic processes are distinguished by the presence of four "horsemen," or signature traits. First, the instigation of an automatic process is often *unintentional*: people do not voluntarily engage it. Once initiated, however, an automatic process is generally difficult for an individual to *control*. This relative lack of control over automatic processes can be traced to their *efficiency* – they require minimal cognitive effort. Finally, automatic processes are often accompanied by a lack of *awareness* on the part of individuals. To be characterized as automatic, a cognitive process must contain one, some, or all of these signature traits (see Bargh 1994). Automaticity, then, is a matter of degree. The basic point, however, is that relative to explicit reasoning, implicit cognition is generally regulated by mental processes characterized by greater degrees of automaticity (e.g., Bargh et al. 1996; Haidt 2012; Leander and Chartrand 2011; Payne et al. 2002).

The automaticity of implicit cognition is nicely illustrated by people's ability to detect, learn, and encode environmental regularities to memory without being aware of how they acquired such knowledge. In one influential study, for example, Olson and Fazio (2001) exposed subjects to randomized information that systematically paired a novel cartoon character with positive or negative words (e.g., *excellent*, *awful*) and images (e.g., *puppies*, *cockroach*). Subjects were found to have developed positive (negative) impressions of the cartoon character, consistent with the valence of the information paired with the object. Critically, however, subjects were unable to recollect the patterns of information that yielded their impressions (see also Dijksterhuis 2004; Gawronski et al. 2014a; Gregg et al. 2006; Olson and Fazio 2002).

As the previous example attests, implicit reasoning allows individuals to draw basic inferences from complex information environments without taxing the more limited cognitive resources of their explicit reasoning system. Yet unlike explicit cognition, implicit reasoning is a more inflexible form of thinking. That is because the inferences it draws are based on stable *recurring* patterns of information. This emphasis on volume and consistency of information means implicit reasoning is relatively slower at adapting to new and novel information. In a series of experiments, for example, Rydell and McConnell (2006) demonstrated that subjects' impressions about a target named *Bob* were impervious to a few pieces of information contradicting these impressions. Only when the volume of contradictory information shifted substantially did subjects' impressions about *Bob* shift.[2]

[2] This does not mean that implicit attitudes are impervious to change. In fact, some research finds that implicit attitudes are sometimes contextually malleable (e.g., Olson and Fazio 2006; Wittenbrink et al. 2001). Against this backdrop, Gawronski and associates (2010) have recently shown that such momentary shifts in implicit attitudes reflect people's heightened attention to counter-attitudinal information. However, individuals generally treat such information as an exception to the "rule," with the initial valence of their implicit attitudes predominating in all other contexts.

The Connection between Explicit and Implicit Reasoning: Diverse and Discordant Views

My discussion to this point reveals a general sense of scholarly agreement that people engage in two types of reasoning, each operating on the basis of different principles. But this redoubt of consensus is surrounded by several organized forces, each with its own theoretical view about the precise interplay between explicit and implicit reasoning. On the one hand, one can interpret this as a "good thing" – a sign of theoretical breadth and maturity. On the other hand, theoretical vibrancy of this type can easily confound, rather than clarify, matters, especially if care is not taken to identify areas of agreement and disagreement, as well as charting new points of synergy going forward. Therefore, in what follows, I discuss three leading psychological models focused on the relationship between implicit and explicit cognition.

Two of these models – the *Associative–Propositional Evaluation* (APE) model and *Motivation and Opportunity as Determinants* (MODE) model – are native to social psychology. I review them because they expressly focus on the interplay between explicit and implicit reasoning and their corresponding cognitive outputs: explicit and implicit attitudes. The third model, *John Q. Public* (JQP), also focuses on the nexus between explicit and implicit cognition. I focus on it because, as far as I am aware, it is the only model of its kind within political science. My discussion of these models will pinpoint their strengths (as I see them), their weaknesses (also as I see them), and – most importantly – their implications for how these forms of reasoning manifest themselves in mass politics. In doing so, my main goal is to begin foreshadowing how the theoretical framework that I propose in the next chapter is an advancement relative to what has been done before.

Associative–Propositional Evaluation Model

The first model I consider is Gawronski and Bodenhausen's Associative–Propositional Evaluation (APE) model (Gawronski and Bodenhausen 2006, 2011). APE acknowledges that people's thinking is organized into two forms, which it dubs associative (i.e., implicit) and propositional (i.e., explicit). Generally speaking, associative thinking entails the activation of mental associations in memory – what APE scholars call "affective gut reactions" and I refer to as implicit attitudes. In turn, propositional thinking consists of validating the information implied by one's implicit attitude through propositions, or what I call explicit attitudes.

APE researchers stipulate that associative reasoning is sparked before its propositional variety, yet the former does not always structure the latter. In some cases it does. But in other instances, propositional thinking overwrites the output of one's associative reasoning, whereas in other cases, associative reasoning countermands the content of one's propositional thinking. APE traces this fluidity to whether propositional reasoning produces output that affirms one's associative thinking. As Gawronski and Bodenhausen (2011: 62–63) explain it:

"[A]ffective gut reactions are translated into the format of a propositional statement (e.g., a negative affective reaction toward object X is transformed into propositional statements such as 'I dislike X' or 'X is bad'). To the extent that this proposition is consistent with other propositional beliefs that are considered relevant for an evaluative judgment, it may be endorsed in a verbally reported explicit evaluation. If, however, the propositional evaluation implied by the affective gut response is inconsistent with other salient propositions that are considered relevant, the inconsistency has to be resolved to avoid aversive feelings of cognitive dissonance..."

Thus, although "gut reactions" – that is, implicit attitudes – are the first element evoked by associative reasoning, APE suggests that people use propositional reasoning to assess the veracity of these responses. From this view, then, the varied correlation between implicit and explicit attitudes often observed by scholars is less intriguing (Greenwald et al. 2009). When these correlations are high, APE suggests it is because people actually endorse the affective response evoked by associative reasoning. And, when these correlations are low, APE suggests it is because people propositionally disagree with the "gut reaction" they experience.

The ability to reconcile the mixed correspondence between implicit and explicit attitudes across different studies and topic domains is APE's main strength. It is also, paradoxically, its primary weakness, especially if we seek a model that explains how implicit attitudes shape *political* thinking. Indeed, for all of its precision in outlining how and why two attitude classes might correspond with each other (or not), APE leaves much to be desired in terms of deepening our understanding about the influence of implicit attitudes on political judgment and choice. Of course, one can simply retort that it is merely a matter of applying APE's insights to the political realm; that if there was ever a domain where propositional reasoning thrives, it is politics, which normatively values deliberation. Yet more than five decades of political science research teaches us that effortful thinking of the propositional type is variable rather than constant, and characterized by a low level of preponderance in the mass citizenry, at that (cf. Converse 1964; Delli Carpini and Keeter 1996; Zaller 1992).

Moreover, and especially relevant for my purposes, APE specifies a populace that is aware of its implicit attitudes. As two leading APE proponents contend: "people usually have *experiential access* to their affective gut reactions resulting from associative processes, and...they often rely upon these reactions in making propositional evaluative judgments (Gawronski and Bodenhausen 2011: 74)." Perhaps this is the case. Yet this claim is based mostly on studies that indirectly consider this matter, which suggests that it might be premature – certainly in political science, I think – to conclude that people are fully aware about their implicit attitudes (see Lodge and Taber 2013). Thus, although researchers should do more to clarify *what* about implicit attitudes people lack knowledge of (cf. Gawronski et al. 2006; Pérez 2013), I will argue that citizens are unaware about possessing implicit attitudes and the influence of these on their political evaluations.

But this is getting too far ahead too soon. Let us first see what additional lessons we might draw from other leading models of implicit and explicit cognition. For that, we turn to another team of social psychologists, this time lead by Russell Fazio.

Motivation and Opportunity as Determinants Model

We just learned that APE scholars see the link between implicit and explicit attitudes as hinging on the degree to which people engage in propositional (i.e., explicit) reasoning. But such effortful thinking, you might have noticed, presumes a degree of motivation to engage in it. And even then, such motivation might be insufficient, as people might also need the opportunity to follow through on it. These are, essentially, the main claims of the Motivation and Opportunity as Determinants (MODE) model (Fazio 1990; Fazio and Towles-Schwen 1999; Fazio et al. 1995; Olson and Fazio 2009).

Although predating APE and the explosion of implicit attitudes research in social psychology, MODE's insights have been usefully harnessed to explain the links between implicit and explicit attitudes (Olson and Fazio 2009). Fazio and his colleagues initially developed MODE to explain the ways through which spontaneous and deliberative processes shaped the connection between attitudes and behavior, where spontaneous processing refers to thinking that is generally automatic and low effort (i.e., implicit), and deliberative processing refers to thinking that is generally controlled and high effort (i.e., explicit).

In MODE's view, environmental cues automatically trigger a person's implicit attitude, which is conceptualized as the association between an object and its evaluation (e.g., Latino–Bad) (Fazio 2007). For some, the attitude is weak, for others it is strong, and for others still, it is somewhere in between. But the key insight here is that stronger implicit attitudes are more easily evoked. And, once they are spontaneously activated, they are ready to color one's subsequent behavior. Whether they do so, however, depends on a person's motivation and opportunity to edit the initial attitude tumbling out of his or her head. For instance, some people in some settings might be motivated to reach a valid decision. Other people in other situations might be motivated to curb a negative reaction against a racial group. In short, some people will feel more compelled than others to edit their spontaneous attitude.

Nevertheless, sensing a personal urge to amend an automatically activated attitude is often insufficient to stave off its influence on "downstream" behavior. Just as important, argue Fazio and his colleagues, is whether one has the opportunity to act on this motivation (e.g., Fazio and Towles-Schwen 1999; Fazio et al. 1995). For example, is there enough information to act on my motivation to reach a valid decision? Do I have enough time to correct an impulsive negative racial attitude, thus allowing me to satisfy a motivation to be racially impartial? As these and other examples attest, people can fully override an implicit attitude only if they have the motivation *and* opportunity to do so (Olson and Fazio 2009).

Compared to APE, then, MODE is arguably clearer about when, why, and among whom implicit attitudes *might* affect people's politics. For instance, whereas APE stresses the role that propositional (i.e., explicit) reasoning plays in shaping the influence of associative (i.e., implicit) thinking, MODE suggests that only some people (i.e., the motivated ones) engage in propositional reasoning – an insight consistent with the variable degree of political awareness in the US mass public (cf. Converse 1964; Delli Carpini and Keeter 1996; Sniderman et al. 1991; Zaller 1992). Moreover, MODE suggests that people will act on their motivation to engage in propositional reasoning *if* they are placed under auspicious circumstances, which might provide the information and resources to follow through on this motivation – an insight affirmed by voluminous political science research on the interplay between predispositions and political information (Taber and Young 2013).

But if MODE appears to have political implications written all over it, the devil is, as they say, in the details. For inasmuch as MODE deepens our appreciation for motivation's moderating influence on the link between implicit (i.e., spontaneous) and explicit (i.e., deliberative) reasoning, the types of motivations that MODE identifies do not seem to be immediately applicable or desirable from the vantage point of political science. Consider the motivation to reach a valid decision. On the surface, this possibility makes sense. Yet a more careful look at contemporary US politics suggests many citizens' political decisions often revolve around "being right" rather than "getting it right" (i.e., motivated reasoning) (Lodge and Taber 2013; Taber and Lodge 2006). Consider, too, a person's motivation to control prejudice (Fazio et al. 1995). This motivation also makes intuitive sense. But it is typically measured via self-report by answering statements like "In today's society, it's important that one not be perceived as prejudiced in any manner," which arguably lends itself to social desirability bias. In fact, consistent with this possibility, some evidence suggests these items tap into more than a motivation to control prejudice.[3] Finally, and perhaps most relevant to political scientists, measures of this motivation have been validated mostly on college students, thus raising strong doubts about their utility among more variegated adult samples.

In short, although MODE takes us some steps closer to understanding how implicit and explicit thinking might shape political judgments, we are not fully

[3] For instance, Dunton and Fazio (1997: 319–320) report that the same factor structure for their seventeen items did not consistently emerge across the three convenience samples they administered them to.

there yet. For that, we will need to return to Stony Brook University and once again heed the insights of two of its leading political psychologists, Milton Lodge and Charles Taber.

John Q. Public

My discussion of APE and MODE reveals that social psychologists have much to say about the ties between implicit and explicit reasoning. Yet despite their useful insights, these models are notably silent about how these forms of thought affect political judgments, if at all. This matters because *political* decision making has peculiar features that caution against a wholesale transfer of these psychological models to politics. For example, APE argues that the degree of correspondence between associative and propositional thinking regulates whether implicit attitudes affect people's judgments. But such cognitive consistency, political scientists teach us, is a very high threshold for most members of the mass public to meet (cf. Converse 1964; Sniderman et al. 1991), which means the political influence of implicit attitudes might be more prevalent than what APE anticipates. In turn, by focusing on motivation and opportunity, MODE claims that the biasing effects of implicit attitudes are limited to some people in some cases. Yet political scientists find that politics often affirm, rather than modify, people's biases (cf. Huddy and Terkildsen 1993; Mendelberg 2001). Hence, MODE also risks mischaracterizing how ubiquitous implicit attitudes are in politics.

In the wake of these blind spots, Lodge and Taber (2013) have undertaken the most comprehensive effort to date to explain the dynamic relations between these forms of reasoning and politics, as enshrined in their *John Q. Public* (JQP) model. I have already extensively reviewed JQP in Chapter 1. My discussion here will therefore serve to compare and distinguish JQP from APE and MODE, while explaining how I think JQP falls short in areas that APE and MODE have greater strengths in. In doing so, my goals are to clarify what we still have to learn about the ties between implicit/explicit reasoning and politics, while outlining some of the ways that the framework I develop in the next chapter improves on these innovating models.

JQP, like APE and MODE, specifies two forms of reasoning, which it labels unconscious (i.e., implicit) and conscious (i.e., explicit). Like APE and MODE, JQP also views implicit reasoning as preceding its explicit variety. Yet unlike these social psychological models, JQP sees a robustly symbiotic relationship between implicit and explicit reasoning, with the output of the former directing the character of the latter. Indeed, JQP goes as far as claiming that explicit reasoning is a rationalization of the spontaneous affective reactions first triggered by one's implicit reasoning (Zajonc 1980; 1984). More precisely, JQP claims that such affective reactions are the first element in citizens' cognitive stream, which matters because affect will color whatever comes after (i.e., *hot cognition*), either by directly shaping evaluations of political objects (i.e., *affect transfer*), or by retrieving considerations from memory that are congruent with this first response (i.e., *affect contagion*). As Lodge and Taber (2013: 21) explain:

> "[C]itizens might...consciously build evaluations of political figures, groups, or ideas from well-reasoned foundations...In the context of hot cognition, affect contagion, and affect transfer, however, such cold evaluations will be exceedingly rare...Far more common...will be the reverse causal pathway from evaluation to deliberation."

Bear in mind, it is not that JQP deems citizens incapable of deliberative reasoning. But the affective response triggered by implicit reasoning happens so quickly and without awareness, according to JQP, that the deck is stacked in favor of implicit reasoning dictating the output of explicit thinking. Indeed, the power of JQP lies in its unequivocal emphasis on unconscious processing. Here, a political stimulus sparks an affective reaction on the order of milliseconds. And, within a few milliseconds more, this affective response biases the sample of additional considerations one retrieves from long-term memory. By the time people are aware about what is going on, it is too late. Citizens simply rationalize their feelings.

These are certainly a powerful set of insights. But some could say they seem deterministic, for unlike APE and MODE, JQP comes quite close to treating implicit and explicit reasoning as unitary rather than distinct. This matters because it implies that explicit reasoning nearly *always* depends on its implicit analog. This view, however, clashes strongly with the empirically grounded insights of APE and MODE, which suggest that the robust correspondence between implicit and explicit reasoning really represents a special circumstance. In APE, this case emerges when one's propositions affirm one's gut reaction (Gawronski and Bodenhausen 2011). In MODE, this case arises when one has no motivation or opportunity to edit a spontaneous response (Olson and Fazio 2009). Yet outside of these limited circumstances, APE and MODE suggest conditions under which the inherent symbiosis in JQP might be broken. For instance, engaging in propositional reasoning might lead to invalidation of one's initial "gut" reaction (per APE). Or, one might have a heightened motivation and opportunity to edit a spontaneously activated attitude (per MODE). All of this is to suggest that there are some conditions under which the strong correspondence between implicit and explicit reasoning can be attenuated. And, insofar as it is, it suggests that each form of reasoning might produce two types of attitudes, each with different observable implications for political judgment and choice. In particular, it is possible (as we will learn in later chapters) that explicit and implicit attitudes can pull individuals' political judgments in countervailing directions.

Let us, then, turn to a more focused discussion of these constructs – explicit and implicit attitudes – and begin defining what they are and revealing how it is that they differ from each other.

Two Forms of Reasoning = Two Types of Attitudes

Explicit Attitudes

Explicit attitudes are verbalized evaluations of objects. In other words, they are people's declarations about how they view or what they believe about a given group, individual, or issue (see, e.g., Eagly and Chaiken 1993: Chapter 1). In the context of public opinion surveys, explicit attitudes are the self-reported opinions people share with researchers (Tourangeau et al. 2000; Zaller 1992).

Explicit attitudes exhibit three characteristics that underscore their origins in people's deliberative system. First, they are verbal expressions that draw directly on language, a higher-order mental process that our deliberative system commands. That is, they involve language in their validation and expression. Second, explicit attitudes require nontrivial amounts of cognitive effort and control, be it in their actual production or in their retrieval and use. For example, to articulate one's attitude verbally, one must be able to retrieve it from memory. And, if one has not formed an attitude about a given object, mental effort is required to cobble one together (Zaller 1992; Zaller and Feldman 1992; see also Schwarz 2007). Third, explicit attitudes entail consciousness. Because retrieving and expressing an explicit attitude is premised on introspection, a significant degree of self-awareness is involved as a person actively recalls a formed attitude from memory or constructs one from scratch.

Implicit Attitudes

In contrast to explicit attitudes, implicit attitudes are basic affective responses to social objects (e.g., Gawronski and Bodenhausen 2006; Hofmann et al. 2005; Payne et al. 2005; Ranganath et al. 2008; Smith and Nosek 2011; see also Spence and Townsend 2008). My description of implicit attitudes as "basic" is designed to call attention to the elementary nature of the evaluations they entail. Steeped in lower-order, associational forms of reasoning, implicit attitudes are nonverbalized appraisals. In rudimentary fashion, implicit attitudes reflect a person's learned but unspoken judgment of objects as *good* or *bad*, *favorable* or *unfavorable*, or *pleasant* or *unpleasant*. The parsimony of implicit attitudes, however, should not be taken as a sign of triviality. Though unrefined on the surface, simple valenced judgments like these are a fundamental way that humans make meaning of their world (Osgood 1962; Zajonc 1980). In the case at hand, implicit attitudes provide individuals with an instant diagnosis of an object: a quick evaluation whose validity is backed by stable and recurring patterns in information about that object.

The immediacy of the evaluative information that implicit attitudes provide is traced to their affective nature. By defining implicit attitudes in *affective* terms, I am directly acknowledging their emotional roots. Here, the seminal work of George Marcus and his colleagues suggests that spontaneous emotional responses to political stimuli can have powerful downstream consequences for citizens' more effortful political deliberations, including the extent to which individuals become politically attentive and engaged (Brader and Marcus 2013; Marcus 2003; Marcus, Neuman, and MacKuen 2000).[4] Emotions, Brader (2006: 51) explains, are "specific sets of physiological and mental dispositions triggered by the brain in response to the perceived significance of a situation or object for an individual's goals (up to and including survival)." Consistent with this definition, implicit attitudes are raw object evaluations that help individuals resolve – rapidly and without deliberation – the challenge of "approach" and "avoidance." That is, implicit attitudes provide people with a quick sense of whether an object poses a possible danger to them.

Neuroscientists have shown, for example, that implicit attitudes (but not self-reported attitudes) are strongly linked to activation of the amygdala – a subcortical brain structure associated with emotional responses to negative stimuli (Phelps et al. 2000; see also Cunningham et al. 2004a, 2004b). The connection between implicit attitudes and amygdala activity has helped scholars to pinpoint when and how implicit attitudes are mentally engaged. As Hofmann and Wilson (2010: 198) explain, the amygdala "has privileged access to incoming sensory information at a relatively crude level of perceptual analysis – before the results of more accurate, but also more time-consuming, high-level perceptual analyses can enter conscious awareness." This suggests implicit attitudes are triggered preconsciously, before one's higher-order mental processes are engaged. This view is highly consistent with the scholarship of Zajonc and others (Lodge and Taber 2013; Murphy and Zajonc 1993; Zajonc 1980, 1984), which shows that basic affective responses to objects can be produced without people being aware of the stimulus or the reaction it generates.

Taken together, these insights converge toward a clear view. Implicit attitudes serve a directive function. In the presence of fitting stimuli, they are spontaneously activated, providing individuals with immediate but nonverbalized diagnostic information. This information is mentally accessible before one's higher-order faculties for thinking are engaged. Consequently, implicit attitudes can structure how the mind responds to the context at hand.

Implicit Attitudes: Are They Really Attitudes? Are They Actually Implicit?

Implicit attitudes are said to be produced through a nonverbalized, associational form of reasoning. Accordingly, people develop spontaneous affective responses to objects on the basis of recurring patterns in information about those objects. Yet some social psychologists have questioned whether these affective responses really qualify as *attitudes*, per se.[5] Rather than reflecting

[4] I say "suggests" because these spontaneous emotional responses are typically gauged via self-reported measures.

[5] For a more detailed overview regarding this point and related issues, see Pérez (2013).

one's own endorsed evaluation of an object, these critics maintain, such affective responses might instead reflect cultural learning. That is, they might capture one's knowledge about how society views or esteems a particular object, but not necessarily one's own personal attitude toward an object (e.g., Arkes and Tetlock 2004; Karpinski and Hilton 2001; Olson and Fazio 2004). For example, given the news media's negative portrayal of African Americans (Gilens 1999; Gilliam and Iyengar 2000), one might learn to spontaneously associate blacks with negative affect. But this association, critics would say, simply reflects a cultural bias against blacks – not one's personal evaluation of African Americans as a group. Indeed, as Devine (1989) has shown, even people who score low on measures of self-reported prejudice toward blacks possess knowledge of negative social stereotypes about African Americans that can be easily called to mind, without necessarily endorsing its content.

There is an intuitive ring to this critique. If, as research suggests, implicit attitudes are hard to voluntarily control, then surely they are not personally endorsed attitudes – they must be artifacts or byproducts of the culture a person is steeped in. Yet one challenge to this view is that explicit attitudes are also acquired through exposure to one's culture (see Nosek and Hansen 2008). And yet, scholars hardly hesitate to characterize self-reported attitudes as being an individual's own evaluation of an object. For this reason, Banaji (2001: 139) suggests that the fallacy in thinking about implicit attitudes as merely cultural residue "may arise from assuming that there is a bright line separating one's self from one's culture, an assumption that is becoming less tenable as researchers discover the deep reach of culture into individual minds..." For this reason, she contends, it is "artificial, if not patently odd, to separate...attitudes into 'culture' versus 'self' parts."

In fact, conceding that people might passively learn implicit attitudes through mass culture does not mean the attitude is not a person's own. As Fazio (2007: 609) reminds us, more important than how an attitude is learned is whether it contains evaluative knowledge about an object. And, in the case of implicit attitudes, this evaluative knowledge is often a robust predictor of people's own *personal* preferences, tastes, and behaviors, a consideration we will revisit in Chapter 5 (e.g., Greenwald et al. 2009; Hofmann et al. 2005).

Think of it this way. Let's say we developed a new self-reported measure of a hypothetical attitude. Many of our social psychology and political science colleagues would expect us to validate this new tool by (in part) establishing that individual differences in this measure correspond robustly with individual differences in measures of other relevant outcomes (e.g., policy preferences). Simple enough, right? But this is exactly what the accumulated record on the predictive validity of implicit attitudes suggests (Greenwald et al. 2009) – individual differences in measures of implicit attitude are robustly associated with individual differences in measures of attitudinal and behavioral outcomes. Thus, notwithstanding their implicit nature, it would appear that the "[t]he associations in our heads belong to us (Nosek and Hansen 2008: 553)."

But for some social psychologists and political scientists, the resistance is not to implicit attitudes as a concept, but rather, to specific measures of this construct. And here, the Implicit Association Test (IAT) stands alone both as the most widely used *and* most thoroughly critiqued measure of implicit attitude. I will reserve a more detailed discussion of this measure's mechanics to Chapter 5, which adapts this tool to the realm of implicit attitudes toward Latino immigrants. But for now, let me simply state that the IAT assesses implicit attitudes by gauging the strength of associations between an object (e.g., Latino immigrants) and positive or negative valence (e.g., Bad) through a timed classification task. This is, for sure, a peculiar way to measure "attitudes." But given that so much of the evidence on the predictive validity of implicit attitudes comes from studies using the IAT, why are there still strong reservations about this measure's ability to capture people's attitudes effectively?

Part of the answer, I think, has to do with a tacit assumption among some researchers that self-reports more faithfully reflect a given attitude, belief, or value. After all, unlike the IAT's timed sorting tasks, we can see the question(s) that are designed to capture an explicit (i.e., self-reported) construct. Nevertheless, this presumption yields a very false sense of security, for the questions we ask to capture explicit attitudes are but indirect indicators of the phenomenon we are interested in observing. The risk of reification is therefore high. Remarking on the logic behind attitude self-reports, Pérez (2013: 276) explains:

> "What we observe are responses to measures of attitudes and, on the basis of those responses, we *infer* the presence of attitudes. This reminds us that assessing attitudes – even explicit ones – is inherently risky. We can read or hear a survey question, yet the underlying evaluation is never seen."

What is more, Taber and Young (2013) suggest that self-reports invite their own, often unacknowledged, challenges and limitations in applied research. In particular, these authors point out that the common practice of using self-reports to predict other self-reports encourages a "shell game" of sorts in studies of political opinion. As they explain:

> "...the more often self-reports are used to predict self-reports; the more often attitudes are used to predict attitudes...the more strongly we step away from *explaining* opinion formation and toward merely *characterizing* the opinions by their associations with other constructs that bear strong resemblances to the opinions themselves." (549)

Against this backdrop, these authors propose that to more fully and accurately understand public opinion, researchers should strive to employ measures of attitudes that are, to the extent possible, devoid of political content and more focused on cognitive processing. Accordingly, they recommend indirect and task-based measures, of which the IAT is but one. Indeed, as a rapid-fire classification task, the IAT is utterly bereft of any political content, reflecting little more than how strongly or weakly one associates a given object with positive or negative valence. Hence, viewed from Taber and Young's (2013) perspective, the IAT stands as a promising measure that can help political scientists establish a more credible connection between "how" people think and "what" they want out of politics.

A slightly different criticism of implicit attitudes involves their actual distinctiveness from self-reported attitudes. This perspective readily concedes that implicit attitudes are personally endorsed evaluations. But it takes issue with how distinct implicit attitudes really are from their self-reported analogs. More to the point, this view contends that implicit and explicit attitudes are really the same underlying phenomenon measured in different ways.

This view's most ardent proponent is the social psychologist Russell Fazio (cf. Fazio and Towles-Schwen 1999; Olson and Fazio 2009). As he explains, implicit attitudes are spontaneously activated, nonverbalized evaluations of objects, while explicit attitudes are controlled and verbalized judgments of objects. These attitudes, he suggests, capture the same evaluation at different points in the cognitive stream (see also Lodge and Taber 2013). Measures of implicit attitude capture one's evaluation early in one's thought process, when the attitude is automatically triggered and difficult to control. Self-reported measures capture the same attitude further "downstream," once one has engaged the ability to verbalize and control one's evaluations. If implicit and explicit attitudes diverge from each other, Fazio reasons, it is because some people are motivated to edit the initial (implicit) attitude tumbling out of their heads (cf. Gawronski and Bodenhausen 2006, 2011).

Some research supports Fazio's claims. Nosek (2005) and others, for example, have found that several individual-level differences shape the degree to which explicit and implicit attitudes correspond. When concern about, say, self-presentation, is low, the correlation between implicit and explicit attitudes increases, suggesting that individual-level motivations affect the degree of correspondence between implicit and explicit attitudes toward an object. In fact, as we learned earlier in this chapter, Fazio and his colleagues have shown that when individuals are given the opportunity to act on motivations like these – for example, more time to complete one's self-reported attitude toward an object – there is increased discordance between a person's implicit and explicit attitude. Such evidence suggests that the often weak association between implicit and explicit attitudes is partly due to how these attitudes are measured, not to differences in the attitudes themselves.

Yet two additional lines of research sit uncomfortably next to the claim that explicit and implicit attitudes reflect differences in measurement, rather than underlying substance. One of these research streams directly examines the role that systematic *and* random measurement error play in the correspondence between implicit and explicit attitude reports. Recall that explicit attitudes are gauged via self-report, while implicit attitudes, as we will learn in later chapters, are tapped through reaction-time measures that assess how fast (usually in milliseconds) people complete sorting tasks. Obviously, the structure of each attitude measure differs. Hence, while the attitude in question might be the same (as Fazio predicts), differences can emerge because of how the attitude is reported (i.e., systematic measurement error). Adding to the illusion of distinct attitudes is the presence of random measurement error, which further cuts down on the correlations between explicit and implicit attitudes (e.g., an ambulance wailing by, thus breaking one's focus as one completes an attitude report).

Studies have shown, however, that once systematic and random sources of measurement error are statistically accounted for, explicit and implicit attitudes remain empirically distinct (e.g., Cunningham et al. 2001; Greenwald and Farnham 2000; Nosek and Smyth 2007). To be sure, the attenuation of measurement error *does* strengthen the correspondence between explicit and implicit attitudes. Yet this enhanced relationship is generally not strong enough to warrant the claim that explicit/implicit attitudes are the *same* concept measured in *different* ways. If anything, this evidence reaffirms the view that explicit and implicit attitudes mainly differ because they are produced by different cognitive processes. As Ranganath et al. (2008: 386) explain, distinguishing implicit/explicit attitudes "by the processes they are presumed to measure (automatic versus controlled) is more meaningful than distinguishing based on ... measurement."

Of course, it is still possible that these empirical differences are without distinction; that each attitude ultimately overlaps with the other in competing for influence on people's judgments and behaviors. Yet psychologists have amassed ample evidence that individual differences in implicit attitude predict individual differences in judgments, evaluations, and behavior across several social domains (e.g., Fazio et al. 1995; Greenwald et al. 1998; Payne et al. 2005), a pattern that is robust to the inclusion of self-reported attitudes toward the same object (Greenwald et al. 2009). Taken together, then, these findings underscore three key points that are important as we move forward, namely, implicit attitudes are (1) a unique type of evaluation; (2) produced by automatic cognitive processes; and (3) consequential to judgments and behavior, independent of self-reported attitudes.

The last misgiving about implicit attitudes that I address is, in some ways, the most open to controversy, particularly because it is less systematically studied than other aspects of implicit attitude. Here, the concern is with the degree to which implicit attitudes are *subconscious*. Up to this point, I have tried to limit my direct labeling of implicit attitudes as subconscious, emphasizing more instead the automatic and inescapable influence that implicit attitudes seem to produce over individuals. This is not because I do not believe that implicit attitudes contain some aspects that might be considered subconscious. Rather, I have done so because, without careful consideration and clarification, I risk giving the wrong impression about how, precisely, implicit attitudes might be considered subconscious.

The insights of Gawronski et al. (2006) are especially instructive in this instance. As these authors carefully explain, there are at least three ways that implicit attitudes might be considered subconscious, though which of these aspects is meant by researchers is typically left unstated and untested. For example, it is plausible that implicit attitudes are subconscious in the sense that people are unaware of the causes of their attitudes, that is, they have no knowledge of how they acquired their attitudes (i.e., source awareness). Another way that implicit attitudes can be subconscious involves knowledge of the actual attitude. Here, implicit attitudes are subconscious insofar as people are unaware that they possess the attitude in question (i.e., content awareness). Third, implicit attitudes might be considered subconscious inasmuch as they shape judgments and behaviors without one's awareness of this influence (i.e., impact awareness) (see also Gawronski 2009; Hahn and Gawronski 2014).

The review of relevant evidence on these aspects of implicit attitudes by Gawronski et al. (2006) suggests that of the three varieties of (sub)consciousness, the third one is the most tenable and empirically supported (i.e., impact awareness). This is not to say that people are fully aware of their implicit attitudes or where they stem from. Rather, in the authors' estimation, the available evidence suggests that source and content awareness weakly discriminate between implicit and explicit attitudes.

But perhaps the bigger lesson imparted by Gawronski and colleagues (2006) is their plea for researchers to specify and test the reputed subconscious aspect(s) of implicit attitudes. As they explain, whether implicit attitudes are unconscious "should be treated as an empirical question, rather than as a methodological dictum" (486). Agreed. And so, to this end, I propose and test the extent to which implicit attitudes in the political realm are subconscious in the sense that people are (1) generally unaware of how these attitudes affect their more deliberative reasoning (i.e., impact awareness); and (2) unaware that they possess this attitude (i.e., content awareness).

Conclusion: Lessons Learned and Moving Forward

The goal of this chapter was to clear the conceptual underbrush surrounding implicit attitudes, to bring them into sharper relief to understand better their cognitive origins and nature, especially in contrast to their more familiar, self-reported counterparts. Thus, I first discussed and explained social (and some political) psychologists' changing views about how the mind reasons. The main lesson emerging from this conversation is that human cognition is characterized by two systems of reasoning. People can and do think deliberately and intentionally. But people also think impulsively and involuntarily. And both types of reasoning faculties, we learned, reside in the same individual, with more impulsive forms of thought preceding one's more effortful and deliberative reasoning. This is not a cognitive glitch in humans. Rather, the distillation of human thought into two systems of reasoning serves an adaptive purpose, enabling individuals to more seamlessly navigate the inherent complexity of their decision-making environments.

Building on this distinction in reasoning forms, I then defined and discussed the characteristics of attitudes produced by each cognitive system: explicit and implicit attitudes. We learned that the former is verbalized, premised on introspection, and steeped in declarative knowledge. The latter, in contrast, is nonverbalized, affective, and automatically called to mind. Given these characteristics of implicit attitude, we concluded that this construct enjoys relative primacy in the unfolding of one's thought processes. It is activated before one engages in more effortful forms of thought, and for this reason, can influence one's actual deliberations.

Because implicit attitudes are thought to play such a key role in human thinking, I focused strong attention on three skepticisms often raised about this construct: whether implicit attitudes merit the label *attitude*; whether implicit attitudes capture evaluations that are different than those obtained via self-report; and whether and to what extent implicit attitudes are subconscious. By many indications, I explained, implicit attitudes are attitudes in the sense that they contain evaluative information that shapes people's own preferences and behavior. Moreover, this evaluative information is distinct both in substance and behavioral consequences from self-reported attitudes. And, so far as my use of implicit attitudes is concerned, I contend that they are subconscious in the sense that people might be unaware that they possess this attitude, and have no knowledge of how it affects their decision-making processes – two claims I test in subsequent chapters.

Taken together, these insights clarify and extend our understanding about human cognition, in general, and implicit attitudes, in particular. But these lessons are nothing more than starting points; theoretical building blocks, as it were, but not a theory proper. Carrying these lessons forward, the objective in Chapter 3 is to develop said theory, which will aim to explain the emergence and influence of implicit attitudes in the realm of immigration politics.

3

Implicit Expectations and Explicit Political Reasoning

We have learned that people's minds are organized into two forms of reasoning that produce two types of attitudes, each with its own attributes. But our discussion to this point has been more psychological than political. We have gained a clearer understanding of the mind's cognitive processes and attitudinal outputs. Yet we have a fuzzier sense about how these psychological insights apply to the politics of immigration: a prominent, group-centric issue that regularly captures the attention of political elites and members of the mass public (Brader et al. 2008; King 2000; Ngai 2004; Santa Ana 2002; Tichenor 2002). Sharpening this sense is crucial, for what we learn about the link between implicit attitudes and immigration politics can help us to understand how the former might affect the politics of other issues with similar features (e.g., antiterrorism, crime).

This chapter fully draws out the political implications of implicit attitudes by explaining why and how impulsive reasoning affects people's more effortful political deliberations. To meet this objective, I draw primarily on Lodge and Taber's (2013) political archetype of unconscious processing – *John Q. Public* (JQP). My goal here is to draw on and expand vital elements of this model to clarify how, exactly, implicit attitudes leave an imprint on people's explicit judgments of US immigration policies. I augment my theory-building efforts here by drawing on some crucial insights from the *Associative–Propositional Evaluation* (APE) model and the *Motivation and Opportunity as Determinants* (MODE) model, which I discussed in the previous chapter. These latter frameworks allow me to anticipate the possibility that under some conditions, people's implicit and explicit attitudes can pull in countervailing directions. In the case of immigration politics, for example, some people might be able to limit the influence of explicit attitude toward Latino immigrants, even as their implicit attitude toward this group boosts their opposition to immigration.

I dub my theoretical explanation "implicit expectations," which refers to the mental process by which automatic attitudes structure citizens' more effortful deliberations about immigration. More precisely, my framework explains how impulsive forms of thought can color people's interpretation of information about a political issue, as well as how that information is deployed in the political judgments they ultimately make. This process begins with recurring patterns in political discourse, which enable citizens to develop implicit attitudes toward protagonists in political debates (cf. Gregg et al. 2006; Rydell and McConnell 2006). Once encoded to long-term memory (LTM), the broaching of political issues is said to spontaneously call forth people's implicit attitudes toward a relevant political object (Lodge and Taber 2013: 17–20). As nonverbalized, affective evaluations, implicit attitudes rapidly inform citizens about how they view a political issue *before* they begin to actively consider relevant information about the political topic at hand. People can, and will, directly draw on these feelings to make a political judgment (Lodge and Taber 2013: 56–58). Moreover, these feelings can, and also will, bias the retrieval of additional considerations in the direction of the affect sparked by one's implicit attitude (Lodge and Taber 2013: 58–59).

Each of these pathways, I argue, leads citizens to judge immigration policies in accordance with their implicit attitudes toward Latino immigrants, even when these subjective thoughts are contradicted by objective information before them. This occurs, I contend, because the interplay between implicit attitudes and explicit political reasoning is subconscious: citizens are unaware about how their implicit attitudes shape their explicit decision making (Gawronski et al. 2006: 491; Lodge and Taber 2013: 3; Pérez 2013: 288–289). In this way, the political mind gets what it implicitly expects – sometimes, despite what citizens explicitly strive toward.

Political Discourse, Associational Reasoning, and the Formation of Implicit Attitudes

Implicit expectations are said to be triggered when the broaching of a policy issue (e.g., immigration) spontaneously calls forth a citizen's implicit attitude toward a relevant political object (e.g., Latino immigrants). But before we can understand how implicit attitudes affect explicit decisions, we must explain why these types of attitudes emerge in the first place. I claim that accumulated discourse on political topics enables citizens to form implicit attitudes through associational reasoning. In particular, systematic patterns in political discourse suggest how political issues should be understood and, most importantly, who the relevant political actors are.

By this view, how policy issues are publicly discussed, and the extent to which these views are disseminated, promote the development of implicit attitudes at the mass level. To be sure, public debate about policy issues can plausibly manifest itself in innumerable ways. It can touch on many, often esoteric, aspects of an issue. It can also speak to an issue from various angles. Yet social and political institutions often serve to tame potentially unwieldy information about politics by narrowing its scope and packaging it into simpler themes with wider mass appeal. This is certainly true of news media. Newspaper stories. Television news segments. Political cartoons. It is through these and other communication media that "citizens are bombarded with suggestions about how issues should be understood" (Kinder 1998: 821). In particular, I contend that news discourse hones political objects while providing a context for their evaluation. That is, discourse makes salient political objects, ties them to policy issues, and implies a specific evaluation of them. Two mechanisms facilitate this sequence: priming and framing (see Iyengar and Kinder 1987).

Priming refers to the process by which political considerations are called forth and put within people's mental reach. By calling attention to some considerations at the expense of others, priming establishes standards by which citizens make political decisions. In politics, news media often perform this priming role (Iyengar and Kinder 1987; Krosnick and Kinder 1990; Stoker 1993). Gilens (1999), for example, has masterfully shown how news media have primed Americans to automatically associate African Americans with the issue of welfare by overwhelmingly focusing on this racial group more than others when reporting on poverty. As he explains: "From 1967 to 1992, blacks averaged 57 percent of the poor people pictured in ... [news] magazines – about twice the true proportion of blacks among the nation's poor" (Gilens 1999: 114; cf. Clawson and Trice 2000).

Framing, in contrast, helps to explain how citizens might evaluate salient political objects on the basis of this very same discourse. Frames provide "a central organizing idea or story line that provides meaning to an unfolding strip of events ... [it] suggests what the controversy is about" (Gamson and Modigliani 1987: 143; see also Druckman 2001: 227). Put differently, frames convey a sense of how political elites understand an issue and what aspects of the issue are deemed most relevant for its evaluation (e.g., Gamson 1992; Iyengar 1991). For instance, Gamson and Modigliani (1989) show how in the wake of the 1986 Chernobyl nuclear accident in the Soviet Union, the majority of US television news stories framed discussions of nuclear energy in terms of either (1) officials' overconfidence in harnessing nuclear power or (2) the hidden dangers of radiation effects in the long run. Yet frames emphasizing greater US energy independence through nuclear power received trivial media attention. This imbalance in frames was consequential. Opinion polls after Chernobyl revealed more negative attitudes toward nuclear facilities.

The success of priming and framing in promoting the development of implicit attitudes at the mass level hinges on the repetition of patterns produced by these processes. By continuously focusing public attention on a political object over others, and by repeatedly framing this object in a particular fashion, citizens are presented with more opportunities to develop and rehearse the evaluative associations of political objects implied by news discourse. As

Rydell and McConnell (2006: 1001) explain, implicit attitudes are rooted in "the totality of the evaluative information associated with an attitude object." Indeed, recall that scholarship suggests people develop implicit attitudes about objects in the direction of the valenced information that attends those objects (Dijksterhuis 2004; Olson and Fazio 2001, 2002). This suggests that if individuals are exposed to information that chronically pairs objects with negative (positive) stimuli, then they will acquire negative (positive) implicit attitudes that reflect those information patterns.

Of course, I readily acknowledge that not all individuals within the mass public ingest information about social objects at similar rates or to the same degree. Some people simply pay more attention to their information environment than others (e.g., Delli Carpini and Keeter 1996; Zaller 1992), with possible consequences for the strength of implicit attitudes, as well as the impact of those attitudes on political judgments. I consider these possibilities in later chapters.[1] But for now, suffice it to say that priming and framing are theorized to influence the content and tone of information about social objects, thus helping to encourage the formation of implicit attitudes.

Contextual Triggers and the Spontaneous Activation of Implicit Attitudes

Through their capacity for associational reasoning, citizens learn to link specific political objects to certain policy domains. Given this connection, I claim that drawing attention to a policy issue will call forth people's implicit attitude toward a relevant political object. This activation occurs automatically. In light of fitting stimuli, implicit attitudes spring to mind involuntarily, with minimal cognitive effort, and with little active direction.

For example, social psychologist Russell Fazio and his associates (1986) have shown that merely presenting an object spontaneously evokes one's affective evaluation of that object (i.e., implicit attitude) (cf. Bargh et al. 1992; Fazio et al. 1995). In one set of studies, Fazio and his team examined how exposure to an object facilitated the speed with which adjectives were classified as having positive or negative connotation. If a person had a negative attitude toward, say, *cockroach*, she was expected to classify a negative word (*terrible*) more quickly than a positive one (*wonderful*) after encountering *cockroach*, because of the shared valence between object and adjective. Across three experiments, Fazio's team found evidence supporting this "automatic activation" hypothesis.

Equally powerful, but more politically relevant evidence of "automatic activation" is furnished by Lodge and Taber (2013; cf. Burdein et al. 2006; Cassino and Lodge 2007). In one of their experiments, subjects read information about a hypothetical congressional candidate, William Lucas. Following this exercise,

[1] Specifically, Chapter 5 examines the extent to which education levels are associated (or not) with levels of implicit attitude. In turn, Chapter 7 investigates the degree to which higher education levels strengthen (or weaken) the link between implicit attitudes and political judgments.

subjects completed an attitude-priming task similar to the one employed by Fazio's team, where the prime was the surname Lucas. Consistent with "automatic activation," Lodge and Taber (2013: 79) found that Lucas supporters reacted more quickly to positive target words (e.g., proud) and more slowly to negative target words (e.g., weak), while Lucas opponents displayed the opposite pattern. These authors then show, through additional studies on additional political concepts, that such reaction time patterns emerge only when the interval between presentation of the prime and a target word is short (e.g., 300 milliseconds), but not when it is long (e.g., 1,000 milliseconds), as the former is too short a window for conscious expectations to develop (Lodge and Taber 2013: 85–86). Finally, and perhaps most crucially, Lodge and Taber (2013: 87–88) demonstrate this general pattern is robust to using target words that are "affectively *un*ambiguous and semantically *un*related" to political concepts, thus cementing their *hot cognition* hypothesis – the notion that automatically activating a concept spontaneously triggers its affective evaluation, thereby infusing the processing of political information with affect from the start.

One additional point merits further attention before moving on. The accumulated work of Russell Fazio, Milton Lodge, Charles Taber, and other social and political psychologists establishes that "automatic activation" emerges when the triggering stimulus is presented subliminally (cf. Burdein et al. 2006; Fazio et al. 1995; Kam 2007; Lodge and Taber 2013) as well as supraliminally (cf. Asendorpf et al. 2002; Egloff and Schmukle 2002; Kim 2003). In jargonistic terms, an attitude can be spontaneously roused by either consciously unnoticed events (type 1 CUEs) or consciously unappreciated events (type 2 CUEs). Whereas the former is "seen, registered, but consciously unnoticed," the latter is consciously recognized but "without realizing its influence on our thoughts, feelings, preferences, and choices (Lodge and Taber 2013: 3). This distinction is a conceptually useful one for my work, as I argue that implicit attitudes are automatically sparked when asking people to consider the issue of immigration. From this angle, then, entertaining the question of immigration reform is a consciously recognized act. What is not recognized, I argue, is the chain reaction that leads people's implicit attitudes to structure their judgments of immigration policies. Let me explain how and why this sequence might unfold.

Mechanisms and Hypotheses: The Political Influence of Implicit Attitudes

I theorize that broaching the immigration issue triggers one's implicit attitude toward Latino immigrants, which is stored in LTM as an object evaluation (Fazio 2007). This configuration simply means the concept "Latino immigrant" is deposited in LTM with a positive or negative affective tag (Lodge and Taber 2013: 30). Thus, evoking one's "Latino immigrant" concept should immediately ignite its evaluative charge (i.e., "good" vs. "bad"), per Lodge and

Taber's (2013) *hot cognition* mechanism. If this reasoning is correct, then this initial phase of a person's decision-making sequence will arouse and introduce affect into their cognitive stream, as their implicit attitude is "pushed" from LTM into one's working memory (WM).

At this stage, implicit attitudes are mentally available to people, ready to serve in subsequent political decision making. I contend that this is when "implicit expectations" are formed. The activation of one's implicit attitude leads citizens to assume that a given political object is relevant to the current judgment. Given the chronic rehearsal between political object and political issue, the individual deems this assumption valid, unproblematic, and – most importantly – familiar. After all, the association between political object and policy domain is a typical occurrence in the information environment – a pattern that citizens' associative thinking has made a mental note of.

I hypothesize that in the wake of their arousal, people's implicit attitudes provide immediate diagnostic information of an affective type. Specifically, citizens now have an unspoken sense of whether they positively or negatively judge "Latino immigrants," and this affective response – via an *affect transfer* mechanism (Lodge and Taber 2013: 56–57) – will directly influence a person's explicit views about immigration. In other words, how one feels about this group will shape how one interprets information related to immigration, as well as what one thinks about specific policy proposals aimed at reforming the immigration system. More specifically, citizens will evaluate information in the direction of their implicit attitude toward Latino immigrants (Lodge and Taber 2013: 58–59). If an individual is negatively predisposed toward this group at the implicit level, then this person will judge subsequent information in a manner that confirms this spontaneous reaction.

Imagine, for example, a person who is asked to indicate her support for increasing the number of visas available to legal immigrants. For argument's sake, let us say her implicit attitude toward Latino immigrants is very negative. Let us also say that in assembling her opinion, this person is given information about the substantial numbers of Asian immigrants who might benefit from a larger pool of immigrant visas (e.g., US Office of Immigration Statistics 2013). This information is novel. Our respondent will attend to it and consider it. She will deliberate, as it were. But at an implicit level, she already has Latino immigrants on her mind. And she happens to hold them in low regard. Her deliberations are shaped by what she implicitly expects. She registers strong opposition to increasing visas for legal immigrants. All of this occurs without her knowing that an implicit attitude has affected her thought process.

This example illustrates how the consequences of implicit attitude might unfold in people's decision making about immigration. And several clues point to its validity, both within social and political psychology (Lodge and Taber 2013: 5–17; cf. Correll et al. 2002; Forgas and Tan 2011). In a lab setting, for instance, Gawronski et al. (2003) asked German subjects to explicitly evaluate the ambiguous behavior of a German or Turkish person they read about. These judgments, the authors discovered, were potently shaped by people's implicit attitudes. In particular, negative implicit attitudes toward Turks led individuals to evaluate the ambiguous behavior of the Turkish target more harshly (e.g., as arrogant and insensitive) compared to the German target. In a similar vein, Fazio and Dunton (1997) asked subjects to evaluate target persons who varied by race, gender, and occupation. When asked to make similarity ratings of these targets, subjects with more negative implicit attitudes toward blacks were more likely to make these evaluations on the basis of race, rather than gender or occupation (cf. Roskos-Ewoldsen and Fazio 1992).

Taken together, the preceding evidence suggests that implicit attitudes should shape political judgments. But I say "should" because the clearest clues about *affect transfer's* influence on decision making, political or otherwise, come from lab studies with college undergraduates (e.g., Fazio and Dunton 1997; Lodge and Taber 2013). Evidence of this mechanism's operation among members of the mass public is therefore still pending. One of my contributions, then, is to marshal empirical evidence from the realm of immigration to bolster this mechanism's external validity for politics.

Besides *affect transfer*, I anticipate that implicit attitudes can influence people's immigration policy judgments by way of *affect contagion* – another mechanism identified by Lodge and Taber (2013: 58–59). Triggering one's implicit attitude toward Latino immigrants does not happen in isolation. As social and political psychologists have taught us (e.g., Collins and Loftus 1975; Lodge and Taber 2013), people's attitudes, beliefs, and values are embedded in LTM in a lattice-like structure of interconnected nodes. Hence, stimulating one's implicit attitude is likely to call forth additional and related considerations via spreading activation. This batch of considerations will flow from long-term to working memory. But this admixture is not a random draw from one's LTM. Rather, it represents those considerations that are congruent with the affective response initially sparked by the arousal of one's implicit attitude. Thus, "reasoning processes that may seem to the citizen to provide reasons for one's evaluative reactions may more often rationalize the initial affect one felt toward the object of evaluation" (Lodge and Taber 2013: 58).

In the case of US immigration politics, I hypothesize that explicit attitudes will – via *affect contagion* – mediate the influence of implicit attitudes on immigration policy judgments (Baron and Kenny 1986). That is, many of the self-reported considerations that people use to judge immigration policy – e.g., partisanship, authoritarian values, and socioeconomic concerns – are themselves affected by one's implicit attitudes toward Latino immigrants. This is another way of saying that people will often draw on their explicit attitudes to evaluate immigration policies in a manner that is generally consistent with the affect initially sparked by one's implicit attitude. And, to the extent that I find empirical support for this hypothesis in the mass public, the external validity of *affect contagion* will, too, be enhanced (McDermott 2011; Sears 1986), since evidence of its political influence is also mainly based on lab studies with college undergraduates (Lodge and Taber 2013).

But just how seamless is the influence from implicit to explicit attitudes? Are there any conditions under which this cognitive sequence is interrupted? Lodge and Taber (2013) suggest that it is incredibly hard to decouple explicit attitudes from the affective charge of implicit attitudes. As they state, "[i]t is possible, though difficult, to override implicit responses" (22), which suggests that one's explicit attitudes will often be consistent with the valence of one's implicit attitudes. I agree that it is incredibly hard to arrest the cascading influence from implicit to explicit attitudes. But I also think of implicit and explicit attitudes as related, yet distinct, constructs that independently influence one's political decision making (cf. Greenwald et al. 2009; Mo 2014; Payne et al. 2010). Hence, identifying those circumstances where these types of attitude diverge is – in my view – a useful theoretical exercise, for it helps to illuminate the boundary conditions to a strong correspondence between implicit and explicit attitudes.

Against this backdrop, I theorize about the conditions under which the political influence of implicit and explicit attitudes might diverge. JQP teaches us that people's political concepts – each with its own affective tag – are stored in LTM, interconnected to each other in associative fashion. Here, implicit considerations will be activated first, with this activation quickly fanning out to other considerations – including explicit attitudes. By the time this activation reaches one's explicit attitudes, people have surpassed their threshold of awareness. That is, insofar as they are entertaining an explicit attitude, they know they are doing so.

At this juncture, JQP expects that the charge of one's implicit attitude(s) will carry over directly into one's explicit attitude(s). People will justify the latter on the basis of the former. Nevertheless, APE and MODE both allow for the possibility that people can manipulate and edit their explicit attitude (because they are motivated to do so) in spite of the original valence of their implicit attitude remaining unchanged. Specifically, the APE model suggests that even if people resolve the cognitive inconsistency that might emerge between a "gut reaction" toward an object (e.g., implicit attitude) and a "proposition" related to that object (e.g., explicit attitude) in favor of the latter, this "does not necessarily deactivate the associations that gave rise to the affective gut response that built the foundation for this proposition" (Gawronski and Bodenhausen 2011: 66). This means that people can edit and adjust the influence of their explicit attitudes, even if their implicit attitudes stay activated and pull in a different direction – what MODE theorists refer to as "mixed processes" (Fazio and Towles-Schwen 1999: 102–103).[2]

[2] This view is also highly consistent with the theoretical work of Timothy Wilson et al. (2000), who propose the notion of "dual attitudes." Here, people can have implicit and explicit attitudes

Applying these insights to the case of immigration politics, I derive a *dueling effects* hypothesis, where some individuals (i.e., highly motivated), under some circumstances (i.e., cued attention to non-Latinos), can suppress the influence of their explicit attitudes toward Latino immigrants even as the influence of their implicit attitudes toward the same group persists. The main implication flowing from this hypothesis is that, if correct, public opposition to immigration is stronger than what verbal self-reports suggest.

The last mechanism that I propose and test concerns social position. To this point, I have couched my theory of "implicit expectations" at a very individualistic level, thus providing a detailed account of how implicit attitudes color a given person's views about immigration. Yet one of the defining features of social and political life is the importance of groups – that is, individual persons as members of larger collectives (Huddy 2001, 2013; Tajfel and Turner 1979). And within the study of politics, one of the more crucial group memberships revolves around race, where current theorizing suggests that this construct leaves a deep imprint on the psychology of individuals' political attitudes (e.g., Dawson 2000; Philpot and White 2010).

Seizing on these insights, I hypothesize that the effects of implicit attitudes on immigration policy judgments are modulated by race – or rather, by the position of one's racial group in America's racial order (Dawson 2000; Kim 2000; Masuoka and Junn 2013). In particular, I expect that the effects of implicit attitudes will be stronger among white Americans, relative to African Americans, as the former are the dominant group in America's racial hierarchy (Fang et al. 1998; Kahn et al. 2009; Sidanius and Pratto 2001). The reasoning behind these differential effects is at once simple and illuminating. As members of a dominant group, whites are motivated to preserve their privileged station in the racial order. Hence, the expression of implicit attitudes against a threatening outgroup (i.e., Latino immigrants) serves as one way for whites to bolster their position in this hierarchy. In contrast, black Americans occupy the lowest tier in the racial order (see Fang et al. 1998; Kahn et al. 2009; Masuoka and Junn 2013). The motivation to maintain a high rank in the order is therefore absent, which suggests that the expression of implicit attitudes might have less relevance for blacks than whites. If true, then this hypothesis implies that "implicit expectations" serve a functional role, which makes the influence of implicit attitudes more pronounced among some segments of the mass public than others.

toward the same object stored in memory, with the former being activated prior to the latter in light of relevant cues. According to this view, people can, with enough effort, manipulate and edit their explicit attitude toward an object, which falls under their awareness and control. But despite explicit attitude change, people's implicit attitude toward the same object can persist.

Implicit Attitude's Political Effects: The Role of Individual Differences

I claim that implicit attitudes can directly and indirectly affect people's immigration policy judgments via the mechanisms I hypothesized about in the preceding text. Critical to these hypotheses is the presence of individual differences in implicit attitudes. As "object-evaluations," implicit attitudes are not a type. It is not the case that one has (or does not have) an implicit attitude. Rather, all of us have implicit attitudes to some degree. For some people, these attitudes are very strong, such that the association between an object and its evaluation (e.g., Latino–Bad) is remarkably robust. For other individuals, these attitudes are anemically weak, with the object evaluation association tenuously held in place, as if by gossamer. For all persons, however, their level of implicit attitude will shape the impact it has on their explicit political judgments and choices.

To some public opinion specialists, this may seem like an uncontroversial and unnecessary point. But it merits emphasis because it contrasts with the constructionist view of (implicit and explicit) attitude formation espoused by Lodge and Taber (2013). Speaking in reference to *John Q. Public*, these authors point out: "[t]he strong implication of this ... model is that all beliefs and attitudes will be constructed in real time from whatever cognitive and affective information is momentarily accessible from LTM" (Lodge and Taber 2013: 33).

But are *all* attitudes really constructed "in real time"? From one perspective, several public opinion specialists teach us that many citizens will form their political attitudes on the basis of immediately salient considerations (Tourangeau et al. 2000; Zaller 1992; Zaller and Feldman 1992). Yet even within this "constructionist" sea, there are islands of scholarship counseling against taking this view too far. One of the more renowned and enduring of these is Phillip Converse's (1964) treatise on the nature of mass belief systems. Although widely famous for revealing the instability and ideological incoherence of most citizens' political thinking, tucked in Converse's (1964) chapter was another, equally provocative insight: that where structure to public opinion exists, one of its foundations is attitudes toward groups. Taken at face value, this insight suggests that some attitudes toward groups are not developed on the spot because people have already formed and stored them in LTM. And one reason why these attitudes are so well-formed and easily elicited is, I suggest, because of stable and recurring patterns of political discourse about groups.

Of course, to argue that some implicit attitudes might be pre-formed and easily stimulated is not to suggest that all implicit attitudes display this character – nor does it imply that Lodge and Taber's (2013) constructionist view is incorrect. A more scientifically productive way to interpret my theoretical proposal is that by establishing that some implicit attitudes are, in fact, preformed, stable, and easily evoked, we can begin to pinpoint when implicit attitudes are formed on the spot, when they are merely drawn out on the spot, and when we will observe a confluence of these perspectives, thus further setting boundary conditions for implicit attitudes' political effects.

Conclusions and Next Steps

This chapter has laid out the theoretical framework that will guide my empirical investigations in the following chapters. In distilled form, this framework traces the development of implicit attitudes to stable and recurring patterns in political discourse surrounding policy issues. These implicit attitudes, my framework suggests, are automatically called forth when a relevant political topic is broached. Once they are made mentally accessible, these implicit attitudes anchor how citizens deliberate about a pending political judgment. This influence of implicit attitudes happens subconsciously, that is, without a person's knowledge that their impulsive thoughts have affected what they explicitly decided.

Using this framework, I analyze contemporary US immigration politics and how citizens' unspoken impressions of Latino immigrants prefigure into how they view and judge immigration policies. To the extent that my framework is valid, several key pieces of evidence must emerge during my investigations. First, a systematic examination of discourse on this political issue must reveal clear patterns in content and focus – patterns that people's associational reasoning can draw on to develop implicit attitudes. In the case of immigration, this means the regularities that emerge in political discourse about this issue should highlight Latino immigrants while encouraging a specific normative view of them. Second, if patterns in immigration discourse lend themselves to associational reasoning, I must find that implicit attitudes toward Latino immigrants exist and that their prevalence matches the regularities in public discussions of immigration. Not only that, but I must also show these implicit attitudes are substantively different than their self-reported counterparts – that they, in fact, offer something new. Third, I must demonstrate that implicit attitudes toward Latino immigrants operate in ways outlined by my theory of implicit expectations. Specifically, I must show that implicit attitudes are easily called forth, and that once mentally accessible, they can shape one's effortful deliberations without one's awareness of this influence.

Meeting these goals necessitates multiple lines of empirical attack. Accordingly, the opening salvo in this investigative assault is also, perhaps, its most fundamental: Does political discourse actually yield stable patterns that might encourage a particular implicit view of Latino immigrants? To answer this question, let us turn to Chapter 4.

4

Ghost in the Associative Machine

> ...[N]ews stories inevitably select only some aspects of reality and leave out others. More important, over time, the specific realities depicted in single stories may accumulate to form a summary message that distorts social reality.
>
> – Robert Entman (1994)

I have argued that associative reasoning enables citizens to develop implicit attitudes on the basis of recurring patterns in political discourse that surrounds policy issues. This claim is informed by several experiments in controlled laboratory settings that suggest an interplay between the valence of information surrounding an object and the development of implicit attitudes toward the object on the basis of this information (e.g., De Houwer et al. 1997; Gawronski et al. 2014a; Gregg et al. 2006; Olson and Fazio 2001, 2002; Rydell and McConnell 2006). In these controlled settings, subjects are experimentally exposed to repeated pairings of novel objects with positive or negative stimuli. Systematic exposure to these pairings, scholars have discovered, leads subjects to develop implicit attitudes toward novel objects in the evaluative direction of the pairings they encounter. Akin to Pavlov's dog, who learned to associate food with the ringing of a bell, people learn to implicitly associate an object with positive or negative affect, consistent with the accumulated information they encounter about the object. What is more, people develop implicit attitudes without retaining explicit memories for the information that promotes these evaluations (Olson and Fazio 2001). People also appear to form implicit attitudes without active control. Gawronski et al. (2014a), for example, have shown that explicitly instructing people to prevent (allow) patterned information from influencing their feelings toward a novel object leads individuals to reduce (increase) their self-reported attitude toward the object, but leaves their implicit attitude unaffected.

This classical conditioning hypothesis has become so influential, many scholars have concluded that implicit attitudes arise from the "accrual of information over time to form and strengthen associations in memory" (Rydell and McConnell 2006: 996; see also Gregg et al. 2006; Olson and Fazio 2002). In laboratory settings, however, the type and volume of information about objects is at researchers' discretion. This level of control enables scholars to shed light on the psychological mechanisms behind the acquisition of implicit attitudes. Yet it also leaves scholars in the dark about actual information flows outside the lab, potentially undermining the external validity of the classical conditioning hypothesis (Shadish et al. 2002). Perhaps this mechanism explains the emergence of implicit attitudes in contrived research settings, a critic might say, but it is unclear whether it reflects how implicit attitudes are actually acquired in the mass public.

This chapter aims to strengthen the hand of the classical conditioning hypothesis by examining the role that news media play in producing and broadcasting information flows that promote the development of implicit attitudes. My focus on news media is deliberate. As Kinder (1998: 821) explains, news media yield an "avalanche of information...that rumbles down on Americans every day." In this way, news content often serves as a conduit for social learning, especially about social groups (Gilens 1999; Kellstedt 2003). Indeed, what journalists report and how they report it can give people lasting mental impressions about what the world is like, what Walter Lippman (1922) referred to as "pictures in our heads."

To this end, I illustrate how news media help to promote the development of implicit attitudes by yoking social objects with an affective charge. I claim that this outcome is produced by two media-level mechanisms: priming and framing. Recall that priming is a process by which news outlets draw attention to some aspects of a topic at the expense of others, thus establishing standards by which citizens make political decisions. In the case of implicit attitudes, I contend that news media prime some political objects over others, thus encouraging the public to associate specific political objects (e.g., groups, candidates) with certain issue domains (e.g., Valentino et al. 2013). In turn, framing conveys a sense of how an issue should be understood and what aspects of the issue are deemed most relevant for its evaluation (e.g., Merolla et al. 2013). In other words, frames organize and provide meaning to a topic (e.g., Gamson 1992; Iyengar 1991).

By systematically priming specific political objects and framing them in a positive (negative) light, I illustrate how news media provide raw material for the evaluative associations that implicit attitudes are said to be. This does not mean that news reports are the only sources of implicit attitudes. Nor am I suggesting that citizens must regularly consume news stories to acquire these types of attitudes. I do claim, however, that news media disseminate affectively rich information that facilitates the acquisition of implicit attitudes toward political objects, in line with the tenets of classical conditioning (e.g., Gawronski et al. 2014a; Gregg et al. 2006; Olson and Fazio 2001, 2002; Rydell and McConnell 2006).

I test this claim by studying longitudinal trends in news reports on Latino immigrants. Specifically, I examine the degree to which Latinos have been discussed in the context of illegal and legal immigration across the last quarter century. The point of departure for my inquiry is the following: the labels *illegal* and *legal* carry strong negative and positive connotations, respectively. By studying the volume and frequency of news coverage on illegal and legal Latino immigrants, I contend that we can unearth a key source of valenced information about this group that promotes the development of implicit attitudes, consistent with the principles of classical conditioning (e.g., Gawronski et al. 2014a; Gregg et al. 2006; Olson and Fazio 2001).

Seizing on these theoretical premises, my analysis establishes that newspapers and television networks overwhelmingly cover Latino immigrants in the context of illegal immigration. Across the last two decades, immigration has ebbed and flowed as a news topic. But when this issue is covered, the focus is frequently on illegal immigration. Moreover, when news outlets report on illegal immigration, the focus is frequently on Latino illegal immigrants. This general pattern, I claim, encourages the development of strong implicit attitudes toward Latinos through the principles of classical conditioning by fostering a distortedly negative image of this group that is regularly and widely broadcast throughout society.

The Salience of Latinos in the Immigrant Stream

The link between Latinos and immigration in the American mind might seem like a given these days. But this association is partly the result of a gradual shift in the regional origins of contemporary immigration to the United States from Europe to Latin America. In this section, I track the historical evolution of this process across the last five decades. Because I am a political scientist and not a historian, my aim here is quite modest. By relying on some of the best historical work available (e.g., King 2000; Ngai 2004; Tichenor 2002), I discuss major pieces of immigration policy in the last fifty years that have facilitated the rise of Latino immigration to the United States in contemporary times. In doing so, this historical sketch establishes some objective benchmarks by which we can judge the accuracy of news coverage on illegal and legal Latino immigrants, which I analyze in later sections of this chapter.

When Immigrants Were European

Until about 1960, immigration to the United States was distinctly European in character (e.g., King 2000; Ngai 2004; Tichenor 2002). This trend was sustained in large part by federal immigration policy, which explicitly favored foreigners from Europe, especially those from western and northern European

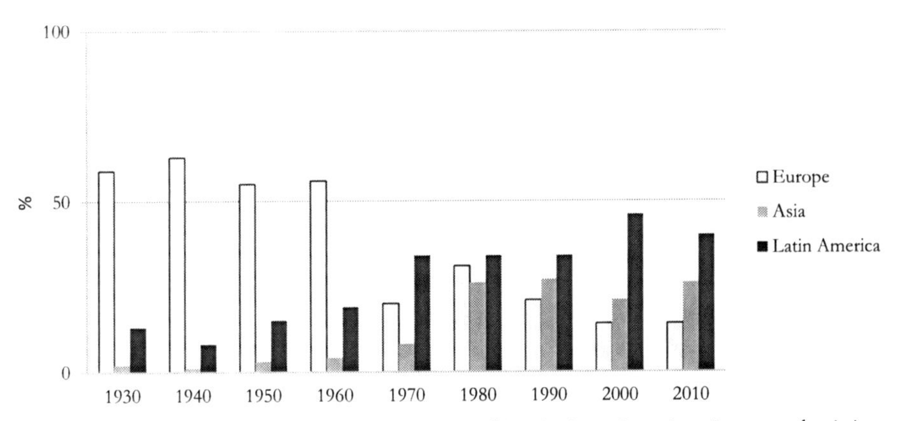

FIGURE 4.1. Percentage of European, Asian, and Latin American immigrants obtaining legal permanent residence (LPR) by decade: 1930–2010. *Note:* Percentages reflect the author's calculations based on raw data for LPRs reported in the *2010 Yearbook of Immigration Statistics*, published by the Department of Homeland Security.

nations such as the United Kingdom, Ireland, and Sweden (e.g., Higham 1981; King 2000). The racial overtones of this policy were no accident. By design, immigration policymakers in the 1920s established a quota-based system that regulated immigrant admissions until 1965 (e.g., Higham 1981; Tichenor 2002). The express goal of these quotas was to admit "desirable" immigrants while excluding "undesirable" ones (e.g., Gerstle 2001; Jacobson 1998). To accomplish the former, quotas were disproportionately allotted to European immigrants, with northern and western Europeans receiving priority above southern and eastern Europeans. In turn, to limit undesirable immigrants, those nations were either allotted fewer quotas or, in the case of most Asian immigrants, legally barred from entering the United States (e.g., King 2000; Ngai 2004; Tichenor 2002).

Figure 4.1 suggests these quotas met their intended goal. There we see graphed the proportion of European, Asian, and Latin American immigration by decade from 1930 to 2010. These proportions represent individuals who received legal permanent residence (LPR) by decade, as recorded by the Department of Homeland Security (DHS). Put differently, they are the percentage of immigrants who received their "green card" in a given decade by major sending region.[1] We can see that until about 1960, Europeans consistently made up

[1] Officially, these data capture the number of eligible immigrants whose residence status has been administratively adjusted by the DHS. Strictly speaking, then, these figures do not capture the actual rate of immigration, which requires accounting for (among other things) illegal/legal migration and temporary migrants. However, consistent with other analysts (e.g., Ngai 2004; Tichenor 2002; Valentino et al. 2013), I use these data to *describe* general immigration trends. Later in the chapter, I report available evidence on actual immigration rates. Those data corroborate the trends displayed in Figure 4.1.

at least half of all foreigners obtaining LPR, with Asians and Latinos trailing far behind. Yet after 1960, European dominance waned dramatically, with Latinos gradually overtaking the lead thereafter. This tectonic shift in US migratory flows can be traced in large part to a dramatic change in US immigration policy: the 1965 Hart–Celler Act (e.g., King 2000; Tichenor 2002).

Dismantling US Immigration Quotas: The Hart–Celler Act

On November 22, 1963, Lyndon B. Johnson assumed the reins of presidential power following the unexpected assassination of President John F. Kennedy. In line with his predecessor's goals, Johnson resolved to aggressively pursue civil rights reform, vowing "to eliminate from the U.S. every trace of discrimination and oppression that is based on race or color" (quoted in Tichenor 2002: 213). The domestic push for civil rights was partly animated by foreign policy objectives. With the United States embroiled in ideological battle with communism during the Cold War, blacks' continued political and economic marginalization was fast undermining US credibility among communist regimes and peer nations. Thus, from the Johnson administration's view, dismantling Jim Crow and extending full political rights to blacks had to be a political priority, a commitment culminating in the 1964 Civil Rights Act.

A similar logic structured the Johnson administration's view of immigration policy, whose quota system increasingly appeared crass, outdated, and detrimental to America's anticommunism efforts abroad and civil rights reform at home (e.g., King 2000; Ngai 2004; Tichenor 2002). As one of Johnson's political aides later recounted, "[t]he President eventually recognized ... existing immigration law, and in particular, national origins quotas created many decades before on racist grounds, as inconsistent with civil rights and racial justice" (quoted in Tichenor 2002: 213). Hence, the Johnson administration also put its political weight behind legislative efforts to reform immigration policy, which yielded the 1965 Hart–Celler Act.

This transformative legislation introduced key changes to US immigration policy, whose consequences reverberate today. Chief among them was the complete elimination of national origins quotas. Henceforth, immigrants would be admitted on the basis of a visa system that privileged family reunification, employment-based criteria, and refugees, respectively (e.g., King 2000; Tichenor 2002). Instead of racial/ethnic quotas, Hart–Celler set yearly ceilings on immigrants from the Eastern and Western Hemispheres. Specifically, 170,000 visas were allotted to Eastern Hemisphere immigrants, with no one nation receiving more than 20,000 visas. In turn, 120,000 visas were allotted to Western Hemisphere immigrants without any nation-specific limits, a plan that "reflected the fact that Mexico and Canada comprised one-half to two-thirds of Western Hemisphere immigration" at the time (Ngai 2004: 258). Critically, spouses, unmarried minor children, and the parents of US citizens were exempt from these guidelines (e.g., King 2000; Tichenor 2002), an allowance marking immigration policymakers' prioritization of immigrant admission on the basis of family reunification.

Hart–Celler advocates intimated to skeptics that these policy changes would remove the racist vestiges of the quota system without drastically altering the European character of immigration. After all, if non-European nations had been contributing fewer immigrants to the United States before 1965, then fewer of them would stand to take advantage of the new law, especially its family reunification provisions. Yet this prediction failed miserably, for Hart–Celler paved the way for two related yet unforeseen immigration trends that matter politically today.

The Shift Toward (Il)-legal Latino Immigration

Rather than maintaining Europe's edge in US migratory flows, Hart–Celler stimulated greater legal migration from Latin America and Asia (see Figure 4.1). In 1960, five years prior to Hart–Celler, Europeans still constituted about 56 percent of immigrants lawfully admitted to the United States in the preceding decade. Yet by 1970, Europe's total dropped to 20 percent while Latin America's climbed to 34 percent. In fact, by 2000, Latin America's share reached a peak of 46 percent of LPRs for the decade prior. Asian immigration also experienced robust growth during this era. And although never larger than Latin America's share in this time period, the growth in Asian LPRs also eclipsed Europeans.[2]

Hart–Celler also had another unanticipated effect: it stimulated sustained increases in unauthorized, or "illegal," immigration. The act, recall, had set hemispheric immigration limits to exercise some regulatory power over immigrant admissions. These limits, however, were based more on political logic rather than acute sensitivity to regional demand for visas. Hence, hemispheric caps – especially those placed on the Western Hemisphere – set artificial ceilings on nations with many potential migrants wishing to *legally* enter the United States. This was especially true of Mexico, which has dominated the legal flow of Latino immigrants since Hart–Celler (Massey et al. 2002; Ngai 2004).

[2] In a report released on June 19, 2012, the Pew Research Center noted that in 2010, Asians overtook Latinos as the largest group of new immigrants to the United States, the culmination of steady growth in Asian immigrants in recent years and a concomitant decline in Latino immigrants mainly due to America's recent economic downturn, especially beginning in 2008. This shift is not reflected in the LPR data because as I explained earlier (see footnote 1), LPR status captures the number of eligible immigrants whose residence status has been administratively adjusted by the DHS. Hence, there is a lag between eligibility for and actual change in LPR status. Whether this change evolves into a stable and lasting pattern is to be seen in the next few years. At any rate, this uptick in Asian immigration does not affect the conclusions drawn from this chapter. For, as will become clear, associative reasoning draws on chronic, long-term patterns of information about political objects – patterns that in the case of contemporary immigration are fixed predominantly on Latino immigrants (Valentino, Brader, and Jardina 2013).

Prior to 1965, Mexican immigrants had enjoyed a peculiar status within America's immigration policy regime. Unlike southern and eastern Europeans and Asians, Mexicans were exempt from national origins quotas. This was the product of intense lobbying by agricultural growers, ranchers, and other southwestern employers, who considered Mexicans an inexpensive, pliable, and – above all – seasonal labor source (Ngai 2004; King 2000). Building on the sojourning nature of many Mexican immigrants, the United States accorded a formal guest worker program with Mexico in 1942. Known as the Bracero Program, this labor pact formally channeled about 200,000 annual Mexican immigrants until the program's end in 1964 (Ngai 2004; Tichenor 2002). Per this agreement, Mexican workers (i.e., *braceros*) signed seasonal contracts to work in the United States for six to nine months. In addition to a set wage, *braceros* were to receive transportation, lodging, and repatriation after their contract's expiry.

The Bracero Program, however, produced inefficiencies in the very labor market it sought to regulate, thus helping to spawn illegal immigration outside the program's official channels (e.g., Massey et al. 2002; Ngai 2004). Potential *braceros*, for example, first had to formally enlist in the program through Mexican officials, a process that often required submitting paperwork to state and federal government agencies separated by thousands of miles. This meant applicants often incurred significant out-of-pocket expenses to complete the necessary paperwork alone. Moreover, on approval, *braceros* were then formally processed at depot centers in major Mexican cities away from migrants' home villages, which meant further costs, often in the form of subsistence while awaiting final authorization.

American employers also faced inefficiencies. Under the Bracero Program, employers were responsible for lodging and transporting Mexican workers once they were authorized. Companies relying on *braceros* also had to wait until Mexican officials formally processed individual workers. This was especially detrimental to some employers (e.g., agro-businesses) who, rather than waiting for Mexican officials to identify and authorize *braceros*, found it easier to recruit potential migrants directly, without the Mexican government as an intermediary.[3] As Mae Ngai (2004: 148) explains:

> ...the bracero program itself encouraged illegal migration. More Mexicans wanted to become braceros than the Mexican government had spaces for. Rural poverty remained the biggest "push" factor in emigration, legal and illegal. On the "pull" side, some growers – especially in border areas like the Imperial Valley of California and the Lower Rio Grande Valley of Texas – preferred recruiting informally near the border to the formal process and cost of interior recruitment.

[3] This was especially the case for employers based in states such as Arkansas, Missouri, and Texas. Mexican officials initially excluded these states as potential destinations for *braceros*, on the grounds that these states racially discriminated against Mexican workers through formal segregation codes (Ngai 2004).

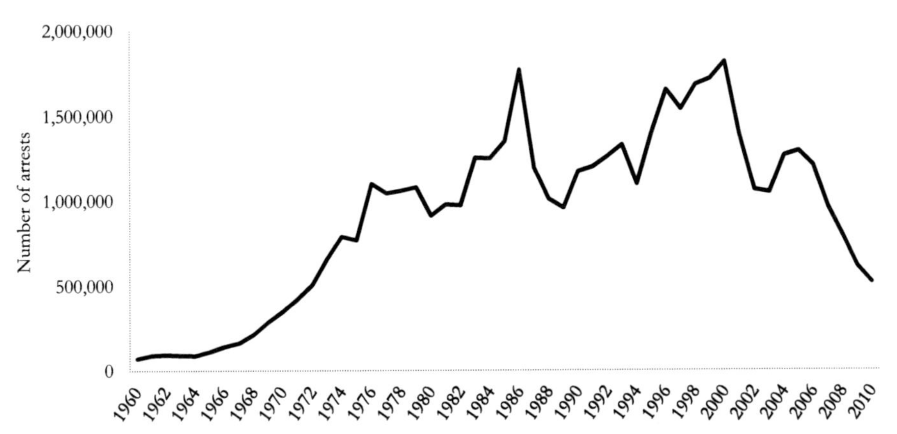

FIGURE 4.2. Annual number of unauthorized immigrants arrested, 1960–2010. *Source: 2010 Yearbook of Immigration Statistics* (Department of Homeland Security).

By 1964, the Bracero Program was formally dissolved, itself, too, a consequence of the liberal tide that was simultaneously pushing civil rights and immigration reform to the top of the Johnson administration's political agenda (Ngai 2004). But by now, the demand for Mexican labor and the informal channels that sustained it were firmly installed. In the absence of the Bracero Program, once regulated flows of Mexican labor were pushed underground. The Hart–Celler Act's hemispheric visa limits further compounded this trend by artificially capping visas available to Mexicans wishing to work legally in the United States.

Though reliable estimates of unauthorized Mexican immigrants during this era are hard to find, yearly estimates for the number of arrests of unauthorized immigrants do exist, which many analysts often use to indirectly assess the scale of illegal Mexican immigration during these years (e.g., King 2000; Massey et al. 2002; Tichenor 2002). These estimates are graphed in Figure 4.2. Consistent with the prior discussion, the number of arrests of illegal immigrants does not exceed 100,000 per year in the years immediately before Hart–Celler. But in the years following this legislation, arrests of unauthorized immigrants climbs steadily and dramatically for the next three decades before beginning a noticeable descent after 2006, a trend abetted by, among other factors, a more sluggish national economy, stricter United States–Mexico border controls, and reduced birth rates in Mexico (e.g., Passel et al. 2012).

Media Coverage of Latino Immigration

The crosscurrents of legal and illegal immigration engendered by the Hart–Celler Act and the Bracero Program have produced a contemporary situation where the same group – Latinos – have contributed the most number of people to each migratory flow across the last four decades. This state of affairs is

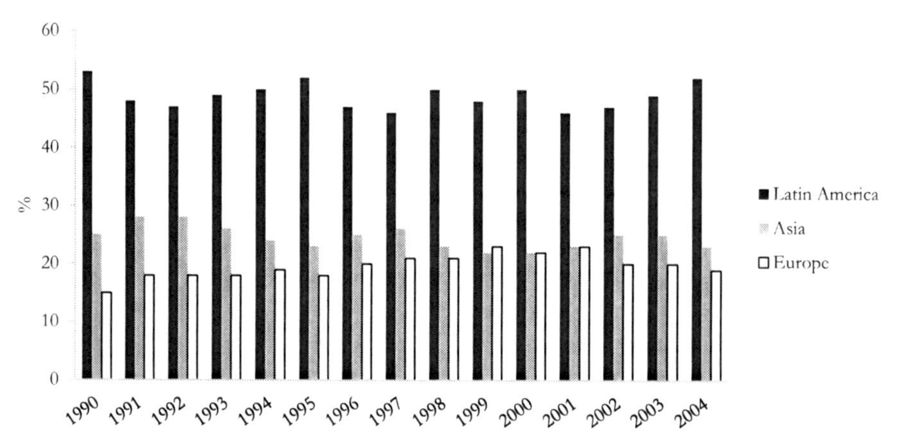

FIGURE 4.3. Proportion of Latin American, Asian, and European immigrants of total immigration, 1990–2004. *Source:* Passel and Suro (2005).

depicted in Figure 4.3, which provides the annual percentage of Latino, Asian, and European immigrants as a total of all incoming immigrants to the United States from 1990 to 2004.[4] These percentages are drawn from Passel and Suro (2005), who estimated annual immigration rates during this time span using available census data and surveys (e.g., Current Population Surveys; American Community Surveys). The advantage of these estimated proportions is that they take into account both illegal and legal immigration inflows, thus providing a reliable representation of *total* immigration to the United States on a year-to-year basis, which the LPR data from Figure 4.1 cannot fully accomplish.

Consistent with our preceding discussion, it is abundantly clear that Latino immigrants have dominated the migrant stream cascading into the United States in recent times. Figure 4.3 shows that from 1990 to 2004, Latino immigrants regularly comprised about half of all immigrants entering the United States legally and illegally. No other immigrant group matches this trend. Asian immigrants – the second largest group in this immigrant stream – regularly makes up no more than 30 percent of all immigrants, while Europeans make up no more than 25 percent in any one year during this era.

How have news media responded to the predominance of Latino immigrants in contemporary US migratory flows? It is difficult to confidently answer this question. The challenge here is not that scholars have failed to investigate this question, but rather, that the evidence yielded so far is fragmentary and incomplete. As a result, inferences about news coverage on Latino immigrants hinge on several caveats, which limit the ability to say whether journalists have provided a balanced portrait of this group. Let me explain.

[4] The category Asian consists of those immigrants identified from census data as Asian Pacific Islanders. The category European contains other white immigrants from former European colonies, including Canada, Australia, and New Zealand.

In 2002, Otto Santa Ana published his landmark study, *Brown Tide Rising*, which examines newspaper coverage on Latinos from 1992 to 1998. By analyzing Latino-focused newspaper articles from the *Los Angeles Times*, Santa Ana amassed evidence that Latinos are negatively portrayed in media discourse through metaphorical language describing Latino immigrants as, inter alia, "invaders," "parasites," and "burdens." These metaphors, Santa Ana explains, injects Latino immigrants with negative connotations (see also Santa Ana 2013).

All seems well and good. But there are complications. Consider that Santa Ana's evidence comes from a single source: the *Los Angeles Times*. This does not mean the trends in this paper are unsystematic. But without comparing coverage in this paper with peer publications, it is difficult to say whether news trends in the *L. A. Times* are peculiar to this outlet, which is based in a key destination city for many Latino immigrants (e.g., 2011 Yearbook of Immigration Statistics). Moreover, Santa Ana's analysis centers on a short period that brackets a key moment in US immigration history: California's passage of Proposition 187, the 1994 ballot measure that excluded illegal immigrants and their children from public benefits and services. Without a longer temporal view, it is difficult to say whether news trends during these years were ephemeral or enduring.[5]

For these reasons, Leo Chavez's book, *Covering Immigration*, is highly relevant. Chavez (2001) examines seventy-six magazine covers focused on immigration from 1965 to 1999. These covers span several magazines, including the *Atlantic Monthly*, *New Republic*, and *Time* magazine. This diversity in magazines and the extended temporal reach of the sample enables Chavez to show that immigration ebbs and flows as a salient news issue. This ebb and flow, moreover, varies in tone, with many magazine covers presenting immigration in alarmist fashion. Indeed, Chavez finds that magazine covers focused on Mexican immigrants especially use alarming imagery to underscore the "illegal" origins of segments of this group (see also Chavez 2008).

But again, there are blind spots in this analysis that matter for what we can confidently say about media coverage on Latino immigrants. Chavez does provide a more expansive temporal view of news coverage. But the exclusive focus on magazine covers yields relatively few time points across this wide time span because magazines do not produce immigration-centered covers each year in the period under study.[6] And, without comparable data on other media sources

[5] More recently, Santa Ana (2013) has examined television coverage of Latinos in four major networks, finding that most stories about this group are negative in both focus and tone. Nevertheless, this newer analysis is limited to one year (2004), which still raises questions about the over-time dynamics of this type of news coverage.

[6] Chavez (2008) has also argued that news stories on Latino immigrants often use a narrative that presents this group as threatening to America's culture, prosperity, and security, among other domains. But here, too, it is hard to gain a firm sense about how lasting this pattern is, as his analysis generally centers on media coverage of a few flashpoints in recent immigration debates (e.g., the 2005 Minuteman surveillance project along the Arizona–Mexico border).

(e.g., television), it is difficult to say how representative these magazine trends are of larger trends in media coverage. Moreover, the strict focus on illegal immigration makes it hard to say how balanced this coverage is, especially with respect to *legal* immigration, the other flow of immigration strongly propelled by Latinos.

The most recent and comprehensive analysis of media coverage on Latino immigration is provided by Valentino, Brader, and Jardina (2013). This research team has tracked the annual number of front-page newspaper stories that mention "immigration" or "immigrant" *and* "Latinos" or specific Latin American countries from 1985 to 2009. Critically, they conduct similar searches for "Asian," "African," and "Muslim" groups. Their analysis shows that in the last twenty-five years, news media have increasingly primed "Latinos" in immigration news reports. Specifically, news stories focused on Latinos have consistently outnumbered those on other groups, especially after 1994, when Proposition 187 grabbed national headlines. This trend, the authors show, partly reflects Latinos' salience in the (legal) immigrant stream.

Valentino et al. (2013) thus show that newspapers generally focus on Latinos when covering immigration, which underlines this medium's ability to prime a specific immigrant group in the context of immigration. But the salience of Latinos in immigration newspaper coverage only tells us why Latinos might be the target of implicit attitudes. It cannot help explain the direction that implicit attitudes will take. Moreover, similar to Santa Ana (2002) and Chavez (2001), this analysis is also unable to show how representative these trends are of other news media, such as television.

In the remainder of this chapter, I bring to bear systematic evidence on both of these fronts. Whereas prior scholarship, especially the work of Valentino, Brader, and Jardina (2013), provides strong evidence that newspaper outlets *prime* an association between Latinos and the issue of immigration, my analysis provides new evidence on how that association is *framed* in the context of illegal immigration (see also Merolla et al. 2013). In doing so, my goal is to show that it is the parallel operation of priming and framing that promotes the development of implicit attitudes toward Latinos through the news media's wide and sustained dissemination of valenced information about this group.

Negative Connotations: Illegal and Legal Latinos in the News

Building on prior work on media priming and Latinos (Chavez 2001; Valentino et al. 2013), I examine how news coverage frames the link between Latinos and immigration across the last twenty years. Specifically, I investigate the media's framing of Latinos in the context of illegal and legal immigration. Given the predominance of Latinos in illegal and legal migratory flows into the United States, which we reviewed earlier in this chapter, I assess the degree to which news coverage reflects actual trends in these interrelated facets of Latino immigration. Doing so, I believe, brings needed traction to the question of what direction implicit attitudes are likely to take, and with what intensity.

Recall that current theorizing proposes that people acquire implicit attitudes via a classical conditioning process, where chronic exposure to negative (positive) information about a social object encourages the development of implicit attitudes consistent with the volume and direction of this information. I reason that insofar as news media generally prime Latinos relative to other groups, while regularly framing Latinos in the context of "illegality" – a label with strong negative overtones – we can more confidently claim that implicit attitudes toward Latinos reflect accrued information about this group (Rydell and McConnell 2006: 1001).

Building on the work of Valentino, Brader, and Jardina (2013), I begin by examining the number of stories across several major US newspapers that mention Latinos in conjunction with the term "illegal (or undocumented) immigration." By the same token, I examine the number of news stories across these same papers that mention Latinos and the term "legal immigration." I conducted these searches through ProQuest®, a database that electronically archives stories from major US newspapers. The papers in this sample are the *New York Times*, *Los Angeles Times*, *Chicago Tribune*, *Washington Post*, and the *Atlanta-Journal Constitution*, which were consistently available from 1990 to 2010, thus setting the time period under analysis. These raw annual story counts allow me to build yearly estimates of the percentage of news stories on Latino immigration that focus on either its illegal or legal dimension. As such, this proportion will serve as a crucial point of comparison to the actual estimated percentage of Latino immigrants who reside in the United States illegally or legally, which I examine in the last part of this chapter.

To retrieve as many relevant news stories as possible, the search term for immigration also allowed the term "immigrant." By the same token, the search terms for Latino included Hispanic and country names identifying major Latin American immigrant groups, including Mexic(o/can), Cuba(n), and (El) Salvador(an) (see Valentino, Brader, and Jardina 2013). News story counts include all news articles and op-ed pieces focused on immigration, but exclude letters to the editor, book reviews, and corrections with the same thematic focus.

Figure 4.4 displays the yearly number of illegal immigration news stories on Latinos from the five papers under study. There we can see that prior to the early 2000s, the *L. A. Times* significantly produced more stories on illegal Latino immigrants than any of the other papers. This is especially true of the years bracketing 1994, when California voters passed Proposition 187. In that year, the *L. A. Times* published an estimated 737 stories on illegal Latino immigrants, with its closest rival (i.e., *Chicago Tribune*) publishing 105 – about seven times less. Beginning in the early 2000s, however, the *L. A. Times* series begins to accord more closely with its peer publications. In fact, in 2006, each paper published about 400 news stories on this subject. This makes sense, as 2006 was a year when immigrants and their children organized nationwide protests

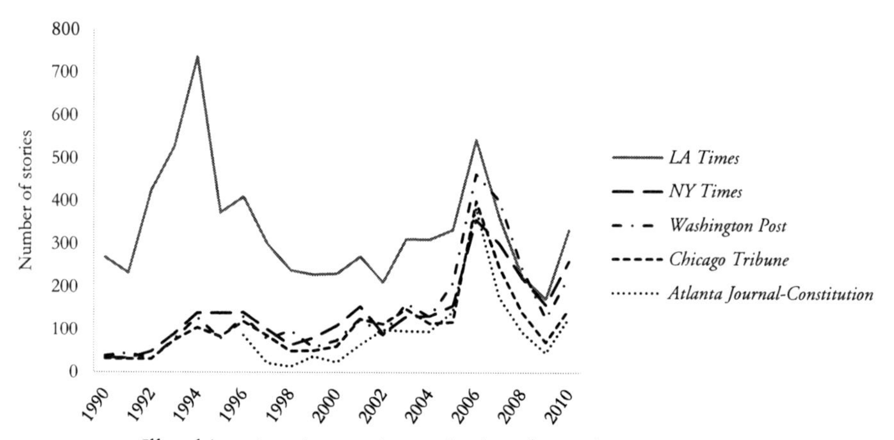

FIGURE 4.4. Illegal immigration stories on Latinos by major newspapers: 1990–2010. *Source:* Estimates based on the author's analysis of electronically archived data, as described in the text.

to call on the US Congress to pass comprehensive immigration reform (e.g., Barreto et al. 2009).

Taken together, these results drive home two points. First, the findings collectively suggest a steady and, at times, torrential supply of news stories on Latinos framed in the context of illegal immigration. Second, these patterns underscore the advantage of collecting and tracking news content across several newspaper outlets (e.g., Valentino, Brader, and Jardina 2013) to minimize possible biases that might emerge by relying on a few or even single print outlet (e.g., Santa Ana 2002). Indeed, in the case at hand, strict reliance on the *L. A. Times* for news content would have led to an overestimate of stories on Latino immigrants framed in the context of illegal immigration.

Turning our attention to news stories on legal Latino immigrants, a different picture emerges. Figure 4.5 graphs the annual number of these stories produced by each paper across the same twenty-year period. Although the *L. A. Times* slightly publishes more stories than its peer publications, all five news series on legal Latino immigrants generally track each other closely over time. Moreover, notwithstanding the ebb and flow of these counts over time, the volume of these legal immigration news series simply pales in comparison to their illegal immigration analogs. For example, in 1994, when the *L. A. Times* published an estimated 737 stories on illegal Latino immigrants, the same publication published only about 199 stories on legal Latino immigrants. Indeed, for most years under analysis, the number of legal news stories is generally between 40 and 60 stories.

Systematic Trends or Vagaries in Single Newspapers?

The over-time movement of the individual newspaper series on illegal and legal Latino immigration suggests that coherent "discourses" exist when it comes

FIGURE 4.5. Legal immigration news stories on Latinos by major newspapers, 1990–2010. *Source:* Estimates based on the author's analysis of electronically archived data, as described in the text.

to each of these two subjects. On their own, however, these raw series cannot tell us just how much of this over time evolution in individual series is shared because they reflect news discourse on illegal and legal immigration, rather than vagaries in single newspapers.

To leverage an answer to this question, I utilize Stimson's (1999) dyad ratios algorithm. This technique is essentially a form of factor analysis for temporal data such as these newspaper series. Accordingly, Stimson's algorithm enables me to assess whether – and to what degree – the separate series of news counts reflect systematic discourse on illegal (legal) Latino immigration, rather than the vagaries of news reporting from five different newspapers. This feat is accomplished by distilling any shared variance from the separate time series, that is, by statistically removing the wheat from the chaff, so to speak. To the extent this common variance exists, it becomes the basis for yearly estimates of news coverage on illegal/legal immigration, *purged* of each newspaper's peculiarities.

Table 4.1 provides the results of this measurement analysis. Each set of news series appears to reflect news discourse on its given topic, an inference supported by two crucial pieces of information. First, the five series on illegal immigration systematically tap into news discourse on this topic, as 77 percent of the variance in these five items is commonly shared. This suggests that the year-to-year movements in the single news series are the product of a shared underlying variable – news discourse on illegal Latino immigration – rather than the incoherent fluctuations of five separate news counts. Second, all five of these series are robustly correlated with the resulting measure, typically at .90 or higher. To be sure, the *L. A. Times* series displays a markedly weaker (though still healthy) correlation than the other series. But this simply means this series is a "noisier" indicator of the variable of interest, that relatively more of its variance can be chalked up to the peculiarities of *L. A. Times* reporting

TABLE 4.1. *Validation of Measures for Illegal Immigration News Coverage (Newspapers)*

Indicator	Correlation with Index of Illegal News
L. A. Times – Illegal	.35
N. Y. Times – Illegal	.97
Chicago Tribune – Illegal	.99
Washington Post – Illegal	.98
Atlanta Journal Constitution – Illegal	.95
% variance explained	77%

on Latino illegal immigration, which our earlier inspection of the raw illegal immigration series hinted at (see Figure 4.4).

Table 4.2 reports the results for a similar analysis of the legal Latino immigration news series. There we can see that these findings are comparable to those discussed above. For instance, 65 percent of the variance in these five items is shared – the product of an underlying variable held in common. Moreover, the correlations between each series and the refined legal immigration series are also all robust, from a low of .54 to a high of .98. Together, these two patterns suggest that these items reliably capture news discourse on legal Latino immigrants rather than the whimsical variation in five separate time series.

The resulting series from the previous two measurement analyses are graphed against each other in Figure 4.6. Essentially, each series provides a refined estimate of annual story counts on (il)legal Latino immigration. These filtered estimates allow us to better see that media discourse on legal Latino immigration has been consistently and markedly lower in volume when compared to news discourse on illegal Latino immigration. In general, news discourse on legal Latino immigrants generally hovers below 50 stories per year. In fact, for the entire 20-year span, news reports on legal Latino immigrants averaged a paltry 23 stories – a stark contrast to the average 131 stories on illegal Latino immigrants produced during the same period. Moreover, whereas legal

TABLE 4.2. *Validation of Measures for Legal Immigration News Coverage (Newspapers)*

Indicator	Correlation with Index of Legal News
L. A. Times – Legal	.54
N. Y. Times – Legal	.83
Chicago Tribune – Legal	.98
Washington Post – Legal	.88
Atlanta Journal Constitution – Legal	.74
% variance explained	65%

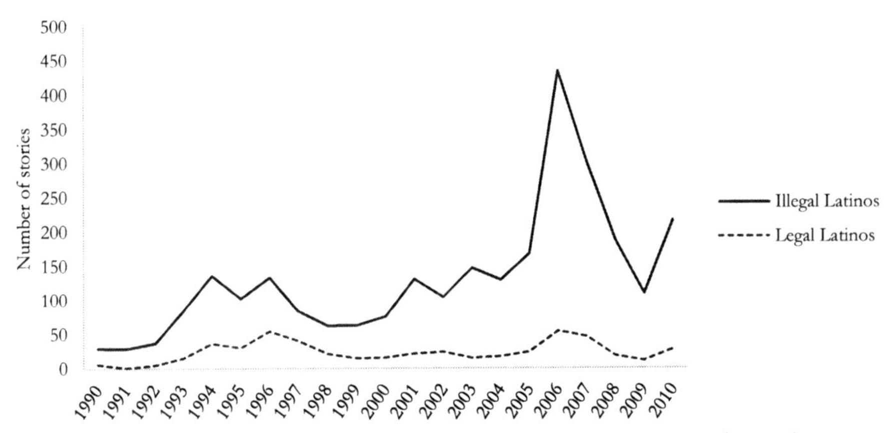

FIGURE 4.6. Estimated number of illegal and legal immigration stories focused on Latinos (newspapers), 1990–2010. *Notes:* Estimates based on series from the measurement analyses reported in Tables 4.1 and 4.2.

immigration discourse varies within a very narrow range year to year, news stories on illegal Latino immigrants have progressively increased, especially in the years after 2000, which experienced the September 11th terrorist attacks and salient public protests in favor of comprehensive immigration reform. Indeed, at its peak in 2006 – when immigration protests took place – discourse on illegal Latino immigrants peaked at about 434 news stories.

What do these patterns imply for the development of implicit attitudes? Recall that implicit attitudes are thought to develop through classical conditioning, where the chronic pairing of an attitude object with positive (negative) stimuli encourages individuals to learn attitudes in the direction of that pairing. This means that an attitude object must be (1) salient and (2) systematically infused with an affective charge. In the case at hand, both of these conditions are met. First, the work of Valentino, Brader, and Jardina (2013) convincingly demonstrates that in the last quarter century, newspaper outlets systematically prime an association between Latinos and the issue of immigration. In other words, in the realm of immigration, Latinos emerge as *the* salient group in news discourse. Second, the findings captured in Figure 4.6 suggest that news stories on illegal Latino immigrants are inordinately more common than news reports on legal Latino immigrants, thereby framing Latinos in a remarkably negative light. Combined, these insights suggest that a search of the American mass public for implicit attitudes toward Latinos should turn up widespread and remarkably negative levels of this phenomenon – a task I undertake in the next chapter.

Newspaper Artifact? Immigration News Trends in Television

The trends in Figure 4.6 suggest that in terms of sheer volume and tone, news media overwhelmingly center on illegal flows of Latino immigrants. But it is

FIGURE 4.7. Estimated number of illegal and legal immigration stories focused on Latinos (television), 1990–2010. *Notes:* Estimates based on measurement analysis reported in Table A4.1 in the appendix to this chapter.

plausible, one might say, that these trends – no matter how systematic – are representative only of major newspapers in the United States. And, because newspapers require reading, these trends really only reflect what some segments of the public – those who are literate and have (or make) the time to read – might encounter about Latino immigrants.

To increase confidence in these news trends and show that they are disseminated on a mass scale, I conduct a similar search of television news content. Accordingly, I draw on the Vanderbilt Television News Archive, which indexes television news broadcast from major networks. Using the same search terms as before for legal and illegal immigration stories on Latinos, I retrieve and count the number of abstracts for television news segments on these two subjects as broadcast on the evening news of the three major networks: ABC, CBS, and NBC. I then analyzed these annual counts using Stimson's algorithm to build over time series for television news discourse on illegal and legal Latino immigrants. The raw results for these analyses are reported in Table A4.1 in the appendix for this chapter. The two series that emerge from this investigation are visually displayed in Figure 4.7.

There we see evidence that largely reproduces the trends uncovered in print media.

Similar to newspapers, television coverage of legal Latino immigrants pales in comparison to coverage of illegal Latinos, with reports on legal Latinos generally hovering below two in most years. In fact, the correlation between the newspaper and television series on legal Latino immigrants correlate at a remarkable $r = .50, p < .05$. This suggests that despite differences in databases and media mode, the anemic volume of coverage legal Latino immigration generally cuts across newspapers and television alike. In other words, it appears

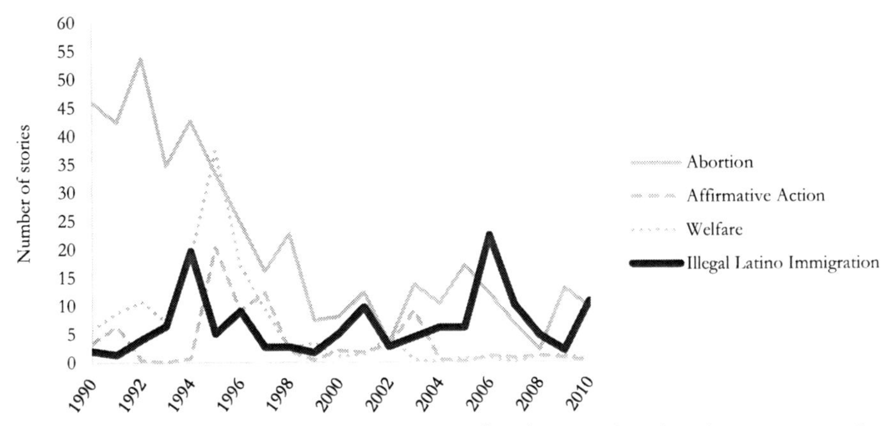

FIGURE 4.8. Estimated number of stories on illegal Latino immigration versus stories on other political issues (television).

that news media in general pay inordinately less attention to legal immigrant flows when covering Latino immigration.

By the same token, television coverage of illegal Latino immigrants replicates the same general trends emerging across print media. As Figure 4.7 shows, the television series on illegal immigration ebbs at precisely the same years as the corresponding newspaper series (i.e., 1994, 2001, and 2006). It is thus unsurprising that the television series on illegal immigration also correlates strongly with its newspaper counterpart ($r = .76$, $p < .05$), thus providing firmer evidence that the chronic focus on illegal Latino immigrants is prevalent across print *and* electronic media.

Nevertheless, even if news stories on illegal Latino immigration overwhelm those on legal Latino immigration, it is possible that coverage of the former is overwhelmed by waves of news coverage on non-immigration issues. After all, I have shown counts of news stories on illegal Latino immigration without a comparison to reports beyond this specific domain. To this end, Figure 4.8 graphs our illegal Latino immigration television series against a count of TV news stories on three contemporary issues: abortion, affirmative action, and welfare.[7]

There we see that, generally speaking, coverage of illegal Latino immigration is comparable in volume to coverage on affirmative action and welfare. In fact, only abortion receives substantially more coverage than illegal Latino immigration, affirmative action, and welfare combined – a trend that changes

[7] Accordingly, I searched the three major networks (i.e., ABC, CBS, and NBC) for story abstracts mentioning "abortion," "affirmative action," and "welfare." Story abstracts were individually inspected to ensure they actually referred to these political issues. Because zero stories were found for some years, the graphed series represent average story counts across the three networks (Stimson's algorithm cannot handle series with zeros).

after 2000, when the abortion series behaves more in line with the other three. Taken as a whole, then, these patterns suggest that illegal Latino immigration is often a salient political issue – at least as salient as other contemporary issues like affirmative action and welfare (and in more recent years, abortion). This suggests the skewed emphasis of news discourse on illegal Latino immigration is unlikely to be lost on many Americans.

Illegal and Legal Latinos: Portrayals versus Actual Numbers

Thus far, my analysis of illegal/legal Latino immigration suggests that both major newspaper and television outlets often cover Latino immigration in the context of illegal rather than legal immigration. But some of this emphasis, one might point out, simply reflects reality. After all, US immigration authorities have regularly published reports showing that Latinos comprise the largest group of illegal immigrants in the United States (e.g., Hoefer et al. 2011). Of course, just because the majority of illegal immigrants in the United States are Latino does not mean most – if not all – Latino immigrants are themselves illegal. Indeed, recall that in the early part of this chapter, I discussed how the 1965 Hart–Celler Act facilitated the unmatched rise of Latinos as the leading group of *legal* immigrants in the last four decades.

So, just how reflective of empirical reality are the results from our news content analysis? Answering this question first requires that we obtain estimates of the proportion of all Latino immigrants who legally and illegally reside in the United States. This task is complicated by the fact that data on the annual number of illegal and legal immigrants entering the United States from Latin America since 1965 is hard to come by. Nevertheless, it is possible to estimate how many Latino immigrants reside legally and illegally in a given year by using publicly available data reported by Passel and Cohn (2012; 2008), and supplementing this with additional data from the US Census *Statistical Abstract* series. From these sources, one can pull together (a) the annual estimated number of foreign-born Latinos residing in the United States, which includes both legal and illegal immigrants and (b) the estimated number of unauthorized Latino immigrants. Using these two quantities, one can estimate the annual percentage of all Latino immigrants that reside in the United States illegally by dividing "b" by "a." In turn, subtracting this quantity from 100 provides the estimated annual percentage of Latino immigrants who reside in the US legally. These estimated proportions are displayed in Figure 4.9 for the last ten years, the longest time span allowed with these data sources.[8]

There we that that across the last decade, the estimated percentage of illegal and legal Latino immigrants living in the United States has been consistently hovering around 50 percent for each subgroup. Yet during the same time

[8] Legal immigrants include those individuals with LPR status, as well as immigrants on temporary visas (e.g., university students) and refugees.

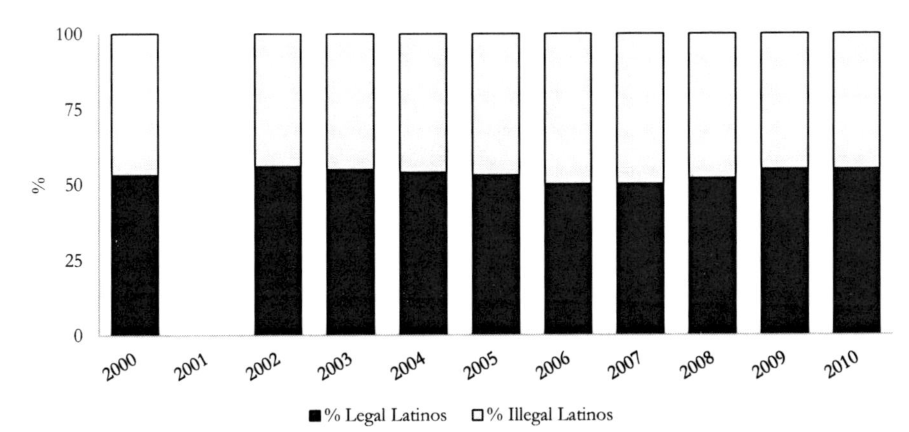

FIGURE 4.9. Estimated percentage of illegal and legal immigrants among Latino foreign-born, 2000–2010. *Source:* Estimates based on data reported by the US Census, *Statistical Abstract: 2000–2012*; and Passel and Cohn (2008; 2012). A 2001 estimate is not reported because the relevant data for that year are incomplete.

period, news coverage about these two flows of immigrants has disproportionately centered on illegal Latino immigrants. Figure 4.10 shows just how disproportionately by graphing the annual estimated percentage of news stories on illegal Latinos (averaged across news media). Although illegal Latino immigrants have generally comprised about half of all Latino immigrants residing in the United States for most years since 2000, about 88 percent of stories on Latino immigration have focused on their illegal origins – a figure that is

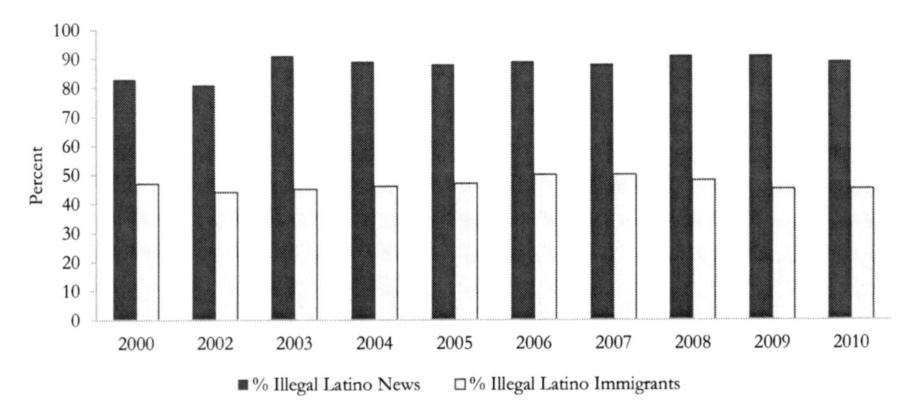

FIGURE 4.10. Estimated percentage of news on illegal Latinos compared with estimated percentage of actual illegal Latinos, 2000–2010. *Source:* Estimates of illegal Latino immigrants based on data reported in Figure 4.9. Estimates of news on illegal Latino immigrants based on average of percentages reported in Figures 4.6 and 4.7. A 2001 estimate is not reported because the relevant data for that year are incomplete.

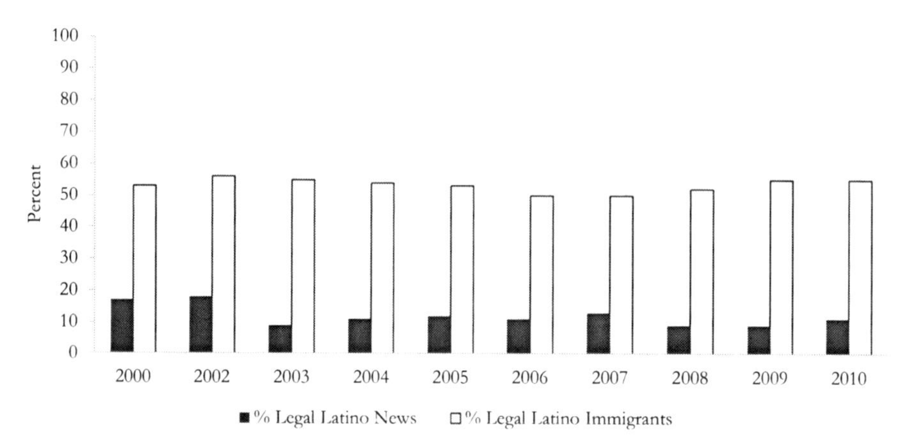

FIGURE 4.11. Estimated percentage of news on legal Latinos compared with estimated percentage of actual legal Latinos, 2000–2010. *Source:* Estimates of legal Latino immigrants based on data reported in Figure 4.9. Estimates of news on legal Latino immigrants based on average of percentages reported in Figures 4.6 and 4.7. A 2001 estimate is not reported because the relevant data for that year are incomplete.

nearly twice the estimated proportion of illegal Latino immigrants during this time span. In contrast, Figure 4.11 reveals that while legal Latino immigrants have also consistently made up about 50 percent of all Latino immigrant in the United States during this same time frame, only 12 percent of stories on Latino immigrants focused on their legal origins – a figure about four times less the actual proportion of legal Latino immigrants.[9] Hence, although the portrayal of Latino immigrants as *illegal* is undeniably systematic, it is also hard to escape the fact that this depiction is only loosely moored to actual immigration trends, a result reflected in analyses of other racial groups in different policy domains (Clawson and Trice 2000; Gilens 1999).

To be sure, one can argue that most news coverage should, in fact, focus on Latino illegal immigrants. It is a sensational topic that can help news outlets drive up audience shares (cf. Gilens 1999), and most unauthorized immigrants in the United States are from Latin America anyway (Hoefer et al. 2011). But even coverage on illegal immigration is askew. Consider that in 2000, 67 percent of the roughly 8.5 million unauthorized immigrants in the United States were from Mexico, El Salvador, Guatemala, Honduras, and Ecuador, in descending order. In that year, the three major television news networks aired an average of five stories on illegal immigrants from Latin America. Nevertheless, in that same year, about 14 percent of undocumented immigrants in the United States were from Asia and about 4 percent from Europe. Yet the same networks did not air one full story on either group in that year.

[9] Again, the figure reflects the estimated annual percentage of news stories on legal Latino immigrants, averaged across news media.

This general pattern prevails in the intervening years leading up to 2010, when 76 percent of the estimated 11 million unauthorized immigrants in the United States were from Mexico, El Salvador, Guatemala, Honduras, and Ecuador, again in descending order (Hoefer et al. 2011). The three major news networks aired about eleven stories on unauthorized Latino immigrants in that year. In contrast, about 9 percent and 3 percent of unauthorized immigrants in the United States during 2010 were from Asia or Europe (Hoefer et al. 2011), yet the same networks, again, did not air a single story on either group. Ultimately, it may be too much to expect news outlets to cover immigration in a way that more fully captures empirical reality (cf. Gilens 1999). But these distortions, I show in the next chapter, are consistent with the prevalence of implicit attitudes toward Latino immigrants.

Conclusions

People are known to develop implicit attitudes toward a variety of objects, including social groups (Greenwald et al. 1998), political figures (Arcuri et al. 2008), cultural symbols (Devos and Banaji 2005), and consumer products (Maison et al. 2004). But on what basis do individuals develop these implicit attitudes? One popular explanation is that people acquire them from the "totality of evaluative information associated with an attitude object" (Rydell and McConnell 2006: 1001). Accordingly, this chapter has shown that plenty of news about Latino immigrants exists on a mass scale to support individuals' development of negative implicit attitudes toward this object, as dictated by the principles of classical conditioning.

Although news media are often thought of as purveyors of political information, they are also business enterprises, strongly driven to report news that increases advertising revenues and audience shares (e.g., Hamilton 2004). And it is this economic logic that can help us to make better sense of the imbalanced coverage of Latino immigration we have discussed in this chapter. As several scholars have observed, reporters often face strong incentives to cover sensational topics in an effort to increase audiences, and therefore, profit margins (e.g., Branton and Dunaway 2009; Patterson 1996). Against this benchmark, a strong media focus on illegal Latino immigration makes sense. This is an emotive subject likely to grab many people's attention (e.g., Merolla et al. 2013). Yet, from another perspective, media focus on sensational topics can also clash with objective reality. Rather than mirroring empirical facts, news media can refract them in a way that distorts how the world is. In the case at hand, it risks promoting the mistaken impression that most – if not all – Latino immigrants are illegal. Hence, for reasons like these, Althaus and his colleagues remind us that "news outlets have neither incentive nor ability to serve as reliable conveyors of social facts" (2011: 1065).

Of course, as I pointed out in the preceding text, it might be unreasonable to expect news content that is empirically accurate (cf. Gilens 1999). Yet, however well that might be true, the mismatch between news coverage and objective reality can still have real consequences. That is because news media are collectively one of the few sources of widely disseminated information. The volume and tenor of news reports is therefore likely to affect what topics we think about, and how we think about them (Iyengar and Kinder 1987). In the realm of immigration, news reports on this topic across the last quarter century have strongly focused on Latino immigrants while chronically casting them in an unflattering light. With society awash in so much negative information about a single immigrant group, it stands to reason that implicit attitudes toward this group should exist on a wide scale and be easy to find. By the same token, if immigration news coverage regularly primes Latinos relative to other groups of foreigners, these implicit attitudes should be strongly tied to people's political judgments of immigration policy proposals. Whether these implications stand up to empirical scrutiny is the subject of the next chapter.

TABLE A4.1. *Validation of Measures for Illegal and Legal Immigration News Coverage (Television)*

Indicator	**Correlation with Index of Illegal News**
ABC – Illegal	.96
CBS – Illegal	.91
NBC – Illegal	.93
% variance explained	87%

Notes: The television legal Latino immigration series is not amenable to analysis using Stimson's algorithm given that in some years, at least one network fails to produce a story on legal Latino immigrants. Unfortunately, Stimson's (2008: 2) algorithm cannot handle series with any zero values. Thus, the television legal Latino immigration series in Figure 4.7 is based on the average of news stories on legal Latino immigrants across networks, on a year-to-year basis. Critically, the correlation between this television measure and its newspaper analog created via Stimson's algorithm is a healthy $r = .50$, $p < .001$.

5

Unstated

The Measurement of Implicit Attitudes

We have seen evidence suggesting that news media can play an important role in promoting associative reasoning by systematically supplying affectively charged information about political objects. Such evidence makes more credible the claim that long-term patterns in political discourse encourage the development of implicit attitudes. But how can we know that these implicit attitudes actually exist and matter for political decisions?

Several obstacles stand in the way of answering this question. But arguably, the most fundamental of these quandaries is this: How does one detect attitudes that are spontaneous, hard to control, and nonverbalized – in a word, implicit? If, as I have explained, implicit attitudes are beyond introspection, then measuring them by asking people about them is a nonstarter. A more creative measure for this task must be found. Yet this measure must be more than just innovative. It must also demonstrate that it can tap into something that other measures cannot. That is, it must capture the evaluative associations about political objects that implicit attitudes are said to be. Yet, just like other measures, it must also show that these implicit evaluations can systematically explain people's explicit political choices.

The goal of this chapter is twofold: first, to propose a solution to this measurement conundrum; and second, to show that what I capture with this proposed measure is politically consequential. My tool of choice is formally known as the Implicit Association Test (IAT).[1] Rather than asking people to evaluate objects, the IAT enables researchers to infer the presence of implicit attitude, not

[1] The IAT is one of many measures aimed at assessing implicit attitudes, including Affective Priming (AP) and the Affect Misattribution Procedure (AMP) (for an overview see Petty et al. 2009). I employ the IAT because relative to other measures, it has been more extensively validated, a point I discuss in length in subsequent pages of this chapter (e.g., Greenwald et al. 2009; Nosek and Smyth 2007; Nosek et al. 2005).

from what people say, but from what they do and how fast they do it. Specifically, the IAT gauges the evaluative associations individuals have about objects by timing people's ability to rapidly sort exemplars of objects (e.g., *Insects, Flowers*), positive attributes (e.g., *wonderful*), and negative attributes (e.g., *terrible*) – all while using different classification schemes on a computer screen. The assumption here is that people will sort exemplars more quickly when their mental associations about objects match the classification scheme they are instructed to use. If, for example, a person has a more negative attitude toward insects than flowers, she should find it easier to sort words when exemplars of insects and negative attributes are classified using the same response key on a computer (e.g., "E") than when flowers and negative attributes share that same key. And, since sorting of these exemplars occurs in milliseconds, the ability to deliberate is minimized. Hence, people's responses are both spontaneous and nonverbalized – features said to define implicit attitudes.

The IAT, as I have briefly described it, appears to provide just the solution that a political scientist interested in measuring implicit attitudes would need. But the IAT is not without its skeptics. Some critics, for example, contend the IAT fails to capture people's own attitudes, that the responses to this measure are an artifact of how the test is completed (e.g., Arkes and Tetlock 2004; Karpinski and Hilton 2001; Rothermund and Wentura 2004). Other critics charge that scores on the IAT are an inconsequential predictor of people's judgments and behaviors and that self-reported attitudes are a more solid basis for individual decisions (e.g., Arkes and Tetlock 2004; Blanton et al. 2009). These types of allegations are ironic, for the IAT has been more extensively studied than any other measure of implicit attitude. Thus, relative to comparable measures, we have firm knowledge about the IAT's validity, including the extent to which responses on this measure reliably capture implicit attitudes (e.g., Lane et al. 2007; Nosek et al. 2007a), and the degree to which these attitudes explain people's decisions and behaviors (e.g., Greenwald et al. 2009; Hofmann et al. 2005).

Of course, knowing more about a measure does not mean we have learned everything about it, nor that it is beyond reproach. And one aspect of the IAT that has received less scrutiny is its relevance to "real-world" phenomena. Despite extensive research into this measure, most IAT analyses utilize data from convenience samples comprised of student subjects or other self-selected populations. Consequently, uncertainty remains over the degree to which IAT responses affect social phenomena beyond the confines of university labs, among people other than "college sophomores" (Sears 1986; see also Henrich et al. 2010).

But what value, really, is there in assessing people's split second attitudes toward political objects? Does it not make sense to simply measure what people expressly report? In a word, no. Self-reported, or explicit, attitudes are a key ingredient in public opinion. But they are conceptually distinct from implicit attitudes. Implicit attitudes are spontaneously evoked, hard to control, and can operate below awareness. They are also fairly immune to social desirability or self-presentational concerns. In turn, explicit attitudes emerge further down a person' cognitive stream, after implicit attitudes are activated. They are easier to control, within introspection, and more easily influenced by social desirability or self-presentational concerns. Given these conceptual nuances, implicit and explicit attitudes demand tailored measurement. In this vein, Gawronski et al. (2014: 1) observe that self-reported measures are often "unable to capture thoughts and feelings that people are either unwilling or unable to report," especially in the realm of racial attitudes, where social desirability can distort what people express (cf. Greenwald and Banaji 1995). "Moreover, the value of self-report measures seems limited for the assessment of thoughts and feelings that are outside of conscious awareness" (Gawronski et al. 2014b: 1), which can color people's interpretation of subsequent information, plus affect their downstream decisions (Lodge and Taber 2013). Measuring implicit attitudes thus positions scholars to obtain a clearer sense of what people spontaneously feel about political objects (devoid of social desirability), and how this shapes their views on immigration.

To these ends, this chapter illustrates the relevance of implicit attitudes to the "real world" of US politics by documenting a robust association between people's IAT performance and their immigration policy preferences. Chapter 4's news content analysis suggests the media's systematic focus on Latino immigrants and their repeated association with negative connotation (i.e., illegal immigration) should produce remarkably negative implicit attitudes toward this group – attitudes that should strongly influence people's thinking about immigration. True, by this reasoning, explicit attitudes toward Latino immigrants should also be just as negative. But given that strong US norms exist against publicly expressing negative attitudes toward racial and ethnic minorities (e.g., Greenwald and Banaji 1995; Mendelberg 2001), social desirability bias should, on average, water down what people openly report about this group, but not what they reveal implicitly.

In the following pages, I marshal several lines of evidence affirming the political importance of implicit attitudes. First, I use the IAT to show that implicit attitudes toward Latino immigrants are pervasive, as well as markedly more negative than self-reported attitudes toward immigrants in general, and Latino immigrants in particular. In fact, although implicit and explicit attitudes toward Latino immigrants are positively correlated, this association is weak, which hints that social desirability pressure might affect how prevalent the former appears to be (cf. Gawronski et al. 2014b). Second, I demonstrate that implicit attitudes are tied directly to Latino immigrants by showing that individual IAT scores are associated with self-reported attitudes toward Latinos, but unassociated with attitudes toward other immigrants. Third, and most importantly, I establish that implicit attitudes toward Latinos reliably predict individual support for exclusionary immigration policies, thereby supporting the *affect transfer* hypothesis explained in Chapter 3 (Lodge and Taber 2013). Specifically, I reveal that the spontaneous and unarticulated affect evoked by one's implicit attitude is directly associated with one's immigration policy judgments, with more negative implicit attitudes producing greater opposition to immigration within the US mass public. This relationship between implicit attitudes and explicit political choices, I show, emerges even after controlling for other predispositions (e.g., partisanship, education) that are relevant to political judgments, thus increasing confidence in the political relevance of implicit attitudes. In fact, my analyses suggest that many of these explicit predispositions mediate, or channel, the spontaneous affective charge of implicit attitudes, thus providing evidence that is consistent with the *affect contagion* hypothesis discussed in Chapter 3 (Lodge and Taber 2013).

But first, let me explain in more detail how the IAT taps into the unspoken evaluative associations we possess about objects – that is, our implicit attitudes.

IAT Basics: Intuition and Mechanics

Implicit attitudes are learned associations about objects. In the presence of fitting stimuli, these associations spontaneously come to mind and serve as evaluative information, telling us whether we feel positively or negatively toward objects. The ingenuity of the IAT is that it retrieves these associations by having people quickly perform sorting exercises. The logic here is that people make faster connections when concepts are consistently linked to negative (positive) affect than when they are not. Let me explain how.

Let us say I am interested in measuring people's evaluative associations about insects and flowers. Let us also say that I hypothesize that people have more negative associations about insects than flowers. The IAT assesses people's evaluative associations about these objects by sitting individuals behind a computer and asking them to rapidly classify words that appear individually and randomly on the center of the screen by using one of two classification schemes. The first of these schemes assumes insects are negatively associated, and flowers are positively associated, in people's minds. In other words, the scheme *matches* my hypothesis about people's evaluative associations about these objects. Thus, the labels **Insect** and **Bad** appear in the upper left corner of the computer screen, while the labels **Flower** and **Good** appear in the upper right corner. This matched scheme is illustrated in Figure 5.1a.

The objective for people taking this IAT is to use this classification pair to rapidly sort single stimulus words that appear on the center of the screen. For instance, if the word is an exemplar of an insect (e.g., bee) or a word with a negative connotation (e.g., terrible), individuals will press the "E" key on their computer. If the word is an exemplar of a flower (e.g., tulip) or a word with positive connotation (e.g., wonderful), individuals will press the "I" key. People eventually sort forty such words, randomly selected and individually presented on the center of the screen. This enables researchers to compute a person's average response time to individual words (in milliseconds), with faster

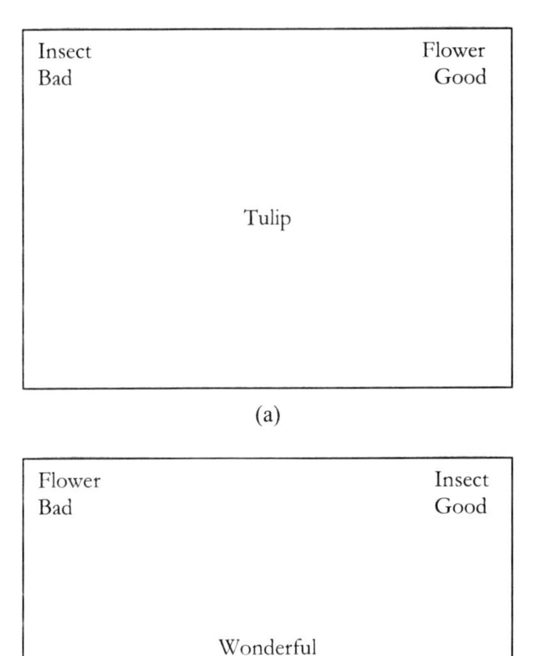

FIGURE 5.1. (a) Hypothetical IAT classification scheme: Insects negatively evaluated and flowers positively evaluated. *Note:* This scheme implies that the object *Insect* is mentally associated with negative connotation (i.e., Bad), while the object *Flower* is associated with positive connotation (i.e., Good). In other words, people have a negative evaluation of insect and positive evaluation of flowers. (b) Hypothetical IAT classification scheme: Flowers negatively evaluated and insects positively evaluated. *Note:* This scheme implies that the object *Flower* is mentally associated with negative connotation (i.e., Bad), while the object *Insect* is associated with positive connotation (i.e., Good). In other words, people have a negative evaluation of flowers and positive evaluation of insects.

responses indicating closer correspondence between the classification scheme and a person's mental associations about these objects.

In the second key exercise, individuals complete another forty words, using the same stimuli and instructions. But this time, the labels **Flower** and **Insect** are interchanged (see Figure 5.1b). Now the classification scheme is *mismatched*, with **Flower** and **Bad** appearing in the upper left corner of the screen, and **Insect** and **Good** appearing on the upper right corner. As before, the quantity of interest is the mean reaction time to single words, with faster times

TABLE 5.1. *Hypothetical Flower–Insect IAT*

Block	No. of Trials	Items Assigned to "E" Key	Items Assigned to "I" Key
1	20	Insect names	Flower names
2	20	Bad words	Good words
3	20	Insect names I Bad words	Flower names I Good words
4	40	Insect names I Bad words	Flower names I Good words
5	40	Flower names	Insect names
6	20	Flower names I Bad words	Insect names I Good words
7	40	Flower names I Bad words	Insect names I Good words

Notes: A trial is the time from the onset of a single stimulus word to its correct categorization. Trials in which an error is made require the respondent to correct the error before moving on to next trial. Most IATs counterbalance the order of blocks 1, 3, and 4 with blocks 5, 6, and 7.

suggesting closer agreement between this classification pair and a person's mental associations.

Armed with the mean reaction time from each block, I can assess the direction and intensity of people's evaluative associations about insects and flowers. If people have negative implicit attitudes about insects (relative to flowers), then they should sort stimulus words faster and with less errors when using the matched scheme (Insect I Bad–Flower I Good) than when using the mismatched scheme (Flower I Bad–Insect I Good pairing). Of course, some people will sort words faster than other individuals, but this simply means they have stronger implicit attitudes. These individual differences are crucial, for they will allow me to assess the degree to which stronger implicit attitudes shape explicit political choices.

The Full Sequence of the IAT

Although these two sorting tasks are the crux of the IAT, the full test involves additional exercises that acclimate people to the measure. In total, the IAT consists of seven blocks, or sets of exercises. The seven blocks for the IAT discussed above are in Table 5.1. In the first, people learn to sort exemplars of two objects, **Insect** and **Flower**. People thus complete twenty trials, or classifications of a randomly selected stimulus word. In the second block, people complete twenty more trials, but this time they practice sorting words connoting **Bad** or **Good**. In the third block, the prior two tasks are combined: **Insect** is paired with **Bad**, and **Flower** is paired with **Good**. People complete twenty more trials using this scheme. After this, the first key block is completed, where the same Insect I Bad–Flower I Good scheme is used for forty trials.

Following this first key block, individuals practice sorting flowers and insects using a scheme that changes the position of the labels **Insect** and **Flower**. Now, **Flower** is on the left-hand corner and **Insect** is on the right-hand corner. After several practice trials, respondents complete a new combined task where **Flower** and **Bad** are associated and **Insect** and **Good** are associated. And, after twenty trials of this combination, individuals go through the second key block and complete forty trials with this new classification scheme.

Three aspects of the IAT merit attention before discussing this measure's validity. First, each key block is preceded by a practice block, which helps to ensure that sorting times are mainly driven by people's own attitudes rather than by unfamiliarity with the measure (e.g., Greenwald et al. 1998). Second, the order of the key blocks and their attendant practice trials are counterbalanced across respondents, which ensures that sorting times are driven by one's underlying implicit attitude, not the order of the key blocks (e.g., Nosek et al. 2007a). Third, IAT response times are transformed into individual attitude scores by subtracting people's average response time on the matched task (Insect | Bad–Flower | Good) from their average response time on the mismatched task (Flower | Bad–Insect | Good) (Greenwald et al. 1998). Higher IAT scores thus suggest stronger associations in the direction of the matched pairing.

In most IAT applications, raw response times are converted into individual scores through an algorithm that utilizes as many response times as possible, while minimizing the influence of error trials. This is mainly achieved by using response times from the key blocks and their attendant practice blocks; eliminating excessively long response times from these blocks; and assessing penalties to trials from these blocks where an error was made (Greenwald et al. 2003). These refined latencies permit researchers to compute individual differences in sorting times between the matched and mismatched tasks from (a) the key blocks and (b) their attendant practice blocks. The results from *a* and *b* are then averaged to yield IAT scores, with higher values reflecting stronger implicit attitude in the direction of the matched task.

What We Know about the IAT's Validity

Compared to self-reports, the IAT is admittedly an unconventional way to capture individual attitudes. People are never asked to express what they think, and their thoughts are inferred from the speed with which they complete a set of tasks. Yet by many scientific standards, the IAT is a valid and reliable measure of attitudes (for overviews, see Lane et al. 2007; Nosek et al. 2007a). To begin with, the IAT yields large effect sizes. For example, subtracting the average response time between key blocks, and dividing this difference by its associated standard deviation produces Cohen's d – a mean difference in standardized units (Cohen 1988). By convention, d values around .2, .5, and .8 are considered small, moderate, and large, respectively. IAT effects often range from large to very large ($d > 1.00$). One virtue of effects sizes this large is that scholars have been able to independently reproduce them across several studies, thus further bolstering confidence in this measure's ability to assess implicit attitudes (e.g., Greenwald et al. 2009; Hofmann et al. 2005).

Research also shows that IAT scores are unaffected by procedural features peculiar to this measure. Individual IAT scores are not driven by people's familiarity with stimulus items (e.g., Nosek et al. 2002; Rudman et al. 1999). Strong IAT effects have been reproduced when people's familiarity with stimulus items is statistically controlled (Dasgupta et al. 2003) or experimentally manipulated (Ottaway et al. 2001). IAT scores are also unaffected by the order of the key blocks and their practice trials, as their sequence is typically counterbalanced to avoid this order effect (e.g., Nosek et al. 2005). The magnitude of IAT effects, moreover, is impervious to whether people are right-handed, left-handed, or ambidextrous (Greenwald and Nosek 2001). Finally, IAT scores are robust to whether words with positive or negative connotations are assigned to the right or left side of the screen.

A vaunted feature of the IAT is its exposure of attitudes that are spontaneous and hard to control (Greenwald et al. 1998). Several studies show IAT scores are hard for people to fake or distort (Kim 2003; Steffens 2004), thus highlighting the IAT's ability to minimize social desirability concerns in attitude reporting. Specifically, accumulating research suggests people often find it difficult to alter their IAT responses even when they are encouraged to do so by researchers (Asendorpf et al. 2002; Egloff and Schmukle 2002; Kim 2003; Steffens 2004). In fact, people can alter their IAT scores only if they have recent experience with the IAT *and* are given detailed instructions on how to adjust their test-taking (e.g., slowing down responses in the key block one finds easier to perform) (Fiedler and Bluemke 2005). Absent these details, individuals are generally unable to alter IAT responses on their own.[2]

The IAT is also a measure with a respectable degree of reliability, especially in comparison to other implicit attitude measures (e.g., evaluative priming; Go/No-Go Association Test; Extrinsic Affective Simon Task) (e.g., Fazio and Olson 2003; Nosek and Banaji 2001; Teige et al. 2004). Indeed, "[p]art of the IAT's acceptance as an implicit measure may be attributable to its achieving greater reliability than other latency-based implicit measures" (Nosek et al. 2007a: 274). Reliability refers to the precision of measurement (e.g., Brown 2006). Technically, it refers to the proportion of variance attributable to the true score of a variable rather than measurement error. Latency tests such as the IAT are often susceptible to low degrees of reliability because varied sources of measurement error can affect the quality and speed of response. For instance, an eye blink, a sneeze, even a cough, can influence how fast (or slow) a person responds to stimuli on a computer screen, *above and beyond* the influence of one's own attitude toward a social object.

Nevertheless, research finds the IAT reliably taps into its intended construct. For example, latent variable analyses of the IAT demonstrate that scores from practice and key blocks are strong indicators of implicit attitude (Cunningham et al. 2001; Ranganath et al. 2008). Item loadings for IAT scores often range at or above .50, far above the .30 threshold used to determine whether an indicator is meaningfully related to an underlying attitude (Brown 2006). In

[2] Emerging research also suggests "faked" IAT scores can be statistically detected and partially corrected for use in applied analyses (Cvencek et al. 2010).

addition, split-half correlations of IAT scores suggest this measure is internally consistent. Split-half correlations are produced by dividing a test into two halves and then correlating (or computing alphas for) these scores. Higher positive correlations (or alphas) indicate a test captures its intended construct. Split-half correlations of IAT scores between .60 and .90 are common, thus suggesting a reasonable degree of internal consistency (Bosson et al. 2000; Greenwald and Nosek 2001; Schmukle and Egloff 2004). By comparison, split-half correlations of evaluative priming measures, which also aim to capture implicit attitudes, have sometimes shown split-half correlations as low as .04 (Olson and Fazio 2003).

Test–retest correlations also suggest the IAT displays a respectable degree of reliability. Here, the IAT is administered to the same individuals at two different time points. Scores from each administration are then correlated. Higher positive correlations suggest the IAT captures trait-related (rather than state-related) variance. Using this approach, Lane et al. (2007) report a stable level of reliability for the IAT, with a median test–retest correlation of .56 across several studies that varied the number of days between time points.

Scholars have also investigated the IAT's predictive validity, finding that IAT scores are systematically related to individual differences in explicit judgments and behaviors. Nosek et al. (2007), for example, find that people's implicit attitudes toward racial, religious, and other social groups are positively and robustly associated with their self-reported attitudes toward these respective groups (see also Amodio and Devine 2006; Jellison et al. 2004; Nosek et al. 2002). Similarly, Maison et al. (2004) have used the IAT to show that implicit attitudes toward soft drinks (i.e., Coca Cola vs. Pepsi) reliably predict individuals' preference for and usage of soda brand (see also Brunel et al. 2004). Furthermore, several studies have found that IAT scores are significantly associated with individual differences in drug use (e.g., Ames et al. 2007), shy and anxious behaviors (e.g., Asendorpf et al. 2002; Egloff and Schmukle 2002), and racial preferences for partners in experimental activities (e.g., Ashburn-Nardo et al. 2003). Capping this stream of evidence, the meta-analysis of Greenwald et al. (2009) shows that IAT scores systematically predict individual differences in behaviors and judgments across these and other domains (average $r =$ .27). Critically, this association between IAT scores and explicit judgments and behaviors is robust to the inclusion of self-reported analogs to implicit attitudes, which suggests IAT scores bear unique leverage over individuals' decisions and actions. In fact, in domains where social desirability concerns are present (e.g., racial attitudes), IAT scores outperform their self-reported counterparts in predicting individual evaluations of and behaviors toward relevant objects (e.g., racial groups).

Blind Spots

The accumulated literature suggests the IAT is a valid and reliable measure of attitudes. Yet there are two relevant and important caveats to these findings.

The first is that while scholars have uncovered robust relationships between implicit attitudes and explicit judgments and behaviors, these associations have often been discovered in self-selected samples of convenience, typically comprised of student subjects. The challenge here is not that we cannot believe the statistical relationships in these data. Rather, it is how representative these relationships are beyond the narrow demographic confines of these samples. Indeed, in his ringing critique of student subject pools for hypothesis testing, Sears (1986: 520) warned that one inherent risk in this research strategy is that the strength of a relationship between variables – say, *y* and *x* – can be misestimated. As he explained, " ...*x* may, in everyday life, not influence *y* much, and/or other variables may influence it more strongly." This raises the possibility that the relevance and strength of implicit attitudes has been under- or even overestimated by relying too heavily on student subjects. Some scholars have addressed this concern by studying implicit attitudes in samples with richer demographic variation, finding results comparable to those gleaned from student studies (e.g., Nosek et al. 2002, 2007b). But, because these more variegated samples are still comprised by *self-selected* respondents, it remains unclear how representative these relationships are of a larger population, such as the adult mass public (but see Pasek et al. 2009).

The second caveat concerns the predictive validity of the IAT. In studies assessing this feature of the IAT, scholars have typically shown that implicit attitudes toward social objects affect judgments and behaviors independently of self-reported attitudes toward the same social objects. This certainly increases confidence in the uniqueness of the attitudes captured by the IAT. But judgments and behaviors are arguably complex, a function of more than implicit and explicit attitudes toward the same social objects. However, without accounting for additional, theoretically relevant considerations, scholars risk misattributing to implicit attitudes what can be better explained by other rigorously measured self-reported predispositions. This danger of omitted variable bias is particularly acute in the realm of politics, where partisanship and other predispositions compete for influence over people's political decisions.

For the political scientist, then, these two caveats might be rephrased in question form: are implicit attitudes politically consequential in the American mass public? The goal in the remainder of this chapter is to persuade you that they can be by examining the relationship between implicit attitudes toward Latino immigrants and mass judgments of immigration policy.

The IAT, Latino Immigrants, and US Immigration Politics

My expectation, set out earlier in this chapter, is that implicit attitudes toward Latino immigrants exist and influence individual preferences for immigration policy. More specifically, per my theoretical discussion in Chapter 3, I hypothesize that the political influence of implicit attitudes will manifest itself via *affect transfer* (i.e., by directly shaping immigration policy judgments) and *affect contagion* (i.e., by indirectly influencing the explicit considerations one brings to bear on immigration policy judgments) (Lodge and Taber 2013). Therefore, in an effort to gauge these implicit attitudes, I designed an IAT that contrasts Latino and white immigrants.

Recall that the IAT is a relative measure of implicit attitude toward objects. This means that in administering an IAT, researchers must make informed decisions about which objects will be contrasted (e.g., Lane et al. 2007; Nosek et al. 2007a). As Pinter and Greenwald (2005: 74) explain, "[b]ecause of the relative nature of the IAT, it is important that the target concept chosen to contrast with ... be selected in a way that is conceptually appropriate for the research question." For reasons I explain in the text that follows, I chose to primarily contrast Latino and white immigrants. Later in the chapter, I also provide evidence that an IAT contrasting Latinos and whites (without the "immigrant" modifier) yields comparable results.

In the annals of immigration, native-born Americans have often compared new groups of immigrants to white immigrants, especially those with Anglo-Saxon origins (Higham 1981; King 2000). These comparisons have revolved around tried-and-true themes, such as whether new immigrants can successfully integrate to American culture (like white immigrants), or whether new immigrants have what it takes to be active, democratic citizens (like white immigrants). Chinese and Japanese immigrants in the late 1800s illustrate this trend. The 1882 Chinese Exclusion Act and the 1907 Gentlemen's Agreement – which limited Chinese and Japanese immigration, respectively – were direct responses to widespread concerns that these groups were incapable of culturally and politically adapting to American norms and practices (like white immigrants) (Saxton 1972; Takaki 1989). In the early 1900s, similar allegations were made against Jewish, Italian, and other southern and eastern European immigrants, who were anything but considered white at the time (Gerstle 2001; Jacobson 1998; Roediger 2005).

I expect this general tendency to hold for Latino immigrants as well. Thus, I employ an IAT that contrasts Latino and white immigrants. This design implies that insofar as individuals have a negative implicit attitude toward Latino immigrants (relative to white immigrants), they should display faster sorting times when using a matched classification scheme (Latino Immigrant–Bad | White Immigrant–Good) than when using a mismatched scheme (White Immigrant–Bad | Latino Immigrant–Good). This IAT's full sequence is detailed in Table 5.2.

Sources of Evidence

Since this IAT version has existed only until recently, I rely on three studies to document this measure's political relevance. The first of these is a laboratory study conducted on college students in July 2007 (henceforth, Lab Study 1). Lab Study 1 ($n = 44$) piloted this version of the IAT to assess whether it actually taps

TABLE 5.2. *Illustration of IAT Sequence: Latino versus White Immigrants*

Sequence	Block 1	Block 2	Block 3	Block 4	Block 5	Block 6	Block 7
Task Description	Concept Classification	Attribute Classification	Practice Combined Task	Combined Task	Reversed Concept Classification	Practice Reversed Combined Task	Reversed Combined Task
Classification Pairs	Latino or White	Bad or Good	Latino/Bad or White/Good	Latino/Bad or White/Good	White or Latino	White/Bad or Latino/Good	White/Bad or Latino/Good
Sample Words	García Johnson Díaz Miller	Horrible Glorious Agony Happy	Smith Terrible López Wonderful	Jones Awful Pérez Joy	Díaz Miller García Johnson	Ramírez Nasty Wilson Laughter	Sánchez Horrible Taylor Love
No. of Trials	20	20	20	40	40	20	40

Notes: Implicit attitude scores are based on data from blocks 3, 4, 6, and 7. The order of blocks 1, 3, and 4 (matched task) and blocks 5, 6, and 7 (mismatched task) were counterbalanced in the study. In other words, some subject first performed the matched tasks, while others first performed the mismatched task. A trial is defined as the time from the onset of a single word to the correct classification of that word. Trials in which an error is made requires a person to correct the error before proceeding to the next trial.

into implicit attitude toward Latino immigrants. By validating this IAT version with a fully controlled experiment, Lab Study 1 also allows me to compare the robustness of this measure when it is employed in settings where researchers have less control over participants and study materials, such as public opinion surveys, which political scientists generally use to examine political attitudes.

Building on Lab Study 1, I designed a national public opinion survey that embedded the piloted version of the IAT (henceforth, National Survey). This survey was conducted online by YouGov/Polimetrix (YGP) during July 16–26, 2008. YGP administers online surveys to respondents from their opt-in panel. These samples are then statistically matched to known demographics of the current population. This matching procedure has been shown to yield representative samples, such that a "...matched sample mimics the characteristics of the target sample" (Rivers 2008: 9). In the case at hand, the YGP sample was statistically matched to be nationally representative of non-Hispanic white adults ($n = 350$).

The national study has several advantages over Lab Study 1. First, the national study yielded a sample with richer demographic variation among respondents. And, because this survey is matched to be nationally representative, we can be more confident that results involving the IAT generalize to a majority of US adults. Second, the national study fielded the IAT alongside several explicit predispositions, including attitudes toward Latino, White, Asian, and Middle Eastern immigrants; authoritarianism; national identity; and – most relevant of all to politics – partisanship. This range of explicit attitudes facilitates a more rigorous assessment of the IAT's predictive validity relative to other predispositions known to shape political judgments, thus increasing faith in the IAT's ability to structure politics.

The third study in my analysis is another laboratory experiment conducted on university students ($n = 122$). The aim of this study (henceforth, Lab Study 2) was to assess whether and to what degree the attitude elicited by this IAT is trained on Latino immigrants in particular, rather than Latinos more broadly. This issue cuts to the heart of my adaptation of the IAT and its conceptual boundaries. One possibility is that Latino immigrants and Latinos are distinct social objects in people's minds, thereby eliciting different implicit attitudes. Yet it is also plausible that these objects are indistinguishable in people's minds, and thus, their implicit attitudes toward them are one and the same. By randomizing two versions of the IAT, Lab Study 2 provides leverage over this question.

But before we get too far ahead of ourselves, let us address the most basic of questions: can the IAT elicit implicit attitudes toward Latino immigrants?

Latino Immigrant = Bad: Strength and Prevalence

I expect to find implicit attitude toward Latino immigrants. Thus, people completing my IAT should sort stimuli faster when using a matched classification

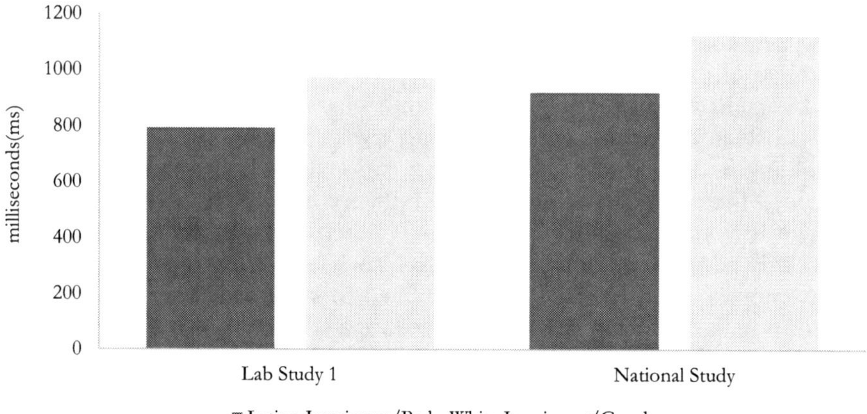

FIGURE 5.2. Average response times by key block in IAT. *Note:* An IAT effect emerges when there is a reliable difference in sorting times between key blocks. Here, people sorted stimuli faster when *Latino Immigrant* was associated with *Bad* and *White Immigrant* was associated with *Good* ($p < .05$, two-tailed). Taking mean response times from the Latino Immigrant/Bad–White Immigrant/Good block and subtracting them from the White Immigrant/Bad–Latino Immigrant/Good block provides the basis of an IAT score, with higher values reflecting negative implicit attitude toward Latino immigrants (relative to white immigrants).

pair (Latino Immigrant–Bad | White Immigrant–Good), than when using a mismatched pair (White Immigrant–Bad | Latino Immigrant–Good). Looking at Figure 5.2, this is exactly what we observe in the data from Lab Study 1 and the National Survey. Subjects in Lab Study 1 sorted words 180 milliseconds faster, on average, when using the Latino Immigrant | Bad–White Immigrant | Good pair. Respondents in the national study similarly sorted words 256 milliseconds faster, on average, when using this same pair. These differences are reliably different from zero ($p < .05$), suggesting that people in both studies have negative implicit attitude toward this group. In fact, dividing each difference by its standard deviation yields Cohen's d values suggesting strong IAT effects, i.e., large differences in sorting times between the matched and mismatched classification pairs (Lab Study 1 $d = .85$; National Survey $d = 1.22$).

Closer inspection of the data in Figure 5.2 suggests that this IAT effect is quite large in the mass public; larger, at any rate, than a convenience sample would reveal. Recall that IAT effects are typically uncovered in lab settings with student subjects. By design, Lab Study 1 mimics this context. The sample is relatively small and displays limited variation in terms of age, education, and political orientation. Yet a large IAT effect still emerges ($d = .85$). However, when I administer the same IAT in the National Survey, an even larger effect emerges ($d = 1.22$). Tellingly, the standard deviation of the mean response time difference in Lab Study 1 (SD = 211) is virtually identical to the one for the National Survey (SD = 210). Thus, IAT scores in both studies are similarly dispersed. What changes across these studies, then, is the size of the difference in sorting times (180 milliseconds vs. 256 milliseconds), which the richer demographic variation of the National Survey allows us to recover.

The Distinctiveness of Implicit Attitudes

Now that we know that these implicit attitudes exist, we can begin to assess the extent to which they are distinct from their self-reported counterparts. In the National Survey, respondents reported their attitude toward Latino, white, Asian, and Middle Eastern immigrants. These reports were provided through standard feeling thermometer ratings (on a 0–100 scale) completed *prior* to completion of the IAT, which means they are uncontaminated by the IAT. Each immigrant rating was recoded so that higher values indicate greater negative feelings, with 50 indicating neutrality. This diversity of reports allows me to create two measures to compare against the IAT: (1) explicit hostility to immigrants in general (i.e., anti-immigrant attitude) and (2) explicit attitude toward Latino immigrants, specifically (i.e., anti-Latino attitude). The former is an additive index of the four group ratings ($\alpha = .84$); the latter subtracts one's rating of white immigrants from one's rating of Latino immigrants.

Figure 5.3a displays the distribution of explicit anti-immigrant attitude. There we see wide variation in this self-reported attitude. Most people, in fact, report what can be construed as mildly positive attitude toward immigrants, as the mean score on this measure, 188, sits just below 200, which marks professed neutrality toward immigrants. Thus, self-reported attitude toward immigrants is remarkable for the restraint it evidently displays.

The distribution of explicit attitude toward Latino immigrants in Figure 5.3b reveals a substantive pattern comparable to the one above. This measure subtracts one's rating of white immigrants from one's rating of Latino immigrants. Figure 5.3b shows that explicit attitude toward Latino immigrants is also characterized by a relatively low mean and wide dispersion of scores. Specifically, respondents on average registered a score of 13.15, which is barely above the 0 value indicating complete indifference toward Latino immigrants. Indeed, if we divide this mean difference in ratings (i.e., 13.15) by its standard deviation (i.e., 23.15), we yield a Cohen's $d = .57$, which suggests a medium effect size for this attitude.[3] Thus, although explicit attitude toward Latino immigrants exists, it is decidedly mild in its negativity.

In contrast to these two self-reported attitudes, the distribution of IAT scores in Figure 5.3c conveys a patently distinct picture. The average score – 256 milliseconds – is well above the zero point indicating no contrast in sorting times.

[3] I do not report Cohen's *d* for explicit attitude toward immigrants because it is an index, not a difference in scores.

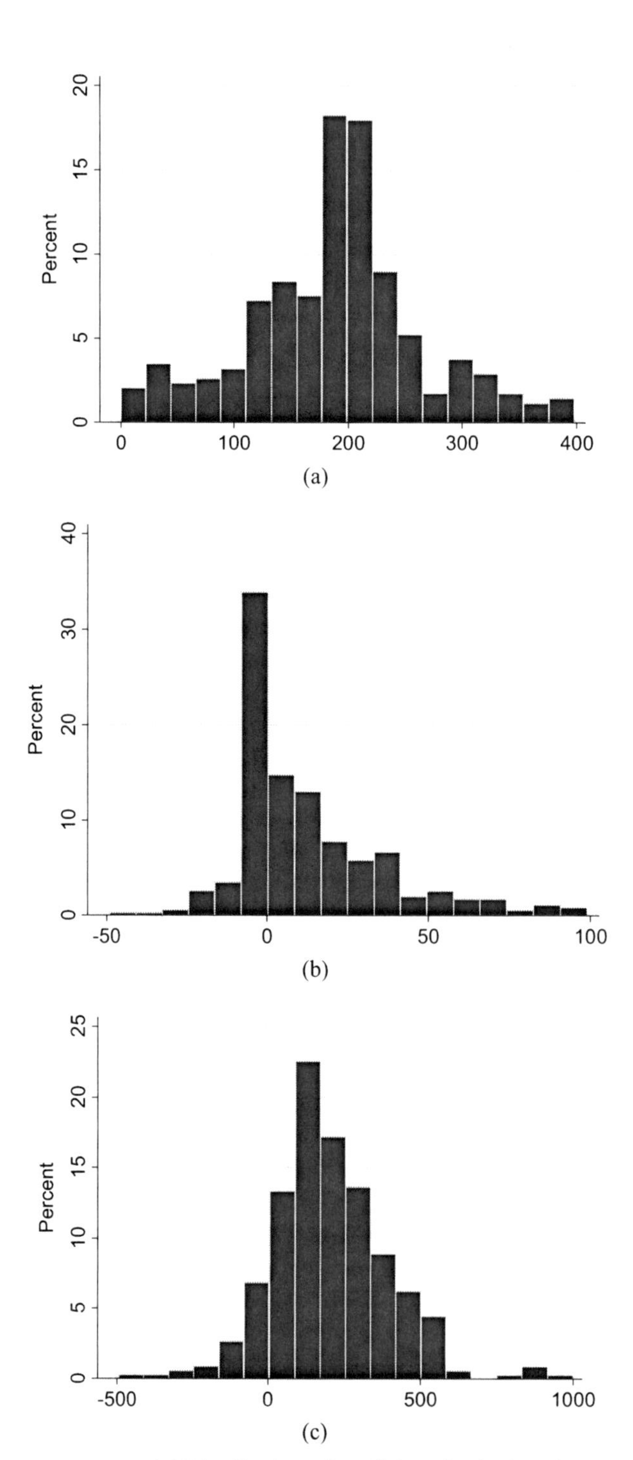

FIGURE 5.3. (a) Distribution of explicit attitude (immigrants) – National Study. (b) Distribution of explicit attitude (Latinos) – National Study. (c) Distribution of implicit attitude (Latinos) – National Study. *Note:* In all three figures, higher values reflect more negative attitude toward the object in parentheses.

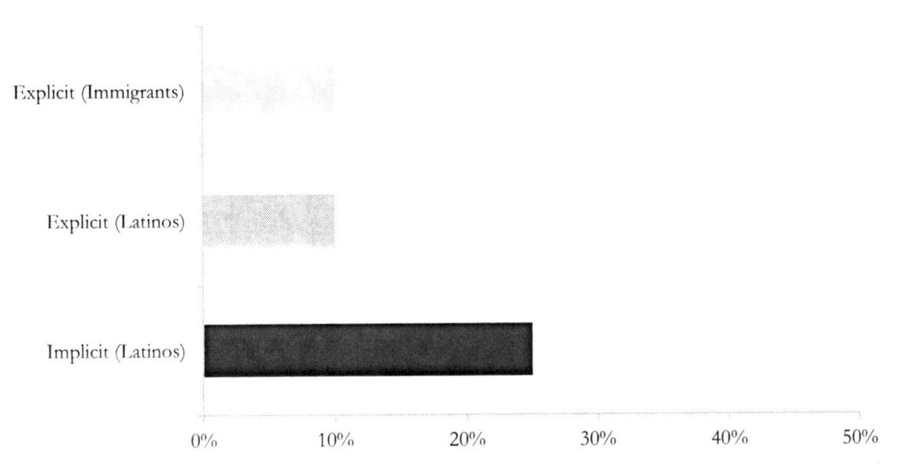

FIGURE 5.4. Proportions of strongly negative explicit and implicit attitudes – National Study. *Notes:* Each measure runs along a 0–1 interval. Proportions reflect the number of respondents scoring in the upper third of the distribution of each variable (i.e., ≥ .66).

Indeed, the Cohen's *d* for this difference in sorting times, you may recall, is 1.22. This suggests that individuals generally possess a remarkably strong and negative implicit attitude toward Latino immigrants. Notice, too, that the dispersion of scores is relatively narrow, with scores generally clustering around that large mean effect. This feature is consistent with my claim that implicit attitude is difficult to control, as greater control should have produced more widely dispersed scores around a lower mean.

Figure 5.4 breaks down the previous distributions into the proportion of people displaying a strongly negative attitude on each measure. To facilitate comparisons between these different measures, each variable was rescaled to run from 0 to 1. Accordingly, individuals are deemed to have a strongly negative attitude if they score in the upper third of the distribution of each variable (i.e., ≥ .66). Based on this configuration of these data, Figure 5.4 shows that about 10% of respondents manifest a strongly negative attitude on the index of anti-immigrant attitude. And, in identical fashion, 10 percent of respondents also express a strong and negative attitude toward Latino immigrants on the measure for this variable. But when we arrive to implicit attitude toward Latino immigrants, a patently different picture emerges. Here, the IAT reveals that about 25 percent of respondents completing this measure display a strong negative attitude toward Latino immigrants – a proportion that is 2.5 times larger than those revealed by the other two measures. This pattern suggests the IAT might be eliciting a different attitude than both self-reports. Indeed, the correlation between implicit and explicit attitude toward immigrants is weak and unreliable ($r = .05, p < .14$), while the one between implicit and explicit attitude toward Latinos is modest but reliable ($r = .22, p < .05$). Thus, even when implicit and explicit attitudes are significantly related in this domain, the

TABLE 5.3. *The Relationship between Implicit Attitude toward Latinos and Social and Political Predispositions*

	Implicit Attitude[a] (Latinos)	Implicit Attitude[b] (Latinos)	Implicit Attitude[b] (Latinos)
Explicit Attitude (Immigrants)	.08	.03	–
Explicit Attitude (Latinos)	.22*	–	.19*
Partisanship (Republican)	.12*	.07	.04
Authoritarianism	.09	.03	.02
American Identity	.19*	.15*	.15*
Socio-economic concerns	.15*	.15*	.13*
Education	.00	.08	.10

Notes: All variables run along a 0–1 interval.
[a] Entries are pairwise correlation coefficients.
[b] Entries are partial correlation coefficients. For all entries, $N = 333$.
* $p < .05$, two-tailed.

two are unlikely to be mistaken for each other, a pattern similar to inquiries in other realms (e.g., for an overview see Rydell and McConnell 2010).

Further evidence of the empirical distinctness of implicit attitude is seen in Table 5.3, which shows the correlations between implicit attitude and several social and political predispositions. A goal of this chapter is to assess the link between implicit attitudes and explicit political judgments; to show, as it were, that spontaneous thoughts can affect our more deliberative opinions. But if I am to persuade you of this, I must also show that implicit attitude is distinct from other predispositions that similarly affect political choice. For starters, this means showing implicit attitudes are distinct from partisanship, that enduring attachment to Democrats or Republicans that structures political opinions across many issue domains (Bartels 2000; Campbell et al. [1960] 1980; Green et al. 2002). In the realm of immigration, it is likely that implicit attitude and stronger identification with Republicans both increase opposition to immigration, because in contemporary times, many Republican candidates have vociferously come out against immigration, especially illegal immigration (Knoll et al. 2011).[4] Yet the correlation between these variables is modest and positive, assuring us that although partisanship and implicit attitude are related, they are also empirically distinguishable.

Another possibility is that implicit attitudes toward Latino immigrants are part of a more general disposition toward intolerance. Recent work suggests

[4] Partisanship is a 7-point scale running from "strong Democrat" to "strong Republican."

that authoritarian values – which emphasize social conformity and uniformity – produce hostile views toward outgroups and public policies related to them. This includes immigration (e.g., Hetherington and Weiler 2009). Yet authoritarianism and implicit attitudes are unrelated to each other.[5]

Next, I consider the relationship between implicit attitude and American identity. National attachments are a powerful determinant of negative attitudes toward immigrants and public opposition to immigration (e.g., de Figueiredo and Elkins 2003; Sides and Citrin 2007). Thus, the influence of implicit attitude on immigration preferences is likely to resemble that of American identity. Empirically, however, the two are also clearly distinct, as evidenced by the modest correlation between these two predispositions.[6]

This leads us to socioeconomic concerns. Several scholars have shown that societal concerns about jobs, public safety, and national culture often contribute to individual opposition to immigration (e.g., Sniderman et al. 2004). These types of concerns, moreover, often cut across several domains. But how similar are these types of socioeconomic concerns to implicit attitude toward Latino immigrants? The answer, again, is modestly. Table 5.3 shows that while higher scores on an index of socio-economic concerns are positively associated with IAT scores, the two are a far cry from being the same phenomenon.[7]

Simple as this correlational analysis has been, it nonetheless increases confidence that the IAT measures a different kind of attitude than other self-reported measures. These correlations are helpful in another regard as well: they enable us to piece together a clearer portrait of the individual-level origins of implicit attitudes. Though psychologists have extensively studied implicit attitudes, remarkably little is known about the determinants of implicit attitudes at the individual level. Some scholars suggest that early developmental

[5] Authoritarianism is measured with three items assessing child rearing preferences. The wording of these items is as follows: "The following are pairs of qualities that one might try to encourage in children. As you read each one, please indicate which one you think is more important to encourage in a child. (1) If you absolutely had to choose, would you say it is more important that a child obey his parents or that he is responsible for his own actions? (2) Is it more important that a child has respect for his elders, or that he thinks for himself? (3) Is it more important that a child follows his own conscience, or that he follows the rules?" People with high levels of authoritarianism prefer a child who "obeys his parents," "has respect for his elders," and "follows the rules." These items were combined into a scale ($\alpha = .69$) where higher values indicate greater authoritarianism.

[6] American identity is measured with a single item that asks individuals: "How important is being American to you? A score of 1 means not at all important, while a score of 4 means very important." Higher values on this measure indicate stronger levels of American identity.

[7] Using a 7-point scale (strongly disagree to strongly agree), respondents answered the following items in random order: Do you think that crime and lawlessness in society is getting worse? Do you think that schools and hospitals are overcrowded? Do you think that the job prospects of Americans are getting worse? Do you think that American culture is endangered? These items are then combined into a counter variable that tallies the number and intensity of these concerns, with higher values indicating greater concern.

experiences, membership in high-status groups, and perceptions of threat each contribute to individuals' development of implicit attitudes (Rudman 2004). Authoritarianism, national identity, and socioeconomic concerns provide useful indicators of these broad umbrellas of explanations. Authoritarian values are thought to be learned early in life (Stenner 2005). The nation often commands strong attachments among its citizenry. And, one might say, socioeconomic concerns betray a broad sense of perceived threat.

The second column in Table 5.3 displays partial correlations between implicit attitude, authoritarianism, national identity, socioeconomic concerns, as well as the other covariates from the previous section. When examined simultaneously, we see that implicit attitudes are associated only with explicit attitude toward Latinos, American identity, and socioeconomic concerns. At this point, one might be tempted to increase the rigor of this analysis by predicting implicit attitudes as a function of these explicit variables in a regression framework. Yet this approach imposes an untenable assumption: that the direction of influence runs from explicit to implicit attitudes. With theory and evidence on implicit attitude suggesting the opposite direction (Bargh et al. 1996; Craemer 2008; Lodge and Taber 2013), it seems less risky (but still useful) to study these associations without making the more questionable claim that explicit attitudes predict their implicit analogs.

Latino Immigrants or Just Immigrants?

So far, we have evidence that implicit attitudes toward Latino immigrants exist. The evidence also suggests these attitudes are remarkably negative and distinct from several political and social predispositions, including explicit attitude toward the same group. But how do we know that these implicit attitudes are really directed at Latino immigrants, specifically? After all, if the IAT is a relative measure that contrasts Latino immigrants with White immigrants, aren't people's attitudes toward both groups tangled with each other?

I have already explained why the relative nature of the IAT makes sense from a theoretical perspective. Yet the IAT's relativity also has a methodological advantage – it prevents the evaluation of Latinos from happening in a vacuum, which helps to guard against an overestimate of how strong this attitude toward one group might be. For instance, a person's implicit attitude toward one group might be indistinguishable from their implicit attitude toward another, even though I claim otherwise. The IAT's relativity allows me to tell whether an implicit attitude toward one group is still there *after* accounting for a possible attitude toward another, which, in the end, is a more scientifically conservative strategy.

But is there a way I can show that the underlying signal breaking through the IAT is directly tied to Latino immigrants? I think I can. Recall that individuals rated Latino and other immigrants prior to completing the IAT, using feeling thermometers. This aspect of the National Survey means I can assess whether people's IAT scores predict their explicit attitude toward these different immigrants. If the IAT, in fact, taps implicit attitude toward Latino immigrants, then people's IAT scores should be related to what they explicitly feel about this group, but unrelated to what they say they feel about other groups. In contrast, if the IAT is associated with people's explicit ratings of several immigrant groups, it would suggest this measure is tapping, not implicit attitude toward Latinos, but rather implicit attitude toward foreigners *in general*.

It is worth noting, however, that some political scientists have criticized feeling thermometer ratings because they can yield response sets through their unique format (Winter and Berinsky 1999). This means that my thermometer ratings of African, Asian, Latino, and white immigrants will be more correlated than is probably true because of the peculiar way in which these groups are evaluated. If this reasoning is correct, then it will be less likely that I find a positive and unique association between people's IAT scores and thermometer ratings of Latino immigrants due to systematic measurement error. So why even use feeling thermometers and not, say, stereotype ratings, which might be less prone to response sets? Well, because stereotypes are not the conceptual analogs of evaluative associations, that is, implicit attitudes. Feeling thermometers, however, are closer in this regard, both in my view and the view of many psychologists (e.g., Amodio and Devine 2006; Dasgupta and Greenwald 2001; Gawronski et al. 2008; Greenwald et al. 1998). For example, like the IAT, feeling thermometers measure affective evaluations of objects (e.g., Latino immigrants). Yet unlike the IAT, thermometer ratings require introspection and explicit reporting of these evaluations.

I therefore predict people's thermometer rating of each immigrant group based on their IAT scores and their level of authoritarianism, partisanship, national identity, and education. Including the latter variables ensures that any observed relationship between IAT scores and immigrant ratings is purged of these factors, which might also affect people's reported feelings about immigrants.[8] At a basic level, then, the test is this: using people's IAT scores to predict their explicit attitude toward Latinos, *without* also explaining people's self-reported attitudes toward the other immigrant groups arrayed around Latinos. Here, with the exception of the immigrant ratings, which run from 0 to 100, all predictors have a 0–1 range.

Table 5.4 provides the results of this analysis, and they are revealing in two key ways. First, IAT scores are related only to people's explicit rating of Latino immigrants. And the effect is sizeable. Going from the lowest to highest level of implicit attitude toward Latinos produces a nearly 31-point shift in people's

[8] Education is a single item ranging from (1) no high school degree to (6) postgraduate degree. Here, higher values indicate greater levels of education. Respondents also rated illegal immigrants. However, about 46 percent of respondents rated these immigrants at 85 or higher (on a 0–100 scale), which I take as evidence of severe ceiling effects. Given such limited variance on this item, I do not include it in this analysis.

TABLE 5.4. *Negative Feelings toward Immigrants by Implicit Attitude toward Latinos*

	Latino Immigrants	White Immigrants	Asian Immigrants	Mid. East Immigrants
Implicit Attitude (Latinos)	30.96* (13.28)	−15.23 (11.41)	13.03 (13.13)	18.21 (12.90)

Notes: Entries are OLS coefficients, with standard errors in parentheses. Models also control for levels of authoritarianism, conservatism, education, and age (see Table A5.1 in the appendix for full model results). All predictors have a 0–1 interval. The dependent variable runs from 0 to 100 in one-point units, with higher values reflecting more negative feelings toward an immigrant group.
* $p < .05$, one-tailed.

explicit feelings about this group, which is about one-third the range of the thermometer scale. Second, this effect is unmatched in magnitude and statistical significance by any of the other relationships in Table 5.4. Each of the remaining shifts in explicit immigrant ratings produced by the IAT is consistently about one-third to one-half the size of the shift produced by the IAT on the Latino immigrant rating. These remaining effects, moreover, are statistically indistinguishable from zero. Third, and perhaps most tellingly, the IAT is unrelated to self-reported ratings of white immigrants. To be sure, the effect is in the expected negative direction, given that I assume this group is positively esteemed by most people. Yet the effect is statistically unreliable. It appears, then, that the signal underlying the IAT is directly tied to Latino immigrants.[9]

Latino Immigrants or Latinos in General?

But is implicit attitude directed just at Latino immigrants or does this attitude encompass Latinos, in general? Recent estimates suggest Latinos comprise about 16 percent of the US population, with about three out of every five Latinos being native-born (Motel 2012). Put differently, most Latinos are *not* foreigners. From one perspective, then, the fact that I have identified Latinos in the IAT as immigrants suggests that even if implicit attitude is strong and negative, it is nonetheless trained on one segment of the larger Latino community in the United States.

But there is another possibility with more troubling implications. From this view, the distinction between Latino immigrants and non-immigrants is too fine

[9] Let us, for the moment, consider what would happen if the uncovered relationship between the IAT and individual thermometer ratings of White immigrants had been statistically significant. Even then, the coefficient for implicit bias is (−15), which is slightly less than half the coefficient for implicit bias when the explicitly rated group is Latino immigrants. In the aggregate, then, the net effect is still being driven by one's implicit attitude toward Latinos, which would be consistent with the claims I have made thus far.

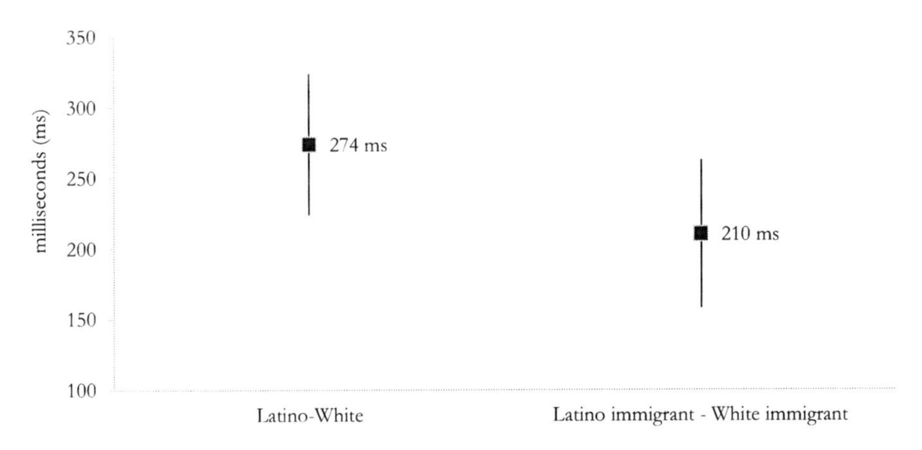

FIGURE 5.5. IAT effect by IAT version (95% confidence intervals). *Note:* $N = 122$. Each IAT effect reflects the mean difference in sorting times between the key blocks in each IAT version. In the Latino–White IAT, the evaluated objects are *Latino* and *White*. In the Latino immigrant–White immigrant IAT, the evaluated objects are *Latino immigrant* and *White immigrant*. Individuals completed either IAT version on a random basis.

grained for most Americans to appreciate. Rather than having distinct implicit attitudes toward Latinos and Latino immigrants, this perspective would argue the two are interchangeable because they are one and the same.[10]

To address these possibilities, I designed an experiment that randomly assigned two IAT versions. The first version is the one we have been analyzing – the one contrasting Latino and white immigrants. The second version compares Latinos and whites *without* identifying them as immigrants. Each of these IATs uses the same word lists as before. Moreover, through the power of randomization, the people completing the IAT in both conditions are alike in every respect, chance variations aside. Thus, any differences in IAT scores can be traced to the description of the contrast categories in the IAT as immigrants or not.

Figure 5.5 displays the average difference in IAT sorting times, surrounded by its 95% confidence interval. There we can see that each IAT elicited a negative implicit attitude toward each Latino group, since both estimates are positive and well above zero. In fact, because the confidence intervals around each estimate do not straddle the zero value, we can be confident these effects are not due to chance. Moreover, though the average IAT effect appears to be smaller in the immigrant IAT (210 milliseconds vs. 274 milliseconds) the overlap between the confidence intervals around each estimate suggests this difference is most

[10] In the jargon of specialists, this means an IAT contrasting Latino and white immigrants and another IAT contrasting Latinos and whites without the immigrant identifier are, in fact, capturing the same latent variable. See, for example, Brown (2006).

likely due to chance. This means these average IAT effects are statistically identical. Thus, implicit attitude toward Latino immigrants appears to be conceptually synonymous with implicit attitude toward Latinos.[11]

Are These Attitudes Really Implicit?

Thus far, we have seen several overlapping layers of evidence suggesting the existence, prevalence, and distinctness of implicit attitude toward Latinos. Yet it remains to be seen whether the attitude captured by the IAT is in fact *implicit* – that is, spontaneous and hard for individuals to control? Recall that one way scholars have addressed this point is by examining the extent to which individuals can manipulate their responses on the IAT. In lieu of detailed instructions, respondents generally find it hard to adjust or distort their scores on the IAT. In the spirit of this work, I devised a simple test to show that implicit attitudes toward Latinos, like implicit attitudes more generally, are spontaneous and hard to control.

Political scientists have taught us that people who are highly educated are more likely to amend their self-reported attitudes toward racial/ethnic groups, thereby reporting lower levels of negative attitude toward these targets (e.g., Sniderman and Piazza 1993; Sniderman et al. 1991; see also Federico 2004: 379–380). And they are more likely to adjust these attitudes, not only because they are sensitive to social norms which frown on the expression of negative racial attitudes, but also because they *can*, as they are more skilled at completing tasks like reporting one's attitudes (e.g., Converse 1964; Luskin 1987; Zaller 1992). Yet if implicit attitudes are really spontaneous and hard to control, then people who have more education should be no better than others at manipulating their responses on the IAT. That, at least, is the expectation I am testing here.

Figure 5.6 displays the average level of explicit attitude toward immigrants, explicit attitude toward Latino immigrants, and implicit attitude toward Latino immigrants by high and low levels of education, with a college education being the cutoff between both groups (Federico 2004). There we see that those with more education do in fact report significantly lower levels of both types of explicit attitude – about 6 percentage points less in each instance ($p < .05$). But notice the pattern for implicit attitude. There we see a statistical dead heat. Highly educated people are no better able to edit their level of implicit attitude

[11] Such a pattern is not due to some vagary related to this study. In my communication with the IAT's developer, Anthony Greenwald, I learned that early tests of this measure showed that attributes shared by two contrasted categories (e.g., immigrant, sex, age) are not used to classify stimuli by individuals completing the IAT. Ultimately, my results show that, if anything, the contrast involving Latino and White immigrants underestimates the level of implicit bias, which works against uncovering any relationship between this measure and, say, immigration policy preferences.

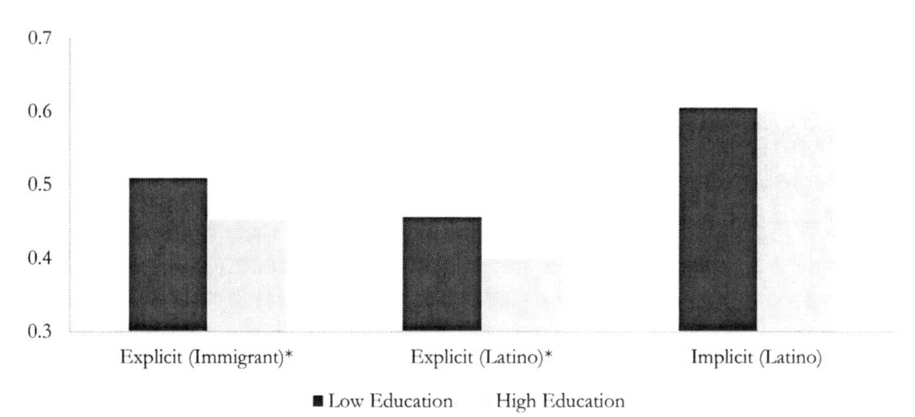

FIGURE 5.6. Explicit and implicit attitude by education. *Note:* $N = 333$. All variables run along a 0–1 interval. High education refers to those individuals with a college education or more. Asterisks denote differences in attitude that are significant at the 5% level.

than those with less education ($p > .10$). It appears, then, that the IAT does capture an attitude that is implicit in the sense that it is hard to control.

Implicit Attitudes and Explicit Political Choices

The IAT appears to capture implicit attitudes toward Latinos. But up to now, I have not demonstrated that these attitudes affect political preferences via my two hypothesized mechanisms, *affect transfer* and *affect contagion* (Lodge and Taber 2013). Indeed, despite its prevalence, what one thinks about Latinos in those early split seconds before expressing an opinion about immigration might matter little, if at all. In the end, one may argue, people's political views on immigration are determined by other factors, such as one's partisan affiliation, one's material self-interest, and whether one has enough education to logically think through one's opinion on immigration (Hainmueller and Hopkins 2014a). And, insofar as intolerance toward immigrants does play a role, it will be the self-reported variety – the type that people control and apply to their political judgments. In fact, once we account for these influences on people's opinions about immigration, it would be remarkable if implicit attitude had any effect at all on one's judgments of immigration.

That is precisely the test I will pursue in the last part of this chapter. I begin this process by first clarifying what we mean by immigration preferences. Analyses of public opinion on immigration often study political opinions on this issue without making formal distinctions between illegal and legal immigration flows (cf. Schildkraut 2013). For instance, one popular question used by scholars asks people whether "the number of immigrants from foreign countries who are permitted to come to the United States to live should be increased, left the same, or decreased." It is plausible, however, that immigration preferences are more nuanced than a question like this allows. Certainly, my analysis of immigration news stories in the previous chapter suggests at least a difference between illegal and legal immigration.

In the national study, individuals were asked about their views regarding illegal and legal immigration policy. To gauge preferences for illegal immigration policy, respondents used a 7-point scale to indicate their support for three proposals: (1) greater efforts to stop illegal immigration, (2) making it easier for illegal immigrants to obtain welfare; and (3) making it more difficult for undocumented immigrants to become US citizens. Similarly, respondents used a 7-point scale to register their support for (1) decreasing the annual number of legal immigrants, (2) making it harder for legal immigrants to become citizens, and (3) increasing the number of visas available to legal immigrants. A confirmatory factor analysis (CFA) of these items (see Appendix Table A5.2) reveals these items tap related but distinct preferences for illegal and legal immigration. With this result in hand, we are set to test the predictive validity of implicit attitudes in these two key policy domains.

Model Specification: Parsimony versus Credibility

Prior work on the predictive validity of implicit attitude suggests its influence on judgments and behaviors is nonredundant with explicit attitudes toward the same social object (Greenwald et al. 2009). Political decisions, however, are often shaped by a confluence of factors involving more than just attitudes toward a set of objects, irrespective of whether these attitudes are explicit or implicit. Primary among these is the influence of partisanship, that "durable attachment, not readily disturbed by passing events and personalities" (Campbell et al. [1960] 1980: 151). Insofar as partisan elites diverge in their views over immigration, partisanship at the mass level should shape public preferences for immigration policy.

But there are other influences as well. And this where challenges begin to arise for the analyst investigating the predictive validity of implicit attitudes within a regression context: How to specify a model that gauges the influence of implicit attitudes on explicit political choices? One common strategy is to employ a seemingly benign "kitchen-sink" approach, whereby a long list of covariates is chosen to control for any extraneous influences beyond the variable(s) of interest. Here, any variable that is correlated with the dependent variable and the independent variable under interest would be entered as a statistical "control" to minimize the challenge of omitted variable bias. This practice, however, can produce challenges of its own, including unstable and even incorrect statistical estimates (Achen 2005).

The more useful strategy, which I adopt here, is to test several credible models that vary in their degree of parsimony. This approach acknowledges that in regression analyses of public opinion, there really is no true or complete model.

As Kinder and Kam (2009) explain, "[a]t this stage of development in public opinion research, there is no such thing, in any domain, as *the* standard model. What we have on offer instead is a family of plausible models" (78). And so, by testing alternative, theoretically driven models, each varying in their degree of complexity, I will reveal that the effect of implicit attitudes on political choice is unique, consequential, and on par with other relevant political predispositions, which aligns with the operation of *affect transfer* in the mass public's evaluation of immigration policies (Lodge and Taber 2013). Further, by showing that explicit considerations like partisanship, authoritarianism, and national identity appear to mediate the influence of implicit attitudes on judgments of immigration policy proposals, I will indicate the presence of *affect contagion* in the mass public's judgments of immigration policy proposals.

I therefore begin by taking the illegal immigration policy factor uncovered by my CFA and regressing it on implicit attitudes toward Latinos. Looking at the Bivariate column in Table 5.5, we can see that implicit attitudes are strongly associated with opposition to illegal immigration, as a shift from the lowest to highest level of implicit attitude yields a reliable 2.08 point increase in opposition to illegal immigration (which ranges from 1 to 7 in one point increments). Building on this bivariate relationship, I then estimate Model 1, which predicts opposition to illegal immigration on the basis of implicit *and* explicit attitudes toward Latinos. This simple model adheres to the general approach used by psychologists testing the IAT's validity, which pits this measure against a self-reported analog (Greenwald et al. 2009). And, consistent with prior work on the IAT, this parsimonious model suggests that negative implicit and explicit attitudes toward Latinos both increase individual opposition to illegal immigration. Specifically, these results indicate that going from the lowest to highest level of explicit attitude boosts opposition to illegal immigration by 1.75 points, which is a strong effect. The coefficient for implicit attitude, in turn, suggests a comparable influence. Here, going from the lowest to highest level of implicit attitude increases opposition to immigration by 1.63 points – which is about one-fourth the range of the dependent variable. Thus, this basic model shows the political strength of implicit attitudes is on par with self-reported attitudes toward the same group. Moreover, it suggests that omitting implicit attitudes from this model would understate the influence of racial attitudes on illegal immigration policy preferences.

The column Model 2 reports a slightly revised model that includes partisanship as a predictor of opposition to illegal immigration. Illegal immigration is a charged political issue, with Republican politicians and aspirants increasingly taking aggressive stances against it (e.g., Knoll et al. 2011). It is plausible, then, that stronger identification with the Republican party heightens individual opposition to illegal immigration. And it does. Going from the lowest (Democratic) to the highest (Republican) level of partisanship boosts opposition to illegal immigration by nearly one point. Yet despite the influence of partisanship,

TABLE 5.5. *The Influence of Implicit Attitudes on Explicit Opposition to Illegal Immigration*

	Bivariate	Model 1	Model 2	Model 3	Model 4	Full Model	Alternate Model
Implicit (Latinos)	2.08*	1.63*	1.44*	1.37*	1.14*	1.05*	1.27*
	(.54)	(.54)	(.55)	(.55)	(.54)	(.57)	(.57)
Explicit (Latinos)	–	1.75*	1.40*	1.32*	1.31*	1.17*	–
		(.39)	(.39)	(.39)	(.39)	(.40)	
Explicit (Immigrants)	–	–	–	–	–	–	1.93*
							(.36)
Partisanship (Republican)	–	–	.91*	.80*	.70*	.81*	.75*
			(.17)	(.17)	(.17)	(.18)	(.18)
Authoritarianism	–	–	–	.55*	.44*	.45*	.33
				(.22)	(.22)	(.24)	(.24)
American ID	–	–	–	–	.69*	.64*	.60*
					(.32)	(.33)	(.34)
Socioeconomic concerns	–	–	–	–	–	.70*	.42
						(.31)	(.31)
Education	–	–	–	–	–	−.24	−.29
						(.21)	(.26)
Income	–	–	–	–	–	.12	.21
						(.26)	(.26)
Estimated R^2	.07	.17	.28	.30	.31	.34	.42

Notes: $N = 333$ for all models. Coefficients and standard errors in parentheses are robust weighted least squares estimates for the latent policy factors derived from the measurement analysis reported in the text (see Table A5.2 in the appendix for the raw results). Each policy factor runs from 1 to 7 in one-point increments. All predictors have a 0–1 interval. Groups inside parentheses refer to the target and direction of a given variable, as in "implicit attitude toward Latinos." The variable Explicit (Latinos) is based on differenced feeling thermometer scores for Latino and white immigrants. The variable Explicit (Immigrants) is an additive index of feeling thermometer ratings of four different immigrant groups.

* $p < .05$, one-tailed.

implicit attitude toward Latinos remains a strong predictor of preferences for illegal immigration policy.

Next, I introduce a model that includes authoritarianism as a covariate. It is possible, one might argue, that implicit and explicit attitudes toward Latinos both stem from a more general disposition toward intolerance of out-groups such as immigrants (e.g., Hetherington and Weiler 2009). If true, then the addition of authoritarianism should diminish the significance and influence of implicit and explicit attitude toward Latinos. Yet the inclusion of authoritarianism does not significantly alter the influence of implicit or explicit attitude.

But perhaps things change dramatically once we account for the influence of national identity on illegal immigration preferences. Sides and Citrin (2007: 479–480) remind us that in "most modern societies, the nation is an object of strong allegiances, so groups perceived to threaten a nation's distinctive identity are likely to elicit hostility." If true, then stronger levels of American identity should engender more restrictive attitudes toward illegal immigration, and thus, possibly diminish the influence of implicit attitude. Model 4 in Table 5.5 shows that moving from the lowest to highest level of national identity shifts opposition to illegal immigration by a little over half a point. Yet despite this relationship, implicit attitude continues to substantively shape individual preferences for illegal immigration policy.

So far, so good. Yet it is plausible that the influence of implicit attitude wanes once we account for people's material interests. As Sides and Citrin (2007: 478) explain, in "interest-based theories of immigration,...competition over scarce resources is the...basis of opposition to immigration. From this view, antagonism towards immigrants is based on the threat they pose to one's material well-being." Accordingly, our Full Model includes income and education as covariates, with higher levels of each expected to reduce opposition to illegal immigration. In addition to these objective indicators, the model also includes the subjective measure of socioeconomic concerns seen earlier in the correlational analysis of the IAT. This model shows that neither income nor education is reliably associated with people's preferences for illegal immigration policy. Only socioeconomic concerns are systematically related to opposition to illegal immigration. Specifically, going from the lowest to highest level of socioeconomic concerns increases individual opposition by about three-fourths of a point. Critically, however, the effect of implicit attitude remains robust and reliably different from zero.

We have, then, two patterns of evidence that emerge from this analysis. First, holding constant the influence of key explicit considerations, implicit attitudes are robustly and reliably associated with people's opposition to illegal immigration. This evidence is consistent with the *affect transfer* hypothesis (Lodge and Taber 2013), as implicit attitudes are reliably and independently associated with Americans' illegal immigration policy judgments. Second, the political influence of implicit attitudes also appears to partly operate indirectly, through the explicit considerations one brings to bear on one's illegal immigration policy judgments. Many explicit predispositions, such as partisanship, authoritarianism, and national identity, are reliably associated with opposition to illegal immigration. Moreover, accounting for many of these explicit attitudes softens (but never eliminates) the correlation between implicit attitudes and these policy judgments. These patterns are suggestive of mediation (Baron and Kenny 1986), whereby one's explicit considerations channel the affective charge behind one's spontaneous implicit attitude.

Nevertheless, although the influence of implicit attitudes remains intact, even after holding constant the influence of explicit considerations, it is possible that my conclusions depend on the explicit racial attitude that I compare implicit attitude against. So far, my evidence suggests that the effect of implicit attitude is independent of self-reported attitude toward Latino immigrants. Yet the latter is a single measure with unknown reliability, whereas the former, recall, is based on an average of two scores. Hence, it is possible that the influence of implicit attitude wanes once we control for explicit attitude toward immigrants in general, a highly reliable measure ($\alpha = .84$). That is the logic of the Alternate Model reported in Table 5.5. And although this measure produces a strong effect, the influence of implicit attitude persists.

The Realm of Legal Immigration

But perhaps the persistence of implicit attitude in judgments of immigration policy is a function of where we looked, namely, the realm of *illegal* immigration. If we turn our attention to the much less controversial domain of legal immigration, maybe implicit attitude loses its grip over people's political views on this issue. Table 5.6 reports the relevant results. To begin, the bivariate association between implicit attitudes and opposition to legal immigration suggests a reliable and substantively large relationship between these two constructs. Indeed, similar to the realm of illegal immigration, a unit shift in implicit attitudes corresponds to a roughly two-point shift in opposition to legal immigration. In turn, Model 1 shows that net of people's explicit attitude toward Latinos, their implicit attitude toward this group still significantly boosts opposition to legal immigration by a smaller but still hearty 1.5 points. Building on this result, Model 2 reveals that the inclusion of partisanship fails to substantially alter this initial finding, as the effect of implicit attitude continues to hover around its initial estimate.

Model 3 displays the results of a model that includes authoritarianism. And there, we see that a shift from the lowest to highest levels of authoritarianism boosts opposition to legal immigration by a little more than half a point. Yet this effect does not significantly budge the influence of implicit attitude. In fact, the influence of implicit attitude persists when we account for the additional influence of American identity (see Model 4), which has no systematic bearing on individual preferences for legal immigration.

The Full Model in this analysis adds our three variables gauging material self-interest: education, income, and socioeconomic concerns. This analysis shows that a shift from the lowest to the highest level of education decreases opposition to legal immigration by about one-third of a point. And, while income does not display a reliable effect on legal immigration policy preferences, one's level of socioeconomic concern does. Specifically, a change from the lowest to highest level of socioeconomic concern increases opposition to legal immigration by nearly one and a half points. Despite these hearty effects for material interests, implicit attitude continues to systematically shape individual views toward legal immigration. Indeed, even when I substitute explicit attitude toward Latinos with the more reliable measure of explicit attitude toward immigrants, the

TABLE 5.6. *The Influence of Implicit Attitudes on Explicit Opposition to Legal Immigration*

	Bivariate	Model 1	Model 2	Model 3	Model 4	Full Model	Alternate Model
Implicit (Latinos)	2.13*	1.57*	1.48*	1.43*	1.36*	1.18*	1.51*
	(.56)	(.57)	(.57)	(.57)	(.57)	(.56)	(.53)
Explicit (Latinos)	–	2.08*	1.99*	1.91*	1.91*	1.50*	–
		(.34)	(.35)	(.35)	(.35)	(.36)	
Explicit (Immigrants)	–	–	–	–	–	–	2.88*
							(.31)
Partisanship (Republican)	–	–	.29*	.17	.14	.35*	.25
			(.16)	(.16)	(.16)	(.17)	(.16)
Authoritarianism	–	–	–	.66*	.63*	.57*	.37*
				(.22)	(.22)	(.22)	(.22)
American ID	–	–	–	–	.22	.06	−.06
					(.32)	(.32)	(.32)
Socioeconomic concerns	–	–	–	–	–	1.45*	1.16*
						(.26)	(.26)
Education	–	–	–	–	–	−.33	−.42*
						(.20)	(.20)
Income	–	–	–	–	–	−.17	−.06
						(.23)	(.23)
Estimated R^2	.06	.16	.17	.19	.19	.29	.43

Notes: N = 333 for all models. Coefficients and standard errors in parentheses are robust weighted least squares estimates for the latent policy factors derived from the measurement analysis reported in the text (see Table A5.2 in the appendix for the raw results). Each policy factor runs from 1 to 7 in one-point increments. All predictors have a 0–1 interval. Groups inside parentheses refer to the target and direction of a given variable, as in "implicit attitude toward Latinos." The variable Explicit (Latinos) is based on differenced feeling thermometer scores for Latino and white immigrants. The variable Explicit (Immigrants) is an additive index of feeling thermometer ratings of four different immigrant groups.

* $p < .05$, one-tailed.

substantive impact of implicit attitude on legal immigration policy preferences endures.

So, once again, the evidence is generally consistent with the *affect transfer* and *affect contagion* hypotheses (Lodge and Taber 2013). In terms of the former, implicit attitudes toward Latinos (which spontaneously evoke a strong sense of affect) are reliably and directly associated with mass opposition to legal immigration. In terms of the latter, many explicit considerations (e.g., partisanship, authoritarianism) appear to mediate the affective charge of these implicit attitudes. More specifically, several explicit predispositions, such as partisanship and authoritarianism, are reliably correlated with opposition to legal immigration. Statistically controlling for these explicit considerations reduces, but does not wipe out, the correlation between implicit attitudes and legal immigration policy judgments. Such patterns hint at mediation (Baron and Kenny 1986), where the association between implicit attitudes and judgments of legal immigration policy is channeled through some of people's explicit considerations. Across two policy domains, then, implicit attitudes are directly and indirectly tied to individual preferences for immigration.[12]

Conclusions

This chapter has marshaled various layers of evidence to document the existence and political relevance of implicit attitudes. Each layer provides a unique clue about this predisposition. And, when pieced together, these clues point to the conclusion that implicit attitude is a political force to be reckoned with. To this end, I first proposed the IAT as a measure of implicit attitude – those evaluative associations we possess about objects. Across three studies, both inside and outside the lab, I demonstrated that this measure effectively captures the unspoken evaluations people have about Latinos. I then showed this implicit attitude toward Latinos is negative, strong and prevalent in society, especially in comparison to people's self-reported attitude toward immigrants in general and Latinos in particular.

Building on these findings, I then documented two key features of implicit attitude toward Latinos. First, I showed that while IAT scores predict people's self-reported attitude toward Latinos, they fail to do the same for other groups, thus underlining the group-specific nature of implicit attitude. Second, I demonstrated that this implicit attitude encompasses all Latinos, not just those who are immigrants. By experimentally manipulating whether the IAT contrasted groups identified as immigrants, I established that the effects emerging from these IATs are statistically identical because they likely capture the same underlying attitude.

The chapter then shifted focus to assessing whether this implicit attitude is implicit at all. Accordingly, I argued that one way to corroborate the implicit nature of this attitude is by seeing whether some people can alter their IAT responses. I showed that they could not. Indeed, although highly educated people report lower levels of explicit attitude toward immigrants and Latinos, they were no better at reporting lower levels of implicit attitude than those with lower levels of education.

Finally, and most importantly, I established that implicit attitude toward Latinos matters politically. I argued that if implicit bias is consequential, it should reliably increase people's opposition to illegal and legal immigration. I also argued that this relationship should hold even after we account for

[12] For comparable, but more in-depth mediation analyses of implicit attitudes toward Latinos, see Pérez (2010).

other factors that affect people's preferences for immigration. Using this logic, I showed that individual opposition to illegal and legal immigration is heightened by implicit attitude toward Latinos, whose influence remains strong even after filtering out the effects of explicit attitude toward Latinos, partisanship, and education, among other things. One major implication of this last finding, which I explore in more detail across the next two chapters, is that implicit attitudes make political compromise harder when the public debates immigration, since many citizens' minds are already made up, in part, on the basis of their spontaneous attitudes toward Latinos.

These are all points that needed to be substantiated, not just asserted. But having corroborated them, they free us to tackle more critical questions. Among them: to what extent does implicit attitude actually bias one's immigration judgments? In the next chapter, I utilize a series of experiments to show that implicit attitude toward Latinos boosts opposition to immigration even when individuals are directed to focus on non-Latino immigrants.

TABLE A5.1. *Negative Feelings toward Immigrants by Implicit Attitude (full results)*

	Latino Immigrants	White Immigrants	Asian Immigrants	Middle Eastern Immigrants
Implicit Attitude (Latinos)	*30.96**	*−15.23*	*13.03*	*18.21*
	(13.28)	*(11.41)*	*(13.13)*	*(12.90)*
Authoritarianism	13.13*	8.37*	10.81*	15.44*
	(5.72)	(4.92)	(5.66)	(5.56)
Partisanship (Republican)	5.63	−2.65	−4.23	5.81*
	(4.07)	(3.50)	(4.02)	(3.95)
American ID	−2.27	−.54	−.32	10.52
	(7.01)	(6.02)	(6.93)	(6.81)
Education	−2.75*	−.18	−2.14*	−.42
	(.91)	(.79)	(.90)	(.89)
Constant	32.99*	44.40*	39.69*	26.29*
	(9.93)	(7.50)	(9.82)	(9.64)
R^2	.08	.02	.04	.08

Notes: Entries are OLS coefficients, with standard errors in parentheses. All predictors have a 0–1 interval. The dependent variable runs from 0 to 100 in one-point units, with higher values reflecting more negative feelings toward an immigrant group.

* $p < .05$, one-tailed.

TABLE A5.2. *Confirmatory Factor Analysis – Illegal and Legal Immigration Policy*

	Illegal Immigration	**Legal Immigration**
Stop illegal immigrants	1.00	
Welfare for illegal immigrants	.99 (.72)	
Citizenship for illegal immigrants	1.09 (.79)	
Decrease legal immigrants		1.00
Citizenship for legal immigrants		.98 (.86)
More visas for legal immigrants		.79 (.70)
CFI	.97	
TLI	.97	
RMSEA	.08	

Notes: Robust weighted least squares estimates. $N = 333$. Each item runs from 1 to 7 in one-point increments. One item loading per factor is constrained to 1.00 to identify the model, thus passing that item's metric to the latent factor (Brown 2006). Cells contain unstandardized factor loadings with standardized estimates in parentheses (which range from 0.0 to 1.0). The correlation between the illegal and legal immigration factors is .66. The item loadings and interfactor correlation are significant at the 5% level or better.

6

Incognito

The Subconscious Nature of Implicit Expectations

Imagine the following scenario. A person sits behind a computer to view two brief movie reels, each one lasting only 16 seconds and presented on a purely random basis. Frame by frame, this individual sees nothing more on the screen than another person's face as it evolves from happiness, to an ambiguous expression, and then to anger. The individual watching these reels is simply instructed to press the space bar the moment he or she senses a shift in the facial expression of the person on the screen, from pleasant-looking to outright menacing. How long do you think it will take someone to detect anger in the face of another?

The answer is that it will depend on that person's level of implicit attitude. More precisely, it will depend on their implicit attitude toward African Americans. For the one difference between the two reels just described is the race of the person that is showcased in each one. In one film, the person is conspicuously African American; in the other, the person is identifiably white.

In fact, when two social psychologists conducted a set of experiments along these lines (Hugenberg and Bodenhausen 2003), they discovered that individual differences in implicit attitude toward blacks (as measured by the Implicit Association Test [IAT]) explained the alacrity with which participants sensed anger in the African American person's face, but not the white person's expression. Specifically, individuals with more negative implicit attitudes toward blacks were about 2.5 seconds faster at detecting a menacing facial expression, even if the face was objectively ambiguous – neither happy nor angry in clearly visible terms. In a manner reminiscent of Mark Lyttle's mistaken deportation to Mexico (Chapter 1), implicit attitude led some individuals to see something that was not really there, without their knowing that it had.

This is, of course, only one report from one research team. Yet dispatches from other studies conducted by other social psychologists suggest similar patterns (e.g., Fazio and Dunton 1997; Gawronski et al. 2003). The cumulative lesson from these laboratory investigations seems to be this: implicit attitude can color how individuals interpret the world around them, and it can do so without people being fully aware of this influence. My objective in this chapter is to establish the presence of a similar psychological dynamic in citizens' political decision making, to show that implicit attitudes structure – subtly, imperceptibly, but indelibly – how citizens interpret and respond to information about immigration, a psychological process I have described as "implicit expectations."

I argued in Chapter 3 that broaching the issue of immigration will spontaneously activate people's implicit attitude toward Latino immigrants, thus making these evaluations mentally accessible to people. Via "hot cognition" (cf. Lodge and Taber 2013), these implicit attitudes rapidly inform citizens about how they feel toward immigration policy, a process that unfolds *before* people begin to actively consider relevant information about the political topic at hand. Lodge and Taber (2013) have established that affective responses like these often bias one's retrieval of considerations from memory, in particular, by recruiting considerations that are congruent with one's initial affective response. I extend this *affective contagion* mechanism to one's processing of political information. Specifically, I hypothesize that people will judge political issues according to the direction and intensity of their implicit attitudes, even when these are contradicted by explicit political information immediately before them. In other words, individuals will interpret political information in a manner that is consistent with the direction of their implicit attitudes. This takes place, I maintain, because the interplay between implicit attitudes and explicit political reasoning is *subconscious* – that is, citizens are unaware of how their implicit attitudes shape the more deliberative aspects of their decision making (Gawronski et al. 2006; Lodge and Taber 2013).

This chapter validates this psychological process and demonstrates its operation in people's political decision making on immigration through two survey experiments embedded within the National Study – experiments that substantively touch on US immigration politics. These experiments provide unmatched inferential leverage in the case at hand. The theoretical allure of implicit attitude is arguably derived in large part from its promise to structure citizens' processing and use of political information – and to do so without one's full awareness. By furnishing me with direct control over the type of information that people are exposed to, these experiments allow me to bore down into some of the psychological mechanisms that underpin individual decision making under different types of conditions. In this case, it allows me to see whether and to what degree implicit attitudes affect one's political judgments when the information one receives is obviously incongruent with the object of one's implicit attitude.

To this end, the survey experiments I analyze in this chapter share a simple but critical feature: they direct people's attention toward individuals and groups who are not Latino – a target of people's implicit attitudes in the realm of immigration (Chapter 5). The logic behind these treatments is straightforward.

It is one thing to show that people's implicit attitude toward Latinos shapes their evaluations of policies relating to this group. It is quite another to demonstrate that people's implicit attitude toward this group affects their judgments of polices relating to those who are non-Latino. The former is unsurprising, while the latter is unintended. But so far as the unintended pattern holds true, it underlines the subconscious nature of implicit attitude. For an attitude that is within full awareness should not affect decision making when the situation one confronts does not match it (Bargh 1994; Gawronski et al. 2006; see also Fazio and Dunton 1997; Gawronski et al. 2003; Hugenberg and Bodenhausen 2003).

Implicit Expectations and Illegal Immigration: The Deportation Experiment

Validating the operation of *affect contagion* in the development of implicit expectations requires very specific evidence. Essentially, I must find a way to show that people's implicit attitudes toward Latinos affect their immigration preferences – not just when the immigrants in question are Latino – but more critically, when they are *not*. This is not to say that implicit attitudes toward Latinos should be unassociated with general immigration attitudes. The correlational analyses in Chapter 5 suggest that they are. But here, with two survey experiments in hand, we can exit the correlational world, where it is harder to say which immigrants people imagine when evaluating immigration policies, and enter a world where we can manipulate the information people have about immigrants prior to judging immigration policies (e.g., Brader et al. 2008; Hainmueller and Hiscox 2010). In undertaking the latter, my goal is to ascertain whether implicit attitudes affect immigration preferences even when people's attention is directed toward non-Latino immigrants – that is, when the information one is exposed to is incongruent with the object of one's implicit attitude.

I begin my search for this evidence by turning to the realm of public opinion toward illegal immigration. My analysis of immigration news content (Chapter 4) suggests that if there is one domain where *affect contagion* will structure the processing of political information it should be here. Indeed, failure to find supporting evidence in this context leaves us hard pressed to look for any further evidence in other areas.

The Deportation Experiment allows me to conduct this crucial test. The logic behind this experiment is this: Are ordinary Americans willing to deport an illegal immigrant, under the same set of circumstances, when he is Latino as when he is not? To begin answering this question, half of the participants in the national study were randomly assigned to a condition that focused their attention on the following undocumented immigrant from Latin America:[1]

[1] In bold, for emphasis.

"Some years ago, ***Juan Hernández left El Salvador*** *to come to the United States in order to find employment. He has been working and living in the U.S. ever since. Recently, however, authorities discovered that Mr.* ***Hernández*** *does not have the proper visa to work in the U.S."*

Following this vignette, people indicated whether it was a good idea or bad idea to deport the individual they were asked about by using a four-point scale running from (1) a very bad idea to (4) a very good idea.[2]

Notice the simplicity of this experimental condition. The individual is clearly Latino. He is also unauthorized to be in the United States. The question for people, then, is whether these circumstances merit the deportation of Mr. Hernández. If they are concerned about the basic violation of law and order that illegal immigration entails, large numbers of them *should* support his deportation. This would be consistent with the public claims of many vocal opponents of illegal immigration, like Jason Woolley: "There's a right way and a wrong way to come into this country. If you are going to come in the wrong way, we're not going to stand for it. That's just how it is."[3]

But if an illegal immigrant is not Latino, how will people react to them? If a concern over law and order is at play, they should react the same, for the only condition that has changed is the person's racial identity. Thus, the remaining half of participants in the National Study was assigned to the following condition, which describes an illegal immigrant in the exact same circumstances. This time, however, he is from Ireland – not El Salvador.[4] Specifically, the vignette read:

"Some years ago, ***David Moore left Ireland*** *to come to the United States in order to find employment. He has been working and living in the U.S. ever since. Recently, however, authorities discovered that* ***Mr. Moore*** *does not have the proper visa to work in the U.S."*

And once again, following the vignette, people had to indicate how good an idea it was to deport this immigrant.

The choice of contrasting an Irishman to Juan Hernández is deliberate on my part. First, it emphasizes that he is European; in other words, not Latino. Second, though most illegal immigrants are from Latin America, Ireland has contributed its share of people to the non-Latino flow of unauthorized immigrants in the United States. Indeed, because of this, US Irish political activists have often been vocal proponents of efforts to regularize the status of illegal immigrants across the last twenty years (Bernstein 2006; Hendricks 2006; see

[2] Specifically, the item read: "Do you think it is a good idea or bad idea to deport this illegal immigrant?"

[3] Mr. Woolley was one of many Murrieta, California residents who publicly protested the transfer of unauthorized immigrant minors for processing at a local US Border Patrol office on July 4, 2014 (Martinez and Yan 2014).

[4] Once again in bold, for emphasis.

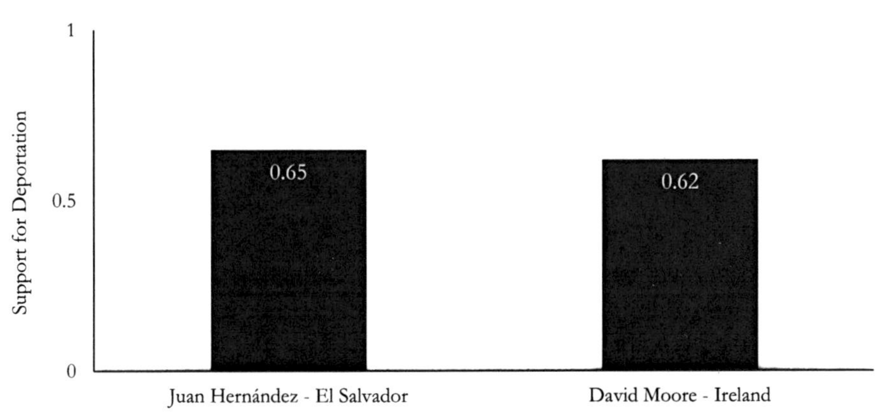

FIGURE 6.1. The deportation experiment. *Notes:* Support for deportation runs along a 0–1 interval. Each experimental condition cued a Latino or non-Latino immigrant. The difference between both experimental conditions is not statistically significant.

also Tichenor 2002).[5] How people react to an undocumented Irish immigrant therefore has implications for the "real world" of politics, as it were.

We have here, then, two illegal immigrants facing identical circumstances. The only difference between them is where they hail from, with one being Latino, the other not. What difference does race make in this instance?

None. At least this is the case so far as the raw experimental results are concerned. Figure 6.1 displays average public support for deportation by each experimental condition. To ease interpretation of these results, responses to the deportation question have been rescaled to run from 0 to 1, with higher values indicating greater support for deportation. When the public is considering the fate of Juan Hernández, average support for deportation stands at .65 on this 0–1 scale. Such a strong level of support should be unsurprising to the extent that we know illegal immigration rankles the American public (e.g., Ngai 2004; Tichenor 2002). But what is noteworthy is that average support isn't even higher. This suggests that even on an issue as controversial as the deportation of undocumented immigrants, there are plenty of Americans for whom deportation is not a good idea, even if the details of the case are clear and unequivocal.

The most remarkable finding, however, involves the comparison of the two conditions, between the individual fates of Juan Hernández and David Moore. On the one hand, you may have expected Americans to be less exclusionary in spirit in the case of the latter immigrant. Sure, Mr. Moore is here illegally, you may have thought, but at least he speaks English and is likely to better understand American customs and culture. Yet those considerations don't seem to

[5] In 2006, for example, it was estimated that about 50,000 Irish immigrants were in the United States illegally (Hendricks 2006).

have structured people's decisions to deport either migrant. Average support for deportation across both conditions is statistically the same.[6] With comparable vigor – .62, to be exact – respondents agreed that Mr. Moore should be deported. In other words, people took both immigrants and treated them even-handedly, notwithstanding the racial differences between the two.

This result seems to drive a wedge into the view that Latinos, by virtue of being Latino, bear special opprobrium from Americans when it comes to the issue of illegal immigration. Indeed, the evidence so far suggests that attitude toward Latinos plays little role in people's decision making in this controversial political domain. And we can be sure that this pattern is not some fluke, a function of the pressure some individuals may feel to offer a polite response to questions involving race. For the people in this study never knew that they were part of an experiment. All they knew was that they were asked (on a random basis) to consider the fate of an unauthorized immigrant. They did *not* know that other individuals in the same study were also asked (on a random basis) to consider the fate of another undocumented immigrant.

I still sense a plausible criticism of this interpretation, however. Perhaps respondents read the deportation question and infer that their fairness is in doubt. Sensing this, they then go out of their way to support David Moore's deportation as a way to show that they are even-handedly opposed to illegal immigration, regardless of where the unauthorized immigrant is from. This is certainly plausible. But if people feel that their fairness is impugned, this sensitivity will be, by virtue of randomization, equally prevalent across both experimental conditions. This should stimulate equally strong support for deportation across experimental groups, just as we have observed.

Digging beneath People's Explicit Reactions: The Role of Implicit Attitudes

So far, the experimental results suggest that people's expressed support for deportation is strong and far from being directed exclusively at Latinos. But there is a catch. While the experimental evidence presented so far is rigorous, it tells us only how people react to different types of information; in this case, to varied *explicit* cues about the national origin of illegal immigrants. Yet what is noticeably missing from these results are the spontaneous, unspoken thoughts that pop into people's minds the moment they are asked to consider the fate of an illegal immigrant. Thus, we have a sense of how people react to direct cues about immigrants, but not how this reaction is conditioned by their implicit attitudes.

But the National Study, you may recall, did measure people's implicit attitude toward Latinos. And it did so early in the survey, well before their completion of the Deportation Experiment, which was one of the last items in the

[6] Which is to say, the difference between the two conditions is statistically indistinguishable from zero.

questionnaire.[7] Thus, with this information in hand, we can see whether – and to what extent – implicit attitude affects people's support for deportation. In particular, we can determine whether implicit attitudes affect people's reaction, not only to Juan Hernández, but more critically, to David Moore. To do this, I will rely on a basic statistical model that enables me to assess the effect of implicit attitude on support for deportation under each experimental condition. Formally, the estimated model is

$$\text{Deportation} = \beta_0 + \beta_1\text{Implicit} + \beta_2\text{David Moore} + \beta_3\text{Implicit} \times \text{David Moore} + \beta_4\text{Explicit Attitude (Immigrants)} \tag{6.1}$$

Per Equation 6.1, β_1 gives us the effect of implicit attitude toward Latinos when people are considering the fate of Juan Hernández. In turn, β_2 yields the estimated effect of explicitly cueing David Moore (rather than Juan Hernández) on people's support for deportation. β_3 gives us the change in the effect of implicit attitude toward Latinos when people explicitly consider the prospects of David Moore. Finally, β_4 captures the estimated influence of explicit attitude toward immigrants on support for deportation. Including this highly reliable index ($\alpha = .84$) helps to ensure that any relationship(s) between implicit attitude and support for deportation is independent of what individuals might self-report about immigrants, Latino and otherwise.

The parsimony of this model derives from a close connection between my theory of "implicit expectations" and the experimental design at hand. My theory predicts that implicit attitude colors one's interpretation and use of information, in this case, explicit cues about immigrants' national origin. The experiment at hand randomly assigns these cues. This positions us to observe whether and to what degree implicit attitude toward Latinos affects support for deportation when immigrants are Latino versus when they are non-Latino. In this way, we can determine whether implicit attitude operates in the face of contradictory information – a key claim behind my theory of "implicit expectations."

For our purposes, the quantities of interest from Equation 6.1 are (β_1) and ($\beta_1 + \beta_3$). The former provides an estimate of the influence of implicit attitude toward Latinos when people are plainly focused on this group; the latter, an estimate of the same implicit attitude when people are directly focused on non-Latinos. Comparing these two estimates will thus allow us to assess the degree to which implicit attitude toward Latinos affects people's responses to congruent and incongruent immigrant cues.

But before getting to the results, it is worth our time to discuss two plausible outcomes and their implications for my claims about "implicit expectations." On the one hand, implicit attitude toward Latinos might affect support for deportation when the immigrant is Latino, but fail to do so when he is not.

[7] The Deportation Experiment was the last item on this fifteen-minute survey.

TABLE 6.1. *Support for Deportation as a Function of Implicit Attitude toward Latinos*

	Support for Deportation
Implicit Attitude (Latinos)	.51*
	(.23)
Experimental Condition: David Moore – Ireland	−.04
	(.21)
Implicit × David Moore – Ireland	.01
	(.35)
Constant	.17
	(.15)
R^2	.08
N	333

Notes: Entries are OLS coefficients, with robust standard errors in parentheses. All variables are rescaled to run from 0 to 1. Model also controls for explicit attitude toward immigrants (not shown).
* $p < .05$, one-tailed.

This would suggest implicit attitude is spontaneously triggered and made mentally accessible, but not necessarily subconscious, since there is no connection between it and people's support for deportation when the immigrant they are asked to focus on is non-Latino.

On the other hand, implicit attitude might affect support for deportation across both experimental conditions, which would suggest implicit attitude is subconscious insofar as it shapes decision-making even when people are explicitly focused on non-Latinos (e.g., Gawronski et al. 2006; see also Bargh 1994; Fazio and Dunton 1997; Gawronski et al. 2003; Hugenberg and Bodenhausen 2003). Indeed, if this pattern emerges, it would underline the point that spontaneously triggered impressions about Latinos can color people's interpretation of the explicit information they are asked to consider, with the interpretation affirming their implicit attitude toward this group.

The Interplay between Implicit Attitude and Explicit Cues

Table 6.1 reports the relevant results of my statistical analysis, where each variable runs along a 0–1 interval. There we see two key pieces of information. First, the coefficient for implicit attitude is positive, large, and statistically significant. More precisely, in the case where people are considering the fate of Mr. Hernández, going from the lowest to highest level of implicit attitude produces a shift of .51 in support for deportation, which is roughly half the range of the dependent variable. This is a strong effect, but it would be surprising if it had not been, as people in this condition are focused on a Latino immigrant.

Second, the effect of implicit attitude does not substantively change in the David Moore condition, as evidenced by the positive and statistically

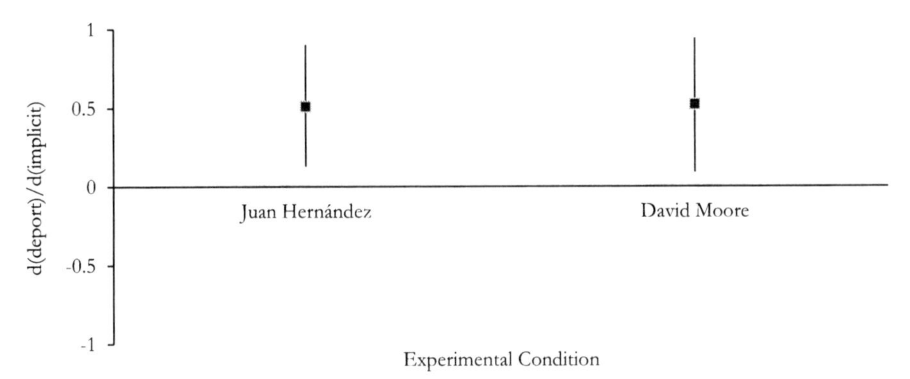

FIGURE 6.2. Marginal effect of implicit attitude by experimental condition (90% confidence intervals). *Note:* In each experimental condition, the displayed effects reveal an increase in support for deportation given a shift in implicit attitude toward Latinos from its lowest to highest level.

insignificant coefficient for β_3 (.01). This means that directing people's attention to David Moore did little to alter the influence of implicit attitude toward Latinos. It *does not* mean, however, that implicit attitude had no effect on people's support for deportation. This can be more readily seen by calculating and displaying the effects of implicit attitude in each condition.[8] For example, in the Juan Hernández condition, the effect is simply .51. For the David Moore condition, the effect is $(.51 + .01) = .52$. These effects, displayed in Figure 6.2, reveal the change in public support for deportation given a shift in implicit attitude under each experimental condition.

Two important points about implicit attitude emerge from this figure. First, we can see that the influence of implicit attitude is positive and reliably different from zero in each condition, as the estimates are above the zero line without the intervals straddling this zero value. Second, we can see these effects are statistically indistinguishable from each other, as evidenced by the overlap between these intervals. This suggests implicit attitude toward Latinos boosts support for deportation, even when the immigrant is David Moore.

Such a pattern is all the more surprising since the IAT is a measure of attitude toward Latino immigrants *relative* to White immigrants. That evaluations of the latter fail to predict judgments of David Moore is consistent with Chapter 4's claim that public discourse on immigration serves to forge a link in people's minds between the realm of immigration and negative evaluations of Latino immigrants. Hence, these experimental results suggest that implicit attitude toward Latino immigrants affects people's judgments without their awareness. Had they been aware, their implicit evaluation of this group should not have predicted their support for deporting David Moore.

[8] More formally, these are marginal effects, or the change in support for deportation induced by a unit change in implicit attitude, holding all else constant (Kam and Franzese 2007).

A plausible objection here, though, is that individuals might be aware of their implicit attitude toward Latinos, as well as cognizant of the greater proportion of illegal Latino immigrants. Yet they nonetheless wish to appear neutral, and so strongly support David Moore's deportation. However, this inclination to appear impartial, if it exists, should be equally prevalent across both experimental conditions through randomization, thus producing strong support for Mr. Hernández's deportation as well. Moreover, if people are in fact aware of their implicit attitude, then just like they adjust their explicit support for deportation to appear even-handed, they should also adjust their implicit attitude to seem impartial. Yet no such adjustment occurs.

The Legal Immigration Experiment

The previous analysis provides initial support for the operation of *affect contagion* in the formation of "implicit expectations." Broaching a policy issue (e.g., deportation) calls forth one's relevant implicit attitude toward an object (e.g., Latinos). Once mentally accessible, the affect evoked by this implicit attitude colors one's interpretation and use of explicit information (e.g., immigrant cues) without one being aware that this influence has taken place.

But however illuminating this evidence might be, it is important to acknowledge that it is derived from a specific context: the realm of illegal immigration. Hence, it is quite possible that the grip of "implicit expectations" holds sway only in this setting, where Latinos and illegal immigration are most discursively linked. Perhaps when considering questions of legal immigration, the influence of implicit attitude dramatically weakens. This begs the question: does implicit attitude also structure people's explicit reactions to legal immigrants?

To address this question, I designed the Legal Immigration Experiment. The advantages of this experiment, also embedded within the National Study, are threefold.[9] First, the direct focus of this experiment is on legal immigration. Indeed, the two treatment conditions emphasize – in no uncertain terms – that the immigrants people are focused on have legal status. In this way, we can confidently rule out that the previous result is an artifact of the realm of illegal immigration, an issue to which Latinos are strongly linked in public discourse (see Chapter 4). Second, this experiment, unlike the previous one, contains a control condition where no immigrants are identified. This will permit us to assess whether – and to what degree – opposition to legal immigration changes as we clarify who immigrants are. Third, and finally, the experiment provides a

[9] These experiments were designed to be orthogonal to each other. In the actual survey, the Legal Immigration Experiment was completed before the Deportation Experiment. In between both experiments, respondents completed a distracter task by answering several items testing their levels of political knowledge (Delli Carpini and Keeter 1996). It is possible, of course, that despite these safeguards, one's completion of one experiment contaminated one's reaction to the other (Gaines et al. 2007). Formal statistical tests of this possibility (Transue et al. 2007) yielded no evidence of such "spillover" effects.

contrast between legal Mexican and legal Chinese immigrants. This is important for two reasons. First, if implicit attitude toward Latinos is indeed about Latinos, then it should display its effects when the immigrants are Mexican as when they are from El Salvador. That is, the effect should not be tied to one particular nationality within the Latino community. Second, if implicit attitude is truly subconscious, we should see it operate once again in the case where an Asian, rather than European, immigrant is cued.

But these are both big "ifs," precisely because the focus of the experiment is on legal immigration, which by design minimizes any tie to the realm of illegal immigration. More importantly, it is quite plausible that implicit attitudes toward Latinos are correlated with implicit attitudes toward other outgroups – implicit ethnocentrism, if you will (Cunningham et al. 2004c) – thus complicating my claims about the former. I nonetheless expect implicit attitude toward Latinos to be a relevant force here. Conceptually, implicit and explicit ethnocentrism do not distinguish between outgroups, which are deemed interchangeable. Yet recent studies show that specific outgroup attitudes, rather than ethnocentrism, are activated when media coverage on political issues strongly focuses on particular groups (recall Chapter 4). Valentino et al. (2013) show that although ethnocentrism shapes immigration attitudes, this impact is driven by attitudes toward Latinos, with attitudes toward Asians and other groups having no effect. Sides and Gross (2013) find a similar dynamic between anti-Muslim attitudes and mass support for the War on Terror. These results suggest that implicit attitudes toward Latinos, specifically, should influence people's views on legal immigration. But to ensure an exacting test of this claim, my experimental analysis once again includes explicit attitude toward immigrants as a covariate, which I construe as an indicator of ethnocentrism in this setting.[10]

To this end, respondents in the first treatment condition read a vignette focusing their attention on legal Mexicans, while the second treatment condition trained people's attention on legal Chinese immigrants. As before, assignment to all three experimental conditions occurred on a random basis. The wording of the vignette in each treatment was:[11]

*Let's talk about legal immigration to the United States. The U.S. has some of the most generous immigration laws in the world, which is why we receive so many foreigners from various countries each year, including tens of thousands of **[Mexican/ Chinese]** immigrants. Some people believe that there are already too many legal*

[10] Indeed, a validating study of measures of explicit and implicit ethnocentrism shows that these are not only robustly correlated ($r = .47$), but that indicators of explicit ethnocentrism display much higher loadings than those for implicit ethnocentrism (Cunningham et al. 2004c). This implies that explicit ethnocentrism is more validly measured, thus further affirming my use of this covariate.

[11] The randomized information appears in bold, for emphasis. Those in the control condition received no information.

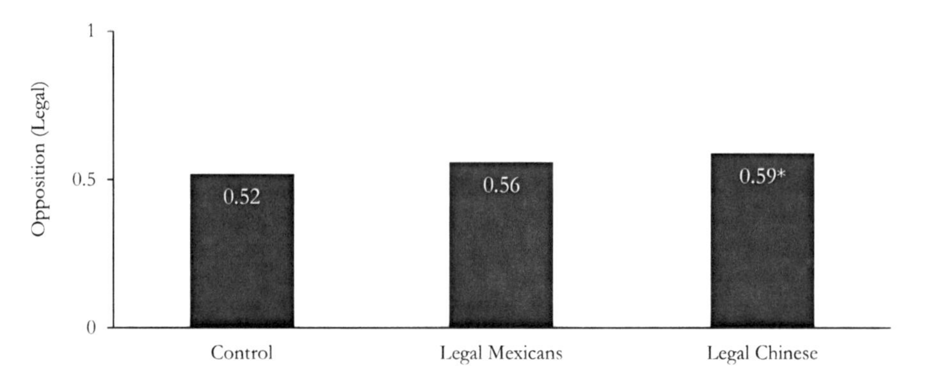

FIGURE 6.3. The Legal Immigration Experiment. *Notes:* Opposition to legal immigration runs along a 0–1 interval. The control group received no group cues, while the remaining experimental conditions cued Latino or non-Latino legal immigrants. There is no reliable difference in opposition to legal immigration between the control group and the legal Mexicans condition. The difference in opposition to legal immigration between the control group and legal Chinese condition is reliably different from zero. $^{*}p < .05$, one-tailed.

*[**Mexican/Chinese**] immigrants in the United States. These individuals believe that we should reduce the number of legal [**Mexican/Chinese**] immigrants to avoid overcrowding in local schools, hospitals, and neighborhoods. Other people, though, believe that the current level of legal [**Mexican/Chinese**] immigration is just fine and should not be tinkered with. These individuals believe that we should continue to allow the same number of legal [**Mexican/Chinese**] immigrants as we have for the last couple of years.*

Following their reading of the vignette, respondents indicated their support for three policy proposals to reform legal immigration – the actual system of immigration that regulates who gets in, from where, and for how long (e.g., King 2000; Ngai 2004; Tichenor 2002). Using a 1- to 7-point scale, respondents indicated their support to decrease the annual number of legal immigrants; to make it harder for legal immigrants to become citizens; and to increase the number of visas available to legal immigrants. Based on the measurement analysis of these items from the last chapter, I combined responses to these questions to form a reliable additive scale ($\alpha = .82$), which runs from 0 to 1, with higher values indicating greater opposition to legal immigration.

Let's begin by examining whether explicit immigrant cues make any difference once we hold constant foreigners' legal status. Figure 6.3 displays average opposition to legal immigration by each experimental condition. Notice, first, that across the board, opposition to legal immigration is relatively more subdued than the type of sentiment we saw expressed in the Deportation Experiment. For instance, in the control condition of the Legal Immigration

Experiment – the condition where people's attention was not focused on any group – average opposition hovers right around the midpoint of this scale (.52). This reemphasizes the point that the domain of legal immigration is a different realm from illegal immigration, at least in the sense that it elicits a relatively milder level of opposition.

Things progressively change once we train people's attention on the national origin of legal immigrants. For instance, prompting people to focus on legal Mexicans boosts opposition by about 4 percent relative to the control condition, though this effect is statistically insignificant ($p > .11$, one-tailed). This suggests that even with clearer prompting, most respondents already have an inchoate sense that legal immigration is tantamount to Latino immigration. Still, it is hard not to notice that this result just misses the $p < .10$ level (one-tailed). Had this effect reached significance at the more relaxed $p < .10$ level (one-tailed), I believe it would suggest that cueing legal Mexican immigrants slightly, but marginally, increases opposition to legal immigration. Such a pattern, in my view, would suggest that the association between Latino immigrants and legal immigration is rudimentary. In contrast, when we turn to the case of legal Chinese immigrants, we observe a relatively larger 7 percent shift in opposition to legal immigration, and this time the increase is clearly statistically significant ($p < .05$, one-tailed). This result is important because it further suggests that people did in fact pay attention to the information they received about legal immigrants.[12]

But what about implicit attitude toward Latinos? Does it subconsciously influence people's opposition to legal immigration? Does it boost support for exclusionary legal immigration policies even if one's attention is directed toward legal Chinese immigrants? To test these propositions, I estimate the following statistical model:

$$\begin{aligned}\text{Opposition (Legal Immigration)} = {} & \beta_0 + \beta_1\text{Implicit} + \beta_2\text{Legal Mexicans} \\ & + \beta_3\text{Legal Chinese} + \beta_4\text{Implicit} \\ & \times \text{Legal Mexican} + \beta_5\text{Implicit} \\ & \times \text{Legal Chinese} + \beta_6\text{Explicit Attitude} \\ & \text{(Immigrants)}\end{aligned}$$

Here, β_1 captures the effect of implicit attitude when no legal immigrants are identified. β_4 gives us the change in implicit attitude when people's attention is

[12] For instance, one could say that the lack of difference between both experimental conditions in the Deportation Experiment arises from the fact that people did not pay attention to the information they received about each immigrant. Though certainly possible, it is highly unlikely given that this experiment replicates previous research using similarly designed experiments around controversial issues (e.g., Sniderman and Carmines 1997: 137; see also Sniderman et al. 2000 and Sniderman and Hagendoorn 2007).

TABLE 6.2. *Opposition to Legal Immigration as a Function of Implicit Attitude toward Latinos*

	Opposition to Legal Immigration
Implicit Attitude (Latinos)	.31*
	(.18)
Legal Mexicans	−.14
	(.17)
Legal Chinese	−.14
	(.17)
Implicit × Legal Mexicans	.29
	(.29)
Implicit × Legal Chinese	.29
	(.28)
Constant	.03
	(.11)
R^2	.27
N	333

Notes: Entries are OLS coefficients, with robust standard errors in parentheses. All variables are rescaled to run from 0 to 1. Model also controls for explicit attitude toward immigrants (not shown).
* $p < .05$, one-tailed.

directed toward legal Mexicans. β_5 gives us the change in implicit attitude when people's attention is directed toward legal Chinese immigrants. And again, the resulting estimates statistically control for people's self-reported attitude toward immigrants (β_6), Latino and otherwise.

The results of this model are reported in Table 6.2. There we find that in the condition where no immigrants are identified, implicit attitude increases opposition to legal immigration by roughly one third the range of the dependent variable (i.e., .31). In the case where legal Mexicans and legal Chinese immigrants are explicitly cued, the effect of implicit attitude increases by .29 in each instance, though these increases are not statistically significant. Yet this does not mean implicit attitude fails to affect opposition to legal immigration under these conditions. Rather, it suggests the effect of implicit attitude is no different when either immigrant is identified than when no immigrant is mentioned.

This can be better appreciated in Figure 6.4, which displays the effect of implicit attitude on opposition to legal immigration under each experimental condition. Going from the lowest to highest level of implicit attitude in the control condition increases opposition to immigration by .31 unit. In the legal Mexicans and legal Chinese conditions, the same shift in implicit attitude increases opposition to legal immigration by .60. It would appear that these shifts get increasingly larger across experimental conditions. Yet the overlap in

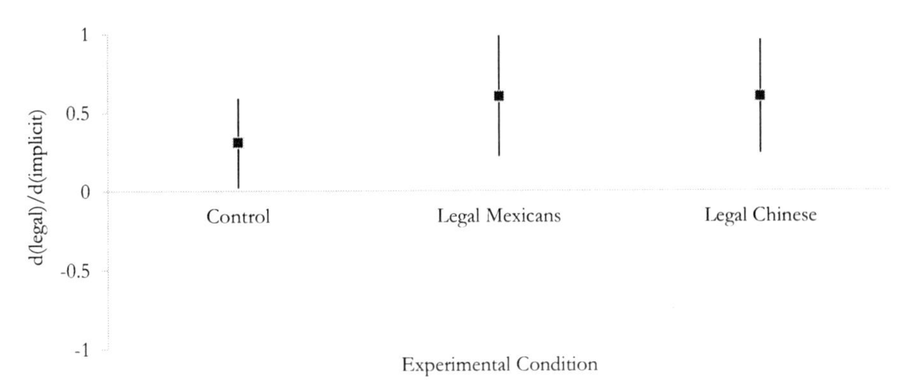

FIGURE 6.4. Marginal effect of implicit attitude by experimental condition (90% confidence intervals). *Note:* In each experimental condition, the displayed effects reveal an increase in opposition to legal immigration given a shift in implicit attitude toward Latinos from its lowest to highest level.

the confidence intervals containing each of these effects tells us they are statistically indistinguishable from each other. This suggests that implicit attitude heightens opposition to legal immigration in similar fashion across all three conditions, even in the case of legal Chinese immigrants.

Of course, it is natural to wonder whether a lack of statistical power limits my ability to detect reliable interactions in this setting. One way to investigate this possibility is by reducing the number of experimental conditions under analysis. Recall from Figure 6.3 that there was no reliable difference between respondents in the control group and those who directly focused on legal Mexicans. Statistically, their support for legal immigration was identical. Hence, I collapse these two groups into one, which I heuristically refer to as the Latino condition. I then re-estimate the model in Table 6.2 by regressing opposition to legal immigration on (a) one's level of implicit attitude, (2) one's assignment to the legal Chinese condition, (3) the interaction between these two variables, plus (4) explicit attitude toward immigrants. These results, displayed in Table 6.3, convey the same substantive story as before. Implicit attitude toward Latinos has a positive and reliable influence among respondents in the Latino condition (.41) – an effect that does not significantly change among those in the Chinese condition (.19, $p < .47$).

Figure 6.5 graphically displays the relevant marginal effects along with their respective 90% confidence intervals. This figure reaffirms my claims about how implicit expectations can influence explicit political reasoning. In this case, implicit attitude toward Latinos boosts opposition to legal immigration, even when respondents are explicitly focused on Chinese immigrants. Hence, implicit attitude appears to have subconscious effects. Once activated, it shapes an individual's interpretation and use of political information without a person's awareness of this influence over their thought process. Had people

TABLE 6.3. *Opposition to Legal Immigration as a Function of Implicit Attitude toward Latinos (Collapsed Latino Condition)*

	Opposition to Legal Immigration
Implicit Attitude – Latinos	.41*
	(.14)
Legal Chinese	−.10
	(.16)
Implicit × Legal Chinese	.19
	(.26)
Constant	−.01
	(.09)
R^2	.27
N	333

Notes: Entries are OLS coefficients, with robust standard errors in parentheses. All variables are rescaled to run from 0 to 1. Model also controls for explicit attitude toward immigrants (not shown).
* $p < .05$, one-tailed.

known about this influence, it should have failed to predict their opposition to legal immigration when considering legal Chinese immigrants. Indeed, these effects are independent of people's explicit evaluations of Latino, Asian, Middle Eastern, and white immigrants – which I have scaled and dubbed explicit attitude toward immigrant (see Equations 6.1 and 7.1). Thus, even after accounting for individual differences in general dislike of immigrants (i.e., ethnocentrism),

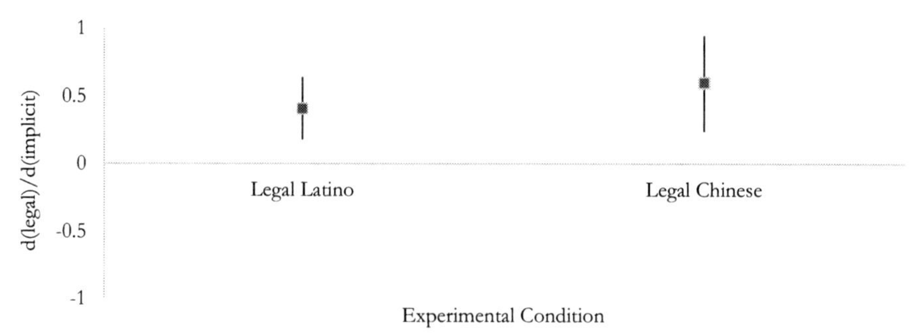

FIGURE 6.5. Marginal effect of implicit attitude by experimental condition (90% confidence intervals). *Note:* The legal Latino condition collapses the control group and legal Mexicans condition in light of the null difference between the latter two (see Figure 6.3). In each experimental condition, the displayed effects reveal an increase in opposition to legal immigration given a shift in implicit attitude toward Latinos from its lowest to highest level.

implicit attitude toward Latinos affects people's immigration policy judgments, even when focused on a non-Latino group.[13]

Summary and Steps Forward

My theory of implicit expectations proposes that citizens' unspoken thoughts can affect the political opinions they openly express. This influence is said to occur via the development of implicit expectations. Here, broaching the issue of immigration automatically calls to mind one's implicit attitude toward Latinos. Once activated, this implicit attitude becomes mentally accessible and its affective charge enters people's cognitive stream. As a result, implicit attitudes stand to color one's interpretation and use of political information via *affect contagion* (Lodge and Taber 2013), a process that occurs subconsciously – that is, without people knowing how their implicit attitude affects their use of explicit information.

To corroborate the subconscious nature of implicit expectations, I proposed that implicit attitude should structure political judgment even when the explicit information one encounters is incongruent with the object of one's implicit attitude. Accordingly, I analyzed two original survey experiments focused on the connection between explicit political information, implicit political attitude, and individual preferences for immigration. Across these experiments, I demonstrated that implicit attitude toward Latinos affects people's opinion about illegal and legal immigration, even if their attention is consciously centered on non-Latino individuals and groups. In the Deportation Experiment, for instance, I explicitly directed people's attention toward an undocumented immigrant who was either from El Salvador or Ireland. With this design, I found that even when individuals focused on an Irish immigrant, their implicit attitude toward Latinos boosted their support for deportation of this non-Latino individual. Building on this finding, I then examined the same dynamic in the realm of legal immigration. In this second experiment, individuals were assigned to a control group that received no explicit cues about immigrants or one of two conditions that centered people's attention on either legal Mexican or legal Chinese immigrants. Similar to the Deportation Experiment, I found that even when prompted to focus on legal Chinese immigrants, people's implicit attitude

[13] Perhaps it is better to control for *implicit* attitude toward immigrant outgroups in addition to (or in substitution of) its explicit form? But this would fatigue respondents, who would have to complete multiple IATs to build such a measure. Conceptually, though, this attitude is what others call ethnocentrism (e.g., Kinder and Kam 2009). And, research shows that implicit and explicit ethnocentrism are robustly associated ($r = .47$) (Cunningham et al. 2004c), with this correlation likely being higher since it does not address method artifact (i.e., variance due to completing self-reports vs. IATs). Thus, using explicit attitude toward immigrants as a covariate should reasonably control for people's dislike of Latino and non-Latino immigrants, which should boost confidence in this chapter's results.

toward Latinos heightened their support for exclusionary legal immigration policy.

Taken as a whole, then, this chapter has met its objective by providing evidence that implicit attitudes affect political judgment without people's awareness. Yet from another angle, the results herein ultimately provide only a useful staging point for the remaining chapters in the book. For on further scrutiny, the general model at hand implies that implicit attitudes structure the political judgments of *most* people in the *same* way. As we will see in the next two chapters, however, there are hidden sources of variation in how this basic model works for different people placed under different circumstances – and often with illuminating insights about how implicit attitudes affect (or do not) political decision-making. Let's begin this undertaking by turning to Chapter 7.

7

In Deliberation's Shadow

Education, (Un)awareness, and Implicit Attitudes

If there was ever a social realm where deliberation seems to matter, politics is one of them. From the electoral selection of lawmakers, to the evaluation of public policies, politics demands from its citizens at least a modicum of attention and reflection to decide between alternatives.

But political deliberation is costly (e.g., Downs 1957). It requires mental energy (e.g., Gailliot et al. 2007). And, the propensity to exert such effort is not uniformly distributed across the polity (cf. Althaus 1998; Delli Carpini and Keeter 1996; Zaller 1992). Certain citizens are simply more motivated than others to engage in the mental effort that deliberation demands (e.g., Sniderman et al. 1991). The end result is that when the public decides, some of this decision is underwritten by people who have meticulously considered their opinions, while some of it is driven by people who have thought less about their views. Seen from this perspective, deliberation is a matter of degree, and this variation among fellow citizens affects the quality of the public's decision making.

Might these differences in people's inclination to deliberate also shape citizens' reliance on implicit attitudes for political judgment?

It is certainly plausible. As I discussed earlier in Chapters 2 and 3, several social psychologists have argued that the connection between implicit attitude and individual judgment is not an all or nothing proposition (e.g., Gawronski and Bodenhausen 2011; Olson and Fazio 2009; Strack and Deutsch 2004; see also Eagly and Chaiken 1993: Chapter 7). Instead, these scholars maintain, the influence of implicit attitude depends on how motivated people are to avoid impulsive judgments, and whether they have enough opportunity to act on this motivation. The study of implicit racial attitudes captures the spirit of this view (e.g., Fazio and Dunton 1997; Fazio et al. 1995; see also Devine 1989). Scholars have shown that although these implicit attitudes can be spontaneously triggered, not all individuals act on this initial impulse. Some people are more sensitive to the prospect of appearing racially biased. Hence, when time or attention is in abundant supply, these individuals can follow through on their drive to remain unbiased by defusing the influence of their implicit attitude.

Whether intended or not, the normative appeal of this approach is easy to appreciate. Sure, implicit attitudes might be spontaneously activated. And yes, these attitudes might be beyond most people's awareness, even if for a brief moment. Yet the same question that I raised about these insights in earlier chapters still remains: how, exactly, do they translate to political judgments?

In this chapter, I examine the extent to which motivation and opportunity shape the relationship between implicit attitudes, explicit attitudes, and political decision making by examining the roles played by individual differences in education and the presence of unambiguous political cues. My focus on education is intentional. Individuals with more education are among the most politically involved within the mass public (e.g., Verba, Schlozman, and Brady 1995; Wolfinger and Rosenstone 1980). They are known to engage in more effortful, deliberative-type thinking (e.g., Converse 1964; Zaller 1992), and they are also acutely sensitive to the expression of racial intolerance (e.g., Sniderman and Piazza 1993; Sniderman et al. 1991). Yet they are also inclined to vigorously defend their attitudes by discounting contradictory political information and more readily accepting material that affirms their predispositions (e.g., Taber and Lodge 2006). Moreover, they are especially adept at connecting their attitudes to relevant political evaluations (e.g., Federico 2004).

Weaving these insights together, I propose and test a pair of contrasting hypotheses about how people's propensity to deliberate affects *who* is more influenced by implicit and explicit attitudes in the realm of politics, and *when*. The first of these predictions anticipates that highly educated citizens can override their implicit and explicit attitudes. This is especially likely if the political information these individuals encounter allows them to act on their inclination to engage in more effortful and reflective thinking; for example, through informational cues that make plain the irrelevance of attitudes toward a specific political object. In the face of such unambiguous cues, highly educated citizens should be able to shake off the influence of their implicit and explicit attitude toward said object.

In contrast, my second prediction – what I dubbed the *dueling effects* hypothesis in Chapter 3 – suggests the effects of implicit attitude become stronger among the highly educated, even as the influence of explicit attitude attenuates among these individuals. By this account, citizens with more years of schooling are predisposed toward more reflective thought. But people's deliberative efforts often enable them to better defend their attitudes in the face of contradictory information (e.g., Taber and Lodge 2006; see also Lodge and Taber 2000), while strengthening their ability to connect these attitudes to actual policy judgments (e.g., Federico 2004; Sniderman et al. 1991). These tensions, I contend, manifest themselves in dueling effects for implicit and explicit attitudes. One distinguishing quality of implicit attitudes, I have argued, is that relative to explicit attitudes, people are generally unaware that they possess the implicit variety (cf. Gawronski et al. 2006; Wilson et al. 2000). This implies that citizens cannot edit, manipulate, or suppress attitudes they fail to recognize.

But is this actually right? Are people generally unable to minimize or eliminate their biases if they closely scrutinize their actions? Patricia Devine (1989), for one, long ago taught us that even people who are low in self-reported prejudice are as knowledgeable about racial stereotypes as their peers who are highly prejudiced. Yet unlike highly prejudiced individuals, those who are low in prejudice invest more personal effort in inhibiting these stereotypes and their possible influence when consciously alerted about it. This suggests that even if implicit attitudes are spontaneously evoked, people are aware of them, just like they are aware of the explicit variety. Hence, those with more education should be better able to inhibit their explicit *and* implicit attitudes – a prediction that is more plausible when we consider that these attitudes are often correlated (see Chapter 5).

That explanation makes sense, but it is not mine. I propose instead that explicit attitudes are more responsive than implicit attitudes to incongruent political information. True, both attitudes are often modestly correlated, which augurs for the view that if people can edit one they should be able to edit the other. Yet Chapter 2 taught us that explicit–implicit attitudes are governed by different mental systems, with a more deliberative/conscious mode *following* a spontaneous/subconscious one. This means explicit attitudes arise downstream from implicit attitudes, placing the former (but not the latter) within introspection (cf. Erisen et al. 2014; Lodge and Taber 2013). It also means a modest correlation arises between explicit and implicit attitudes, not because they are mentally juxtaposed, but because forces like social desirability can intervene between the mental systems regulating each attitude (Gawronski et al. 2014b). Given that people with more education are not only more sensitive to norms about race, but also more skilled at (dis-)connecting their attitudes to political judgments, they should be better able to counteract the effects of racial attitudes entering their ken of awareness. This suggests that broaching the immigration issue by cueing a non-Latino group should enable the more educated to censor their explicit attitude. But if implicit attitudes are beyond introspection and relatively immune to social desirability concerns, then the more educated will bolster the connection between this attitude and their opposition to immigration (just like they would if their attitude is within awareness but relatively immune to social desirability).

To test these theoretical propositions, I revisit Chapter 6's Legal Immigration Experiment. The substantive focus of this experiment on legal, rather than illegal, immigration optimizes the opportunity individuals have to override their implicit attitude by asking for their evaluations of immigration policy in a domain where Latinos are a weak focus of public discourse (Chapter 4). This opportunity is further enhanced by the experimental manipulation involved, namely, a direct focus on a clear non-Latino group: legal Chinese immigrants. In these ways, the Legal Immigration Experiment positions me to assess whether and to what degree highly educated individuals are able to counteract their implicit attitudes toward Latinos when the focus of attention is non-Latinos.

My analysis reveals evidence that is consistent with the *dueling effects* hypothesis. Specifically, when people's attention is directed toward legal Chinese immigrants, individuals with more education are able to minimize the link between their explicit (i.e., self-reported) attitude toward Latinos and their opposition to legal immigration. Yet the same is not true of their implicit attitude toward this group. Even when citizens' attention is drawn to Chinese immigrants, implicit attitudes toward Latinos continue to affect the immigration policy preferences of the most educated segments of the US polity. This pattern serves to underscore the fact that many people are often unaware that they possess an implicit attitude. For if highly educated individuals had knowledge of this evaluation, they would have suppressed it the way they censored their self-reported evaluation of this group.

Taken as a whole, the evidence in this chapter suggests the grip of implicit attitudes is stronger among those citizens who are most inclined toward the political arena. Implicit attitudes, these findings suggest, do not fall under the strict purview of individuals some might consider boorish or uncouth. Rather than being confined to the margins of the polity, the current of implicit attitudes runs most strongly through its core, among the most politically engaged citizenry. For this reason, implicit attitude is more than a psychological curiosity. It is a phenomenon with palpable political consequences.

Education and Political Deliberation: One Coin, Two Sides

For political scientists, education holds a special place in the study of mass politics. Across the years, scholarship has taught us that greater years of schooling increases the likelihood that one will vote, heightens one's awareness about political figures and events, and improves one's chances of becoming involved in political causes and campaigns, among other things (Delli Carpini and Keeter 1996; Sniderman et al. 1991; Verba et al. 1995; Wolfinger and Rosenstone 1980). In these ways, educated individuals are thought to embody the temperament of the idealized democratic citizen: thoughtful, attentive, and incredibly engaged.

And not only does education enhance those qualities many of us admire about the idealized democratic citizen. It also appears to diminish some of those qualities many consider normatively undesirable, if not socially repugnant. Most relevant for our purposes is intolerance toward racial and ethnic minorities. In this regard, research has found that more years of education – especially a college education – encourages people to develop a more tolerant outlook toward racial and ethnic groups (e.g., Bobo and Licari 1989; Lipset 1960; McClosky and Zaller 1984; Sniderman and Piazza 1993; Sniderman et al.

1991). By directly and intensely exposing people to social norms that frown on negative racial attitudes, higher education leads people to acquire an acute sensitivity to expressing these types of attitudes. The highly educated person therefore learns that society generally disapproves of negative racial attitudes, endorses this position as his own, and does everything in his power to adhere to this norm (e.g., Sniderman and Piazza 1993; Sniderman et al. 1991). In these ways, education is believed to blunt the force of negative racial attitudes in society.

At the same time, however, greater levels of education impart another, often overlooked, quality to individuals: an improved ability to make a connection between their attitudes and their support for public policies (e.g., Federico 2004; Sniderman et al. 1991). The educated individual, always more attentive to the happenings of the political world, is more skilled at putting "two and two" together when forming their political opinions (e.g., Converse 1964; Zaller 1992). Immersed in the discourse about political issues, the highly educated individual is just better at connecting their attitudes to the policies he is considering – and often in the ways suggested by political debate (e.g., Gilens 1999). In fact, research on motivated skepticism suggests that individuals with greater cognitive sophistication are more inclined to process political information in a way that affirms their preexisting attitudes (Taber and Lodge 2006). Specifically, they are more likely to disregard contradictory political information, while more readily accepting facts that support their prior views.

In the realm of racial attitudes, Federico (2004) has established that this improved ability among the highly educated to link one's attitudes to relevant policy judgments can have paradoxical effects. To this end, he demonstrates that although education leads individuals to report lower levels of racial animus, these same individuals are more effective at applying such attitudes toward specific policy judgments (see also Federico and Sidanius 2002). This occurs, not only because highly educated people are more cognitively adept at connecting their attitudes to their evaluations of public policies, but also because political discourse links specific policies to certain racial groups (e.g., Gilens 1999; Valentino et al. 2013). Indeed, as Federico's (2004) experimental analysis illustrates, highly educated people are more likely to join their attitude toward African Americans to judgments of welfare proposals only when people are primed to think of black Americans as a beneficiary of such policies.

Putting Education in Context

It is obvious from the previous discussion that education can propel citizens to engage in more effortful and reflective political thought. But it is also clear that the consequences of those deliberations also depend, in part, on the characteristics of one's decision-making environment. Indeed, as Federico's (2004) work suggests, it might hinge on the quality of political information one has access to.

In this regard, social psychology has plenty to say about how differences in individuals and the evaluative contexts they face affect the relationship between deliberation and judgment (e.g., Devine 1989; Fazio and Dunton 1997; Fazio and Towles-Schwen 1999; Fazio et al. 1995; Olson and Fazio 2009; see also Gawronski and Bodenhausen 2011; Strack and Deutsch 2004). This perspective has been most forcefully and parsimoniously put forth by Russell Fazio and his collaborators. In their view, human behavior is underpinned by automatic (impulsive) and controlled (deliberative) mental processes, what I have labeled implicit and explicit reasoning, respectively. According to Fazio and his associates, the balance between automatic and controlled processes in shaping individual behavior is tipped in favor of the latter when two conditions are met: (1) people are motivated to engage in more effortful and controlled thought; and (2) people have the opportunity to follow through on this motivation. Across several studies, focused primarily on implicit racial attitudes, Fazio and his colleagues have shown that people placed in these circumstances display behaviors characterized by greater mental effort and reflection – in a word, by deliberation.

Despite the decidedly non-political focus of the studies yielding these insights, the lessons themselves are laden with implications for how we might think about the association between implicit attitudes and citizens' political decision making. Perhaps the most obvious one of these is that the influence of implicit attitude in the political arena depends not only on some citizens' penchant for deliberation (i.e., motivation), but also, on the clarity of information that forms the basis of people's deliberations (i.e., opportunity). Indeed, this potential interplay between motivation and opportunity suggests that implicit attitudes seep into political evaluations, not because – as the previous chapter suggested – they operate without people's awareness, but because certain people have not been made enough aware about the contradiction between their implicit attitudes and the political decision at hand.

Reprise: The Subconscious Nature of Implicit Attitudes

The preceding discussion rekindles the issue of awareness as it pertains to implicit attitudes. In the last chapter, we learned that citizens are unaware of their implicit attitudes insofar as they have no knowledge about how these leave an imprint on their political judgments. Specifically, we saw that citizens' implicit attitudes affected their judgments of immigration policy, even when the political cues they received were incongruent with the target of their implicit attitudes (i.e., Latinos). Yet nothing in this pattern of evidence suggests that people are unaware that they *possess* this implicit attitude (Gawronski et al. 2006). Indeed, people can know that they have this attitude, and yet still remain in the dark about how it affects the mental processes that give rise to their political judgments. In the case at hand, people can be aware that they negatively esteem Latinos without having knowledge about how this evaluation affects their views of immigration policy.

Not surprisingly, evidence demonstrating that people have no knowledge of their implicit attitude has proven difficult for researchers to produce. And, what evidence has been marshaled in favor of this claim has been deemed unpersuasive by skeptics (e.g., Gawronski 2009; Gawronski et al. 2006). For instance, scholars have noted that implicit and explicit attitudes toward the same object often display weak to modest correlations; a sign, they claim, that people are unaware of the former. Critics have countered, however, that these correlations sometimes strengthen when individuals are encouraged to reflect further on their attitudes (e.g., Akrami and Ekehammar 2005; Hofmann et al. 2005). Thus, although further reflection might increase mean values of explicit attitudes, critics maintain that it is hard to imagine how the same efforts also increase the *correlation* between explicit attitudes (which people are aware about) and implicit attitudes (which people are presumably unaware about) (e.g., Gawronski 2009).

This is difficult to imagine, but not impossible. For example, one plausible explanation for this pattern of strengthened correlations between implicit–explicit attitudes is that further reflection attenuates the volume of measurement error in self-reports, thus increasing the correlation between explicit and implicit attitudes (e.g., Brown 2006). However, in suggesting this counter explanation, it is important not to miss the larger point of this line of criticism. Namely, that a strong claim – that people do not know that they possess implicit attitude – requires strong evidence; stronger, at any rate, than what has been on offer. Let us see if we can improve on this front.

Laying Out the Alternatives

Our discussion so far can be distilled into four separate points. First, citizens differ in their propensity to deliberate in the political realm, as indexed by their level of education (i.e., motivation). Second, citizens face varied opportunities to act on this inclination, as in the clarity of political information they receive (i.e., opportunity). Third, this interplay between individual differences in education (i.e., motivation) and clarity of cues (i.e., opportunity) should structure the ability of citizens to override their implicit attitudes. But, fourth, the success of minimizing the political influence of implicit attitude will depend on whether citizens are actually aware that they possess this evaluation.

Is there a way to unify these insights into a set of coherent and testable hypotheses? I think there is. And it involves pulling the theoretical levers of individual motivation and opportunity to see how people's political decision making is shaped by both implicit *and* explicit attitudes toward the same object.

Let's begin with explicit attitude. By most accounts, explicit attitudes are fully within a person's awareness (Tourangeau et al. 2000). Accordingly, people can control, manipulate, and edit these attitudes. Citizens should therefore be able to censor the influence of their explicit attitude toward a target to the extent that they are motivated and have the opportunity to do so. Applied to the case of immigration politics, this means citizens with greater levels of education will be motivated to defuse the influence of their explicit attitude toward Latinos. After all, highly educated individuals are acutely sensitive to norms governing the expression of such racialized attitudes (Federico 2004; Sniderman et al. 1991). And, they will be more likely to do so when the political information they have access to calls into question the relevance of this explicit attitude for their evaluation of immigration policies.

Of course, this is not to say that more educated people do not possess racial attitudes. Such individuals are sensitive to norms governing the *expression* of racial attitudes, not their acquisition. As Federico (2004) shows, people with lower and higher levels of education both hold racial attitudes; the latter simply express them less than the former. Indeed, "it is clear that education by no means eliminates intolerance altogether, even though it does reduce the overall proportion of people who endorse intolerant ideas" (376). These insights align with the view that people with more education are among the most politically aware segments of the polity (e.g., Converse 1964; Zaller 1992), which means they should be more aware of the connection between Latinos and negative information about them. Yet such persons should also show more restraint in expressing a negative view of this group because highly educated persons are more likely to internalize social norms and, given their enhanced cognitive skill, more likely to "recognize the logical implications of the norms they internalize and act in accordance with them" (Federico 2004: 375).

But what happens to implicit attitude in these same circumstances? The answer will depend on whether people are, in fact, aware of their implicit attitude (Gawronski 2009; Gawronski et al. 2006; Hahn and Gawronksi 2014). Insofar as citizens have knowledge of their implicit attitude, those who are predisposed toward more reflective thinking, and who have the chance to recognize the inapplicability or undesirability of this attitude, should be able to lessen its impact on political judgment. Indeed, such a pattern of decision making would provide clear evidence that people are in fact aware of implicit attitudes because they are able to avoid its influence under propitious circumstances.

But, if citizens are truly unaware that they possess an implicit attitude toward Latinos, its effect on judgments of immigration policy will persist, even among those who can stave off the influence of explicit racial bias, thereby producing *dueling effects* for implicit/explicit attitudes. In fact, the influence of implicit attitude might even become stronger, as highly educated people, you may recall, have a more acute ability to join their attitude to relevant policy judgments (e.g., Federico 2004; Taber and Lodge 2006).

Figures 7.1a through 7.1c capture the essence of these three propositions. There we see illustrated the anticipated relationship between explicit (implicit)

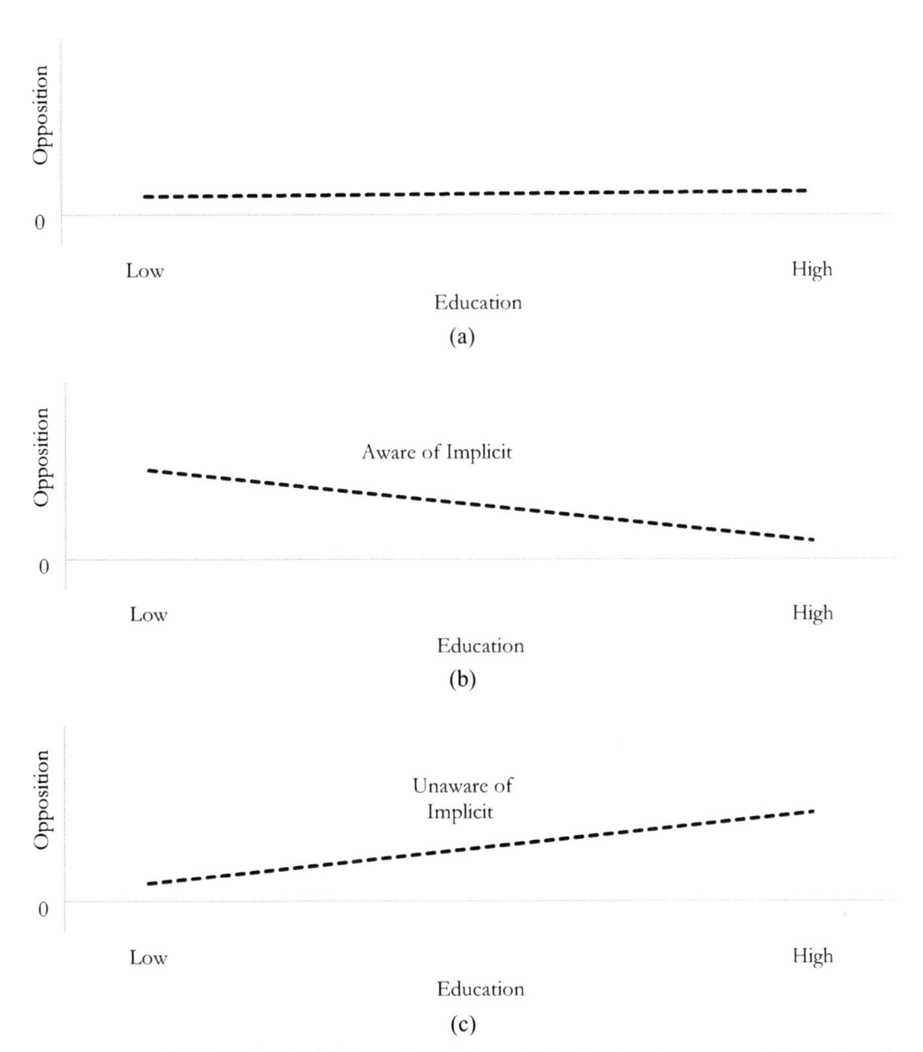

FIGURE 7.1. (a) Hypothetical effect of explicit attitude (Latinos) on opposition to immigration when non-Latinos are cued. (b) Hypothetical effect of implicit attitude (Latinos) on opposition to immigration when non-Latinos are cued. (c) Hypothetical effect of implicit attitude (Latinos) on opposition to immigration when non-Latinos are cued. *Notes:* The top panel shows that when non-Latinos are cued, explicit attitude toward Latinos is unrelated to opposition to immigration across all education levels. The middle panel shows that when non-Latinos are cued, more educated individuals minimize the impact of implicit attitude toward Latinos on their opposition to immigration, which implies awareness of implicit attitude. The bottom panel suggests that when non-Latinos are cued, the link between implicit attitudes toward Latinos and opposition to immigration grows among the more educated, who can better connect their attitudes to political judgments. This pattern implies a lack of awareness of implicit attitude.

attitude toward Latinos and opposition to immigration by levels of education when people are focused on a non-Latino group of immigrants. In each of these hypothetical scenarios, the x-axis runs from low to high levels of education and the y-axis runs from weak to strong opposition to immigration.

Figure 7.1a depicts the relationship between self-reported attitude toward Latinos and opposition to immigration when the focus of people's attention is a non-Latino group. There we see a virtual flat line. This is meant to suggest that explicit attitude toward Latinos should be essentially unrelated to one's opposition to immigration in this key circumstance because there is a clear *mismatch* between one's explicit attitude and the immigrant cues one is exposed to. And, because people have knowledge of their self-reported attitude, they are able to seize on this mismatch to keep at bay the influence of their self-reported attitude toward Latinos.

In contrast, Figure 7.1b depicts a downward- sloping line in the same circumstance (i.e., non-Latino cue). This is meant to suggest that although implicit attitudes are spontaneously triggered, people are nonetheless aware of this attitude, for its influence noticeably declines among people who are more predisposed toward reflective thinking. Thus, as people's level of education increases, so does their ability to arrest and minimize the political effects of their implicit attitude.

Finally, Figure 7.1c depicts the relationship just discussed, but it relaxes the assumption that people are aware of their implicit attitude. Actually, it makes the assumption that people have no knowledge that they possess an implicit attitude toward Latinos. In the absence of this knowledge, cues directing attention on a non-Latino group fail to counteract the effects of implicit attitude toward Latinos. In fact, as the figure shows, the influence of implicit attitude strengthens across levels of education, a pattern that simply reflects the greater ability of educated individuals to link their attitudes to policy evaluations (e.g., Federico 2004; Sniderman et al. 1991).

On paper, all three of these propositions seem viable. But which of these perspectives actually captures the gist of *who* is influenced by implicit attitudes and *when* within the US polity? For an answer, let us turn once again to the Legal Immigration Experiment in the National Study.

Empirically Assessing the Possibilities

If you recall, the Legal Immigration Experiment from Chapter 6 revealed that relative to a control condition with no immigrant cues, focusing attention on legal Mexican immigrants had no effect on opposition to legal immigration, while directing attention toward legal Chinese did. Based on this finding, the experiment reduces to two conditions: (1) a Latino condition that collapses respondents from the control and legal Mexicans conditions; and (2) the Chinese condition that focuses attention on legal Chinese immigrants. Hence, the key test for our purposes will involve how levels of education condition the effect of implicit attitude toward Latinos in that second condition, when people's attention is trained on non-Latino immigrants.

But before we get to that critical test, it is important to ascertain whether levels of education actually perform in any of the ways we have discussed in the previous pages. Indeed, if this key individual difference does not operate in a way that is consistent with prior work, it makes little sense to engage in a more elaborate modeling strategy that takes fuller advantage of the Legal Immigration Experiment. In particular, it is important to answer here two related questions. First, does education mitigate or amplify the influence of explicit attitude toward Latinos? Second, does education similarly affect the influence of implicit attitude?

To answer these questions, I estimate the following statistical model:

$$\begin{aligned}\text{Opposition (Immigration)} = {} & \beta_0 + \beta_1\text{Explicit} + \beta_2\text{Implicit} + \beta_3\text{Legal Chinese} \\ & + \beta_4\text{Education} + \beta_5\text{Explicit} \times \text{Education} \\ & + \beta_6\text{Implicit} \times \text{Education} \\ & + \beta_7\text{Legal Chinese} \times \text{Education} \qquad (7.1)\end{aligned}$$

In this model, we are particularly interested in β_5 and β_6, which will give us a sense of whether and how education affects the connection between people's opposition to legal immigration and their levels of explicit attitude and implicit attitude. In other words, how does the influence of explicit and implicit attitude change – if at all – as one's level of education increases? To facilitate the interpretation of these and subsequent results, opposition to legal immigration runs on a 0–1 interval. In contrast, explicit and implicit attitude are transformed to have standard deviation units, while levels of education is left in its raw metric.[1] In this way, the coefficients from this initial model will reveal the percentage increase in opposition to legal immigration that is produced by a standard deviation shift in explicit (implicit) attitude as we move *across* increased levels of education.

The raw results of this analysis are reported in Table A7.1 in the appendix. Based on these results, I then depict the relevant effects in graphical form. What, if anything, do we learn from this initial analysis of the data? Figure 7.2 displays the influence of explicit attitude toward Latinos on public opposition to legal immigration across people's level of education. There we can appreciate two interrelated patterns suggesting that education enables people to reduce any connection between their explicit attitude toward Latinos and their opposition to legal immigration. First, notice that among those individuals with the lowest level of education – that is, those without a high school diploma – explicit attitude has a positive and strong effect. These are the individuals who embody some of the conventional wisdom on racial intolerance – parochial and hostile

[1] Specifically, education ranges from 1–no high school to 6–postgraduate education.

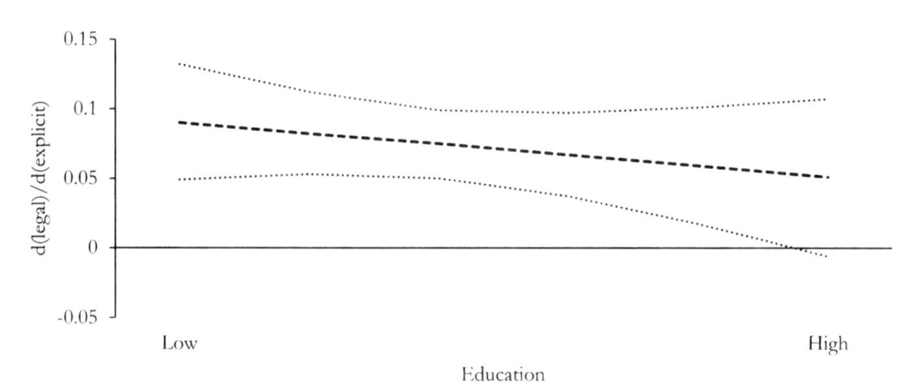

FIGURE 7.2. Explicit attitude and opposition to legal immigration by level of education (90% confidence intervals). *Note*: The figure reveals the change in opposition to legal immigration in light of a standard deviation shift in explicit attitude toward Latinos, across levels of education.

to minorities, in this case, Latinos. And embody it they do. Among these individuals, a standard deviation shift in explicit attitude toward Latinos actually increases opposition to legal immigration by about .09. But notice what happens as we move from left to right across higher levels of education. As people's level of education increases, they begin to behave more in line with the view of education as a corrective to racial intolerance. Simply put, having more education chips away at the effect of explicit attitude toward Latinos on people's opposition to legal immigration. In fact, at the highest level of education, the effect of this explicit attitude is essentially zero, because the confidence interval surrounding this estimate straddles the zero value.

But what about *implicit* attitude toward Latinos? How does education affect its influence, if at all? A critic could argue that implicit attitude toward Latinos is really nothing more than explicit attitude measured in a fancy way. Hence, education should also diminish its influence. To convince this skeptic, then, we would have to show that the force of implicit attitude pierces through a person's political thinking even as the effects of explicit attitude are contained. Figure 7.3 displays the effect of implicit attitude on public opposition to legal immigration across levels of education. There we see evidence that, rather than minimizing the effect of implicit attitude, higher levels of education actually heighten its effect. In other words, the more educated one is, the stronger the effect of implicit attitude on one's opposition to legal immigration. In fact, the effects of implicit attitude are strongest and most reliably estimated for the highest levels of education. Among those with a postgraduate education, for example, a standard deviation shift in implicit attitude increases opposition to legal immigration by about .09. Ironic as this may be, it is nevertheless consistent with the view that people with higher education have stronger attitudes that they are better at connecting to their policy stances. It is also consistent

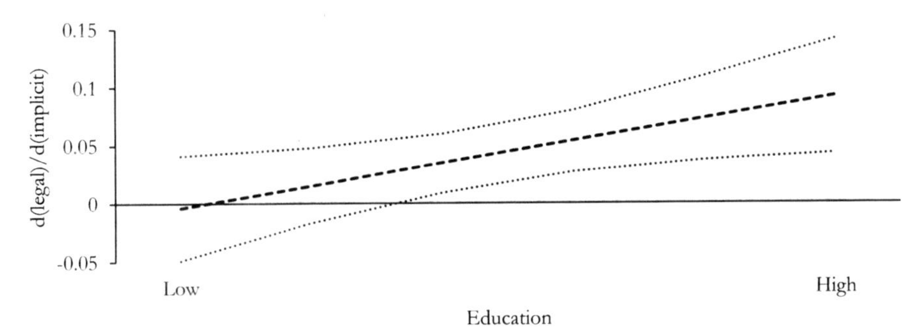

FIGURE 7.3. Implicit attitude and opposition to legal immigration by level of education (90% confidence intervals). *Note*: The figure reveals the change in opposition to legal immigration in light of a standard deviation shift in implicit attitude toward Latinos, across levels of education.

with the claim that people are unaware of their implicit attitude, as education fails to dampen its influence the way it was able to minimize explicit attitude toward the same group.

Taken as a whole, this evidence suggests that greater levels of education can lead citizens to engage in more deliberative thought. In turn, this further reflection appears to enable these individuals to correct those attitudes they wish to avoid – but only if they are aware of these evaluations. Translated to the realm of immigration policy, this implies that people at the center of politics – the more educated – are substantially more tolerant than their counterparts on the periphery of politics – the less educated. At an implicit level, however, the more educated display some signs of the very intolerance they work so vigorously to avoid.

Making the Most of Deliberation: The Role of Opportunity

The evidence so far suggests people are unaware of their implicit attitude, and this attitude is more likely to influence the political judgments of the most – not the least – educated segments of the polity. Deliberation, it seems, can only help people correct attitudes they have knowledge about.

Or does it? In one crucial respect, the pattern of evidence presented thus far can be said to be incomplete. I have shown that people with more education can suppress their attitude toward Latinos if they are aware of it. But, what I have not examined is whether and how this pattern changes when we clarify the information people have about immigrants. One could reasonably argue, for example, that the preceding analysis makes it hard – too hard, actually – for educated people to correct their implicit attitude because they don't have the opportunity to do so (e.g., Fazio and Towles-Schwen 1999; Olson and Fazio 2009). Simply put, there is an inherent ambiguity as to who the immigrants in question are when people are asked to judge policies toward legal immigration.

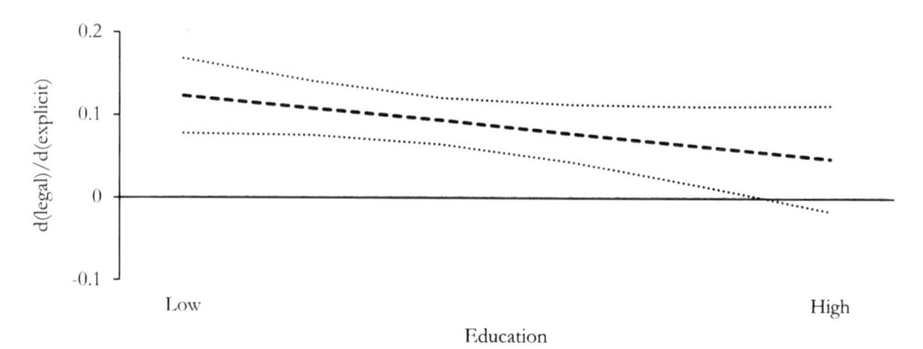

FIGURE 7.4. Explicit attitude and opposition to legal immigration by level of education – Latino condition (90% confidence intervals). *Note*: The figure displays the change in opposition to legal immigration across education levels, given a standard deviation shift in explicit attitude toward Latinos when Latino immigrants are cued.

People therefore default to assuming Latinos are the group in question. But perhaps if we direct people to focus on a non-Latino group, highly educated individuals can override the impulse behind their implicit attitude toward Latinos. With their attention plainly trained on non-Latinos, the more educated should be more likely to appreciate the mismatch between the information they have just received and the object of their implicit attitude. Thus, implicit attitude toward Latinos should fall by the wayside among educated individuals in this crucial circumstance.

To wrestle with this possibility, I modify the statistical model from the previous section in one crucial way. Whereas the previous model allowed us to see how explicit and implicit attitude toward Latinos operates among people with higher and lower levels of education, this modified model allows us to see this same pattern when people are focused on either Latino or non-Latino immigrants. This added layer will put us in a better position to determine whether the deliberative effect of education itself hinges on the opportunity to act on people's more reflective thoughts. Table A7.2 in the appendix reports the raw results of this model. But once again, I visually depict these findings in order to facilitate their interpretation.

I begin with the influence of explicit attitude across levels of education when people's attention is trained on Latinos. How does this information affect the connection between explicit attitude and levels of education? Consider Figure 7.4. Because people in this condition are directed to focus on Latinos, we should expect explicit attitude to have some effect. And it does. But notice that as levels of education increase, this influence wanes. Among those individuals with the highest levels of education, explicit attitude against Latinos has no hold whatsoever on their opposition to legal immigration. So, even in the most obvious of cases – when people are considering Latino immigrants – people with more education are still less likely to rely on their explicit attitude toward this

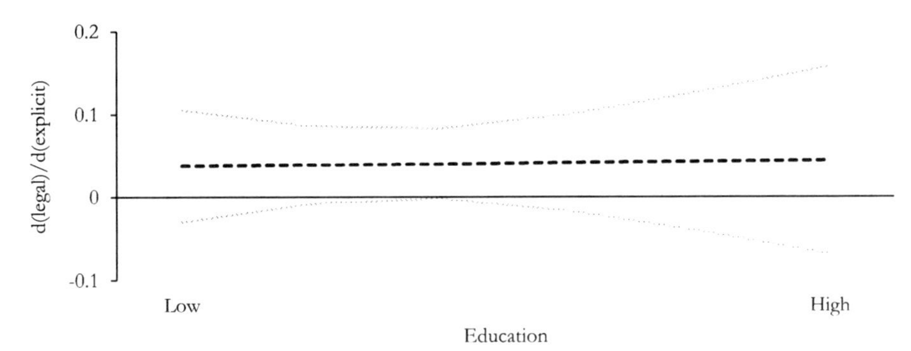

FIGURE 7.5. Explicit attitude and opposition to legal immigration by level of education – Chinese condition (90% confidence intervals). *Note*: The figure displays the change in opposition to legal immigration across education levels, given a standard deviation shift in explicit attitude toward Latinos when Chinese immigrants are cued.

group. The inclination toward more reflective thinking, it appears, enables more highly educated to lessen the impact of negative racial attitude on their political judgment.

This pattern is even more compelling in the case where people are focused on non-Latinos, that is to say, legal Chinese immigrants (Figure 7.5). There we see explicit attitude striking a flat note across all levels of education. In other words, explicit attitude toward Latinos fails to affect people's opposition to immigration in this condition *regardless* of people's level of education. Thus, any connection between the latter and people's opposition to legal immigration is completely minimized.

Now let us turn to implicit attitude and its influence across levels of education under both of the experimental conditions we just saw. What do we find then? In the Latino condition (Figure 7.6) we see evidence that implicit

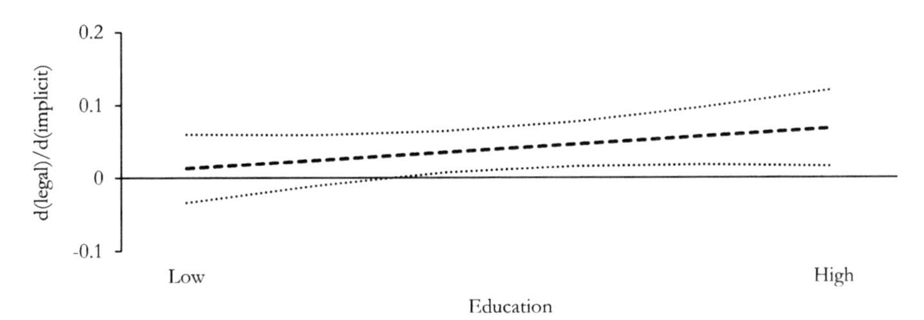

FIGURE 7.6. Implicit attitude and opposition to legal immigration by level of education – Latino condition (90% confidence intervals). *Note*: The figure displays the change in opposition to legal immigration across education levels, given a standard deviation shift in implicit attitude toward Latinos when Latino immigrants are cued.

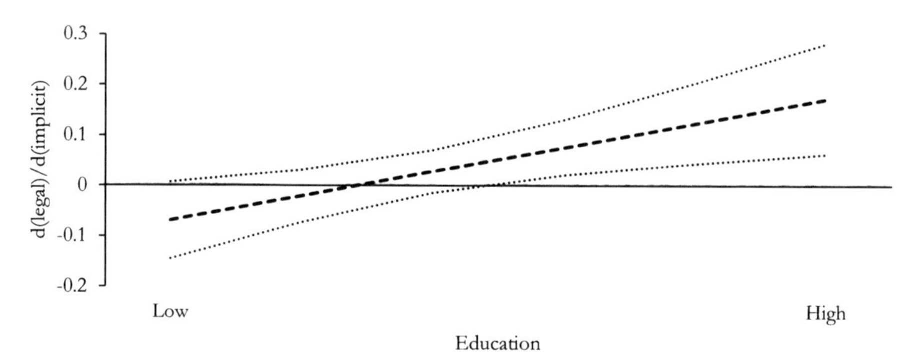

FIGURE 7.7. Implicit attitude and opposition to legal immigration by level of education – Chinese condition (90% confidence intervals). *Note*: The figure displays the change in opposition to legal immigration across education levels, given a standard deviation shift in implicit attitude toward Latinos when Chinese immigrants are cued.

attitude toward Latinos gets stronger – not weaker – with greater levels of education. In other words, in the case where people are directed to focus on Latinos, it is the more educated who are most influenced by their implicit attitude toward this group as they form their opposition to immigration. This is consistent with the view that highly educated people are more effective at connecting their attitudes to policy support. It also aligns with the stronger claim that highly educated people can only correct those undesirable attitudes they know about.

You might have noticed, however, that those with the lowest levels of education failed to reliably connect their implicit attitude to their immigration policy judgment. Is this surprising? Not when viewed against the backdrop of research on cognitive sophistication and public opinion (Althaus 1998; Bartels 1996; Delli Carpini and Keeter 1996; Zaller 1992). In his now classic chapter, Converse (1964) taught us that much of mass opinion is awash in a sea of noise, as many people do not possess coherent opinions on most matters, answering survey questions haphazardly. These are precisely the kind of people who possess lower education levels and, by extension, less cognitive sophistication. Consequently, they often have difficulty in consistently linking their attitudes to judgments or evaluations, and the patterns we just observed mesh with this insight.

But what happens when we turn to the more critical condition, where people are focused on non-Latinos – more specifically, legal Chinese immigrants. Do highly educated people behave any differently then? Figure 7.7 suggests they do not. In fact, what it suggests is that they behave identically as before. Although their attention is trained on legal Chinese immigrants, the more educated are still more likely to rely on their implicit attitude against Latinos to form their opposition to legal immigration (with the least educated once again displaying an unreliable pattern). This bears repeating, for it is the case that the same people who correct their explicit attitude toward Latinos are the same ones who are most likely to succumb to their implicit attitude toward this group *in the same exact circumstance*. Perhaps without meaning to, a highly educated person forges a stronger link between an implicit attitude toward Latinos and his or her opposition to immigration, even when concentrating on an obviously non-Latino group of immigrants.

Conclusions

We began this chapter with a simple question: do individual differences in the propensity to deliberate affect how people's political views are shaped by implicit and explicit attitudes? The evidence in this chapter suggests "yes," through a process that we might describe as *dueling effects*.

Education, I explained, often performs as a palliative in the realm of public opinion, especially when citizens' racial attitudes are concerned. Predisposed toward more reflective thought and acutely sensitive to the expression of racially intolerant views, a highly educated person is sometimes presented as a potential bulwark against racial bias, especially when placed in the right circumstances – for example, by highlighting the irrelevance or undesirability of racial attitudes in political judgment. And we learned that there is, in fact, some merit to this claim. When induced to focus on non-Latino immigrants, the highly educated respondents in the Legal Immigration Experiment were able to soften the blow of their explicit attitudes toward Latinos on their opposition to immigration.

In sharp contrast, however, the highly educated were unable to arrest the influence of implicit attitude toward Latinos on their judgments of legal immigration. Two reasons were proffered ex ante for this pattern of evidence. First, although education does promote more deliberative thought, it also imparts an improved ability to connect one's attitudes to political evaluations. Second, implicit attitude not only operates without one's awareness; it also potentially exists in one's mind without one's knowledge. When synthesized, these insights suggest, even if paradoxically, that people with greater levels of education will more effectively connect their implicit attitude to their political judgments – even if one encounters direct information to the contrary.

Taken as a whole, these findings provide yet another reason for why political scientists should care about implicit attitude, its presence in the mass public, and the extent of its political reach. As the results make plain, implicit attitudes are not confined to the margins of the polity. Instead, their influence reverberates most strongly among those citizens who are most likely to determine the course of politics.

At this point, some might be tempted to conclude from this chapter that implicit attitudes reflect the "true" nature of people – what they really think about political objects, such as racial groups. Indeed, how else can somebody explicitly feel one way, but implicitly in another? But the deeper lesson is that what people declare about political objects and what they leave unstated are both unique evaluations, with one being more relevant than the other among some individuals, some of the time. To be sure, it is no doubt disquieting to discover that some forms of attitude can affect individuals who we least suspect. Yet it is perhaps even more disquieting to insist that this cannot be the case when, in fact, the evidence suggests otherwise.

TABLE A7.1. *Opposition to Legal Immigration by Explicit Attitude, Implicit Attitude, and Levels of Education – Pairwise Interactive Model*

	Opposition to Legal Immigration
Explicit Attitude – Latinos	.10*
	(.03)
Implicit Attitude – Latinos	−.02
	(.04)
Experimental Condition – Legal Chinese	.18*
	(.07)
Education	−.02*
	(.01)
Explicit Attitude × Education	−.01
	(.01)
Implicit Attitude × Education	.02*
	(.01)
Legal Chinese × Education	−.04*
	(.02)
Constant	.62*
	(.16)
R^2	.19
N	333

Notes: OLS coefficients, with robust standard errors in parentheses. The dependent variable runs on a 0–1 interval. Explicit and implicit attitude have been transformed to have standard deviation units.

* $p < .05$, one-tailed.

TABLE A7.2. *Opposition to Legal Immigration by Explicit Attitude, Implicit Attitude, Education, and Experimental Condition – Fully Interactive Model*

	Opposition to Legal Immigration
Explicit Attitude – Latinos	.14*
	(.04)
Implicit Attitude – Latinos	.00
	(.04)
Education	−.02*
	(.01)
Experimental Condition – Legal Chinese	.20*
	(.07)
Explicit × Education	−.02*
	(.01)
Explicit × Legal Chinese	−.10
	(.07)
Education × Legal Chinese	−.04*
	(.02)
Explicit × Education × Legal Chinese	.02
	(.02)
Implicit × Education	.01
	(.01)
Implicit × Legal Chinese	−.12*
	(.07)
Implicit × Education × Legal Chinese	.04*
	(.02)
Constant	.62*
	(.04)
R^2	.20

OLS coefficients, with robust standard errors in parentheses. The dependent variable runs on a 0–1 interval. Explicit and implicit attitude have been transformed to have standard deviation units.

* $p < .05$, one-tailed.

8

In Black and White

Race, Group Position, and Implicit Attitudes in Politics

Across the last few chapters, we have seen various layers of evidence affirming the political influence of implicit attitudes among individual citizens. By necessity, these efforts have centered on the psychological processes behind implicit attitudes. Yet by focusing on the inner recesses of the mind, the fact that individuals are embedded within a larger social structure has been minimized, if not eliminated, from our investigations so far. This can potentially give the wrong impression about implicit attitudes. At its worst, it insinuates that implicit biases like these are strictly a matter of individual predisposition or temperament, mostly, if not completely, divorced from the social landscape in which he or she is inserted. This chapter endeavors to correct this omission by shedding light on the social foundations of implicit attitude: a feat I accomplish by centering on the role of race.

Race has often been at the center of America's politics and institutions (e.g., Marx 1998; McClain and Stewart 2005). At America's inception, for example, race was used to systematically exclude black Americans from the nation through active denial of citizenship (Smith 1997). This policy continued through the Civil War until passage of the 14th Amendment, which broadened the definition of citizenship to include this group. Yet in spite of constitutional reforms, informal institutions and practices (e.g., Jim Crow) sustained many of the same attitudes, norms, and practices that had thrived under de jure racial exclusion. Race continued to matter. In fact, even today, nearly five decades after the 1964 Civil Rights Act officially ended discriminatory practices like housing segregation and voter fraud, race *still* matters. For many individuals, their outcomes continue to be profoundly shaped by whether they happen to be black or not, as evidenced by the starkly higher rates of incarceration and poverty within the larger African American community, for example (Brown-Dean 2007; Conley 1999).[1]

Of course, this is not to say that American race relations have not genuinely changed. Progress has been made – and is being made – on many, if not all, of these fronts. We are definitely not the nation of yesteryear. But to focus exclusively on aggregate improvements in the standing of African Americans is to risk missing an enduring but critical insight about black individuals. Even in the face of collective progress, race continues to leave an indelible imprint on many aspects of their personal lives. This axiom applies with special force in the realm of politics, where scholars continue to amass evidence that blacks' status as racial minorities affects the formation and expression of their political attitudes (e.g., Dawson 1994; Harris-Lacewell 2003; Nunnally 2010; Philpot and White 2010; Philpot et al. 2010; White 2007).

Building on these insights, this chapter examines how race influences the manifestation and bearing of implicit attitudes in the political realm. The renowned political scientist, Michael Dawson, has astutely observed that although racial groups in the United States are clearly ordered in a descending hierarchy of status and privilege, this "American racial order is a phenomenon with which many researchers are loathe to deal" (2000: 344). Mindful of Dawson's point, the following pages strive to show how the location of one's racial group within this hierarchy affects the acquisition and use of implicit attitudes among individual Americans – what I refer to as the *social position* hypothesis (e.g., Bobo and Hutchings 1996; Kim 2000; Masuoka and Junn 2013; Sidanius and Pratto 2001). Accordingly, I draw on psychological scholarship establishing a strong connection between social hierarchies, power, and individual attitudes toward outgroups. Cognitive researchers have demonstrated that being in a social position of relative power leads individuals to pay less attention to individuating information about their subordinates (Fiske 1993; Goodwin et al. 2000). The reason for this is straightforward: people in more powerful positions do not depend as much on subordinates for their own outcomes. A supervisor's prospects, for instance, depend less on her underlings than the other way around. Similarly, a teacher's fortunes hinge less on her students than vice versa. Power asymmetries like these, scholars have learned, lead individuals to develop negative, coarse, and inflexible attitudes toward the larger categories that subordinates belong to (e.g., employees, students). Indeed, in intergroup settings, where people derive much power from group membership, these attitudes can serve as a way for members of advantaged groups to justify the unequal stratification of disadvantaged groups (Goodwin et al. 2000;

[1] The case of African Americans is instructive, but not anomalous. Recall the legal exclusion of Chinese immigrants and other foreigners from Asia from the late 1800s to the middle of the twentieth century (Takaki 1989). Consider, too, the systematic disenfranchisement of many Mexican Americans in the wake of the 1846 US–Mexico war (Gutiérrez 1995).

Richeson and Ambady 2003; see also Masuoka and Junn 2013; Sidanius and Pratto 2001; Sidanius et al. 2000).

A key implication from this scholarship is that the position of one's racial group within America's racial order might be a key influence over an individual's implicit attitude. More specifically, it suggests that race might modulate the intensity and relevance of these attitudes for people's political decision making. Seizing on these insights, I examine the degree to which African Americans judge immigration policy on the basis of implicit attitudes toward Latinos. Accordingly, I draw on an oversample of black respondents who completed the Legal Immigration Experiment in the National Study.

My investigation reveals evidence that is consistent with my *social position* hypothesis. African Americans, like white Americans, possess implicit attitudes toward Latinos. That is, many members of both racial groups have learned to negatively evaluate Latinos at an implicit level. Black Americans, however, exhibit discernibly lower levels of this implicit attitude relative to whites: a difference I attribute to blacks' minority position within America's racial hierarchy. This "racial gap" in implicit attitudes is politically consequential. In contrast to white Americans, whose preferences for immigration policy are spontaneously shaped by implicit attitude, African Americans do not connect their implicit evaluations of Latinos as readily to their explicit political judgments. Together, these twin results underline the role that social structure – in this case, racial hierarchy – plays in the development and expression of implicit attitudes within the mass US public, thus providing finer-grained insight about where the political force of implicit attitude is stronger – and, just as importantly, where it is significantly weaker.

But before we get to these findings, let's begin by further explaining why one's position within a larger social order might affect the intensity and relevance of implicit attitudes, a task that involves confronting the often underappreciated role of power and individual decision making.

The Interface between Power and Individual Attitudes

Talk of power can make many a good political scientist wince. And for good reasons. To speak of power is to easily slip into the use of normatively laden terms – a faux paus in the eyes of many empirically oriented political scientists. Indeed, the word power itself connotes, among other things, strength, dominance, and privilege – all phenomena that many scholars rightfully sense are involved in politics, but that ultimately feel judgmental, if not polemical, when brandished in scholarly discussions.

Adding to this discomfort is the conceptual fuzziness of power itself. The fact that power can refer to so many different things at once – money, status, information, etc. – appears to undermine its utility as a unified scientific concept. During the late 1950s and early 1970s, for example, political scientists engaged in fierce debates about power as concept (e.g., Bachrach and Baratz 1962; Dahl 1961; Morriss 1972; Polsby 1960; Riker 1964). The opening salvo in this exchange was Robert Dahl's (1957: 203) effort to clarify and make empirically testable the notion of power, which he defined in relational terms as the ability for one person to get another to do something that he or she would not otherwise do. It was a parsimonious and seemingly tractable definition, one aimed at studying the one-on-one influence that politicians and other notables have over each other. But in the span of just a few years, critics picked apart Dahl's conceptualization. Bachrach and Baratz (1962), for example, lamented Dahl's failure to consider the power of agenda setting – that is, influence over the issues and problems that powerful actors actually haggle about. Riker (1964), in turn, sensed ambiguity in the causal direction of power between actors. And Morriss (1972: 459), to note another skeptic, cited Dah'ls neglect to consider veto players in power relations: people "whose approval is essential for the proposal to pass (or the opposition to succeed)." Hence, even if, as these critics recognized, power is essential to the study of politics, it still feels like a concept in search of a way to identify it empirically, especially if one is interested in how power shapes the political evaluations of ordinary individuals in the mass public.

In the end, there is little that can be done about the judgmental overtones of the word power, other than to employ a thesaurus, perhaps. But the conceptualization of power can be addressed more concretely, thus better equipping political scientists to study its role and possible influences on people's political decision making.

In this regard, social psychologists have blazed a promising trail in the study of power and individual judgment. There, scholars have discovered that humans possess a universal need to control (or have a sense of control) over their own prospects, fortunes, and opportunities – in a word, over their own *outcomes* (e.g., Brehm 1993). Against this backdrop, power boils down to the control one has over the outcomes of other people (e.g., Fiske 1993; Goodwin et al. 2000; Richeson and Ambady 2003; Rodríguez-Bailón et al. 2000). In essence, powerful individuals have more sway over the prospects and fortunes of their subordinates. Or, to put it in a different light, individuals with less power exert a weaker influence over their own outcomes.

By this metric, power is a matter of degree, not an absolute. It is not the case that some people have it and others do not. Rather, it is the case that some people have more power relative to others. In this way, power should not be confused with individual agency. Although all people have individual agency, not all people share a uniform level of power to exercise this self-direction.

Scholars have found that powerful individuals – that is, those with more influence over the outcomes of others – generally face weak incentives to individuate among the less powerful. Powerful people weakly depend on subordinates for their own outcomes. Hence, those with more power often pay less attention to, and make minimal distinctions between, those with less power.

In one illustrative study, for example, Fiske (1993) found that undergraduate students who were invested with greater power to judge summer job applications from high school students were less likely to pay attention to nuanced information about these applicants. In a similar experiment, Goodwin et al. (2000) showed that besides attending less to individuating information about subordinates, powerful individuals were also more likely to focus on stereotypic information about those with less power (see also Rodríguez-Bailón et al. 2000). Richeson and Ambady (2003) demonstrate these tendencies in the realm of implicit attitudes. In their experimental research, these authors found that white individuals who were invested with more power over a black subordinate during an experimental task displayed more negative attitudes toward African Americans in general. As these authors explain, higher-position whites were more inclined to attend to category-based information about their African American subordinates; that is, information about blacks as a group, rather than blacks as individuals. Consequently, high-position whites expressed more bias against blacks via an Implicit Association Test (IAT) than lower-position whites.

Taken as a whole, scholarship like this suggests that individuals with more power develop and express negative attitudes toward the less powerful as a way to maintain and justify their privileged positions (e.g., Goodwin et al. 2000; Rodríguez-Bailón et al. 2000; see also Blumer 1958; Sidanius and Petrocik 2001; Sidanius et al. 1997). But power is not a strict individual affair. As Richeson and Ambady (2003: 177) remind us, "power is often confounded with ... group status." Thus, there is often a tight correlation between a person's power and the social groups to which they belong. More precisely, there is often a strong correspondence between a person's power, the social groups to which they belong, and the position of these groups relative to others (e.g., Blumer 1958; Bobo 1983; Bobo and Hutchings 1996; Kim 2000; Sidanius and Pratto 2001). The end result here is that many times power at the individual level accumulates into power asymmetries between groups. And once these imbalances emerge, they become difficult to change. Members of groups that enjoy a privileged position within a stratified order strive to preserve this arrangement (e.g., Bobo and Hutchings 1996; Jost et al. 2004; Sidanius and Pratto 2001).

Indeed, the example often used to illustrate this point is the case that is the focus of this chapter – race, or more precisely, racial hierarchy in the United States (e.g., Sidanius and Petrocik 2001; Sidanius and Pratto 2001; Sidanius et al. 1997; see also Jacobson 1998; Kim 2000; Masuoka and Junn 2013). By this account, whites are positioned as an ascendant group, collectively attended by relatively more resources and higher status than several racial minority groups, including African Americans. Within this racial order, negative attitudes toward outgroups become a means for many white Americans to preserve and justify their dominant position within this social structure (e.g., Bobo 1983; Kim 2000).

Race, Power, and Implicit Attitudes

Race is power, or so our discussion implies. But if this is actually the case, how exactly does the simple fact that one belongs to a more (or less) powerful racial group affect one's implicit attitudes? I propose two specific pathways, both of which require us to revisit and extend some of the fundamental operating principles behind implicit attitudes that we discussed earlier in this book.

Implicit attitudes, you may recall, are underpinned by automatic cognitive processes. In the face of fitting stimuli, these attitudes are spontaneously called to mind, made mentally accessible, and applied to relevant judgments and behaviors. Yet there is a specific reason why such spontaneity works so seamlessly, at least for some individuals. And that reason has to do with how important an implicit attitude is to a particular person. Importance, in this context, has a very specific meaning. It refers to the *relevance* of one's implicit attitude. Implicit attitudes that are important are, to paraphrase the social psychologist Russell Fazio, "regularly rehearsed" (e.g., Fazio 2007). Thus, when a person has possession of an important implicit attitude, it means he or she chronically draws on it to inform their decisions and behaviors. In this way, implicit attitudes that are important serve as critical guides in people's everyday navigation of the world around them.

Seen from this perspective, the reason implicit attitudes become "automated" is that people continuously rely on them. Indeed, in a series of clever experiments, Fazio et al. (1982) experimentally induced subjects to repeat their evaluation of several puzzles, which served as attitude objects. Fazio's team discovered that those who rehearsed their evaluation of these objects subsequently displayed faster reaction times on a test gauging the automaticity of their attitudes toward these puzzles (see also Fazio et al. 1986). In other words, practice made perfect – or, at the very least, practice made people's implicit attitude more spontaneous.

So, how does this tie to my claims about race, power, and implicit attitude? Individuals with more power, we have learned already, face less incentive to individuate among their subordinates and more incentive to rely on category-level information about them as a way to maintain their privileged position. In an intergroup setting like America's racial order, this means that people from relatively advantaged groups face stronger incentives to develop and use implicit attitudes toward outgroups as a way to buttress their more privileged position. The use of implicit attitudes toward this end leads individuals to more regularly practice or rehearse these attitudes, thereby imbuing them with greater importance. Consequently, implicit attitudes become *relatively* more automated for members of socially powerful groups. In other words, although members of both powerful and less powerful groups generally acquire some level of implicit attitude, the joining of these attitudes to relevant judgments and behavior is less impulsive among individuals who are less advantaged.

By the same token, this also means that in intergroup settings, individuals from less advantaged groups should form lower levels of implicit attitudes; lower, at least, than those in more advantaged positions. That is because individuals from less powerful groups do not have as privileged a position to maintain. Thus, they are less likely to rehearse these attitudes in the service of preserving such a status. In fact, to the extent that their group shares a relatively less powerful position with a potential outgroup, this shared status might make for interdependent outcomes between groups, which means individuals from less advantaged positions will face even weaker incentives to acquire a high level of implicit attitude toward an outgroup (e.g., Richeson and Craig 2011; Rodríguez-Bailón et al. 2000).

When applied to the case of black and white Americans and their implicit attitudes toward Latinos, this line of reasoning suggests the following. First, relative to whites, African Americans should display significantly lower levels of implicit attitude toward Latinos. Second, if the relatively milder levels of implicit attitude among African Americans emerge from the fact that these attitudes are less relevant to blacks given their group's relative positioning in America's racial order, then individual differences in implicit attitude should weakly predict blacks' opposition to immigration.

Evidence on both counts is needed to support my *social position* hypothesis – the notion that racial hierarchy – and one's position in it – modulates the connection between implicit attitudes and political judgment. But this is a challenging feat. On one level, examining implicit attitudes among African Americans has obvious merits. They are a racial minority that occupies a lower tier – some say *the* lowest tier (e.g., Dawson 2000; Kahn et al. 2009; Sears et al. 1999) – within America's racial order. However, although their position as minorities hints at a shared status with Latino immigrants, that very same location often puts African Americans in tension, rather than harmony, with this group (Diamond 1998; McClain et al. 2006; Shankman 1982). Many African Americans share the same labor markets as Latino immigrants and their kin (e.g., McClain et al. 2007). Many black Americans also reside in inner-city neighborhoods increasingly populated by Latinos (e.g., Gay 2006). Black families, moreover, often send their children to public schools where Latino enrollment has swelled (e.g., Meier et al. 2004). And, politically, African American voters often find themselves competing with Latinos over local government positions and electoral spoils (Kaufmann 2003; McClain 1993; McClain and Karnig 1990).

This substantial overlap between the social and economic worlds of blacks and Latinos, and the friction it sometimes produces, thus suggests an alternative hypothesis: that African Americans might be more likely – even justified, you may say – in displaying more negative implicit attitude toward this group in comparison to whites. By this account, the ordering of racial groups matters to blacks' implicit attitudes, but it is not the asymmetry between the powerful and less powerful that is crucial. Instead, it is the position of blacks next to Latinos, a group which is also socially, economically, and politically less powerful relative to whites. If correct, this reasoning suggests that shared disadvantage will actually induce blacks to develop higher levels of implicit attitude toward Latinos, and to more effectively connect these attitudes to political judgments, in an effort to establish even modest gains within a smaller hierarchy of less powerful groups.

For these reasons, then, a focus on African Americans provides a critical and rigorous test of how race conditions (or does not) the role of implicit attitude in political judgment.

Race and the Manifestation of Implicit Attitudes

The question before us is this: are black Americans, by dint of their position within America's racial order, less likely to express and utilize negative implicit attitude toward Latinos? There are several ways to tackle this question, but I begin by looking at what African Americans actually say about immigrants. You may find this a peculiar way to start. My primary claims are about the unspoken thoughts blacks may have about foreigners. And yet, here I am about to analyze a record of African Americans' *spoken* thoughts about immigrants. But there is a logic to this choice. If African Americans, as members of a less advantaged racial group, face weaker incentives to acquire implicit attitudes, this general tendency should affect not only what they neglect to say about immigrants, but also what they are willing to say about them. Hence, by first examining what Blacks report about immigrants, we can get a sense as to whether there is any basis to the much stronger claim that African Americans are less implicitly biased than whites.

To this end, I draw on an oversample of African American respondents in the National Study (n = 350). Like their white counterparts in this survey, these individuals also registered their feelings toward Latino, white, Asian, and Middle Eastern immigrants, which allows us to explore the extent to which black and white Americans differ in their level of explicit attitude toward foreigners in general. The measure for this task is the additive index of average ratings of these different immigrant groups, which we have seen in previous chapters. Scores on this index, you may recall, are coded to run from 0 to 1, with higher values indicating more negative attitude toward foreigners in general.

To test for racial differences in explicit attitude toward immigrants, I regress this measure on a dummy variable indicating one's self-reported race as well as respondents' level of education and the interaction between these two variables. By including race and its interaction with education, I ensure that any racial gap that emerges in this attitude cannot be attributed to differences in education between both racial groups (e.g., Federico 2004; Sniderman and Piazza 1993;

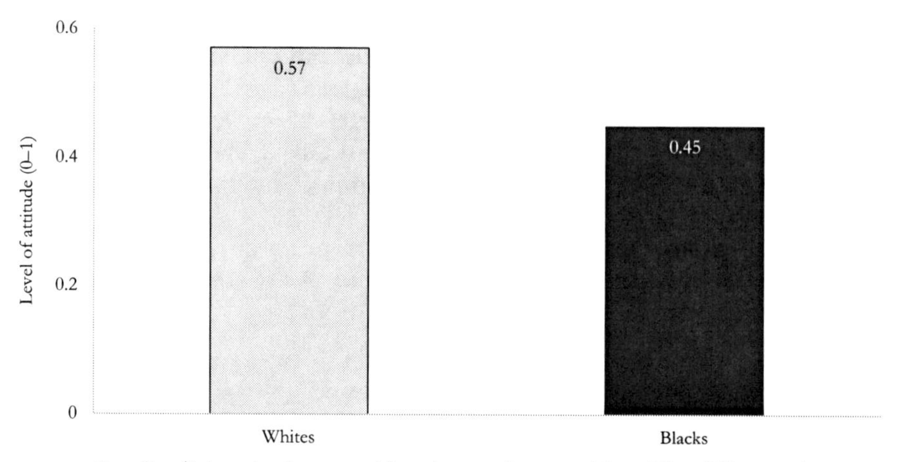

FIGURE 8.1. Explicit attitude toward immigrants by race. *Note:* The difference between both scores is reliable at the 5% level.

Sniderman et al. 2004). Figure 8.1 displays the relevant results. There we see that on average, white Americans score .57 on this 0–1 scale, which places them just above the midpoint of the scale. This suggests that generally speaking, whites report what can be considered a mildly negative attitude toward immigrants in general. When we turn to African Americans, however, we find that these individuals score about 12 percentage points *lower* than their white counterparts, or .45, to be exact. In other words, holding constant black and white differences in education, African Americans self-report, on average, a mildly *positive* attitude toward foreigners. This substantive gap in explicit attitude toward immigrants is significant at conventional levels ($p < .05$), and it is consistent with the broader claim that African Americans, by virtue of their less powerful position in America's racial order, are less likely to express negative attitude toward other racial outgroups, in this case, immigrants.

But perhaps African Americans only appear to express weaker levels of explicit attitude because the measure we used is too blunt. If we ask African Americans to report their attitude toward Latino immigrants – a group that shares the same labor and housing markets as many Blacks – stronger levels of explicit attitude will emerge. Indeed, when we consider that African Americans are more likely than whites to live and work alongside many Latino immigrants and their families (Gay 2006), it is possible that Blacks are in fact *more* explicitly biased against this group, as African Americans are more likely to experience the negative repercussions of a Latino presence.

To assess this possibility, I repeat the same regression analysis as above, but this time substitute in explicit attitude toward Latinos as the dependent variable, which also runs on a 0–1 scale. This measure, if you recall, consists of one's rating of Latino immigrants relative to white immigrants, with higher values indicating more negative attitude toward the former group. Figure 8.2

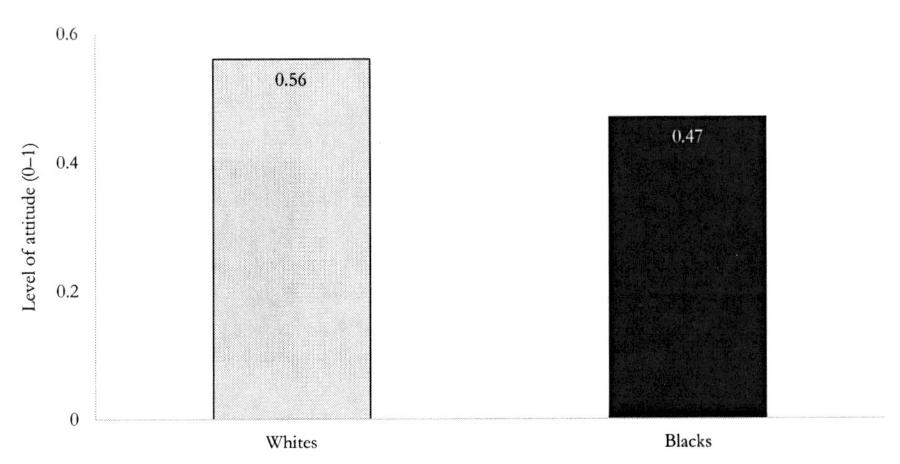

FIGURE 8.2. Explicit attitude toward Latinos by race. *Note:* The difference between both scores is reliable at the 5% level.

displays the relevant results. Once again, we see that black Americans hold weaker explicit attitudes toward Latino immigrants. In this particular instance, whites on average score .56 on this index of explicit attitude toward Latino immigrants. In contrast, African Americans register an average score of .47, which produces a significant difference of about 9 percentage points ($p < .05$). On both self-reported measures, then, black Americans manifest relatively lower levels of explicit attitudes.

The position of one's group within America's racial order appears to matter in the anticipated manner. African Americans report less negative attitudes toward Latino immigrants, just as our discussion on hierarchy and social power leads us to expect. Yet the operative word in these analyses is *reported* attitudes, that is, those attitudes that people are able and willing to share with researchers. Thus, there is an obvious counter-explanation to this pattern of findings so far. Rather than being less explicitly biased, African Americans, more than whites, have merely learned to take the "politically correct" stance when it comes to expressing racial attitudes. In other words, Blacks feel what whites do, but because they are racial minorities themselves, they are uneasy about expressing negative attitudes toward another racial minority. By this account, African Americans feel obliged to express, not what they really think or feel about another racial minority, but what they think society expects them to say, precisely because they themselves are members of a racial minority.

The key question, then, is whether the previous racial differences in explicit attitudes translate in any way to the realm of one's implicit evaluations. Throughout the previous chapters, I have shown that implicit attitude toward Latinos is both spontaneously activated and hard to control. This suggests that if black and white differences in racial attitudes are driven by stronger social pressures among African Americans to offer politically correct responses, such

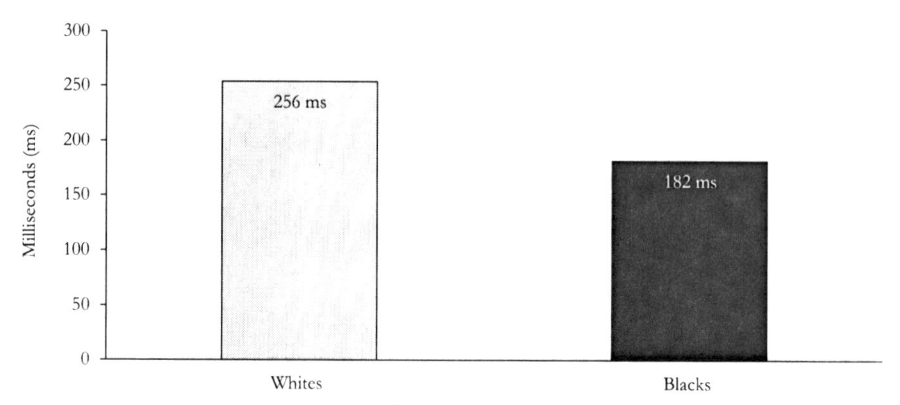

FIGURE 8.3. Mean reaction time differences in IAT by race. *Note:* The difference between both scores is reliable at the 5% level.

differences should evaporate when we examine black and white responses to the IAT – our measure of implicit bias against Latinos. That is because the IAT, by design, short-circuits people's ability to modify their attitudes before reporting them. Thus, if blacks score similarly to whites on the IAT, we will have strong disconfirmation that the position of one's group within the larger racial order has an effect on the intensity of implicit attitudes that spring to people's minds. By the same token, however, if Blacks reveal lower levels of implicit attitude than whites, we can be more confident that racial hierarchy, and one's position within it, does shape the strength of implicit attitude. In fact, if this account has any credibility to it, African Americans *should* display lower levels of implicit attitude than whites.

Which of these perspectives is correct? Figure 8.3 reports the average response time differences on the IAT by race, where larger differences indicate more negative implicit attitude toward Latino immigrants (relative to white immigrants). Two important patterns stand out. First, members of both groups display the anticipated "IAT effect," where higher millisecond scores reflect an easier (and thus, faster) ability to sort stimuli when using the matched classification pair (i.e., Latino Immigrant–Bad|White Immigrant–Good). Second, the IAT effect is larger among whites than blacks. For whites, the average difference in response time is 256 milliseconds; for blacks, it is 182 milliseconds. This difference is significantly different from zero ($p < .05$), and it suggests that whites have a stronger implicit attitude toward Latinos than do African Americans. Indeed, to put this racial gap into clearer perspective, the relatively smaller reaction time among Blacks suggests individuals from this group found it less easy to sort stimuli on the IAT when using the matched classification pair (i.e., Latino Immigrant–Bad|White Immigrant–Good). Hence, although African Americans are not immune to the development of implicit attitudes toward Latinos, the tone of these attitudes is decidedly less negative than whites.

Spot Check: Do Blacks *Really* Display Less Implicit Attitude?

The previous evidence suggests implicit attitude toward Latinos is less acute among Blacks than whites, a finding I assign to the relative positioning of both groups within America's racial order (e.g., Bobo and Hutchings 1996; Dawson 2000; Kim 2000; Sidanius et al. 1997). But are these findings real, or are they artifacts of how we measured implicit attitude among both racial groups?

Recall that in the IAT, black and white respondents are contrasting Latino immigrants to white immigrants. Given this set-up, one might reason that blacks score differently than whites, not because they are less implicitly biased, but because blacks are contrasting two non-black groups and whites are contrasting a non-white group to a white group. This is a reasonable skepticism and a damaging one if it is true, for it suggests that any differences in implicit bias between blacks and whites are due to a deficiency in our measure of this attitude – the IAT – not to actual differences in the attitude itself.

This view, however, rests on a very strong assumption; namely, that whites are comparing Latino immigrants to members of their *own* racial group. Yet previous scholarship shows that many whites are also hostile to white immigrants, just as they are hostile to non-white minorities – which is to say, they do not automatically view white immigrants as part of their racial group (e.g., Sniderman and Carmines 1997; see also Higham 1981; Ignatiev 1995; Jacobson 1998; King 2000). Thus, for blacks and whites taking the IAT, both targets in this measure are meant to operate as outgroups. Conceptually, then, the IAT is designed to operate in the same way among African Americans and whites.[2]

But does the IAT, in fact, perform as expected? To formally test this assumption, I rely on a modified version of an analysis completed in Chapter 5. This analysis aims to answer two key questions. First, does the IAT predict blacks' and whites' explicit attitude toward Latino immigrants without also explaining their explicit attitude toward other immigrants? If it does, we can be more confident the IAT is picking up an implicit attitude directed at Latinos, specifically, across blacks and whites. Second, holding constant other important differences among blacks and whites, does one's race affect the degree to which the IAT explains one's explicit attitude toward Latino immigrants? If it does not, this would suggest the IAT is picking up the same attitude, to the same degree, among Blacks as it is among whites. This would reassure us that black and white scores on this measure are comparable, and any differences between them, meaningful.

What we are about to do, then, is predict respondents' explicit attitude toward several immigrant groups as a function of their IAT scores, holding constant their levels of authoritarianism, partisanship, national identity,

[2] One might argue that if the IAT operates similarly across blacks and whites, there should be cases where this measure produces no racial differences. There are (e.g., Devos and Banaji 2005; Nosek et al. 2007b).

TABLE 8.1. *Negative Feelings toward Immigrants by Implicit Attitude and Race*

	Latino Immigrants	White Immigrants	Asian Immigrants	Middle Eastern Immigrants
Implicit Attitude	30.92*	−15.10	13.04	18.11
	(13.84)	(11.16)	(11.46)	(12.79)
Black	−7.85	−8.67	−1.30	6.36
	(12.20)	(11.45)	(10.23)	(12.15)
Implicit × Black	−8.74	12.72	−8.67	−4.19
	(17.73)	(15.48)	(14.91)	(16.16)

Notes: N = 639 for all equations. OLS coefficients with standard errors in parentheses. Models also control for levels of authoritarianism, partisanship, national identity, education, and the interactions of these with race (see Table A8.1 in the chapter appendix for full model results). All predictors have a 0–1 interval. The dependent variable runs from 0 to 100 in one-point units. *$p < .05$, one-tailed.

education, and being African American.[3] This analysis, moreover, also accounts for the possibility that the influence of the IAT and the remaining factors are themselves conditioned by whether one is Black or not.[4]

Table 8.1 reports the relevant results (the full results of this analysis are located in Table A8.1 at the end of this chapter). There we see two striking and relevant findings. The first is that the IAT is significantly related to one's explicit attitude toward Latino immigrants. But – and this is critical – this same relationship is not reproduced for one's explicit rating of white immigrants, the other immigrant group contrasted in the IAT. Moreover, IAT scores are generally unrelated to people's ratings of the remaining groups of foreigners. Across blacks and whites, implicit attitude toward Latinos uniformly increases one's negative attitude toward Latino immigrants, while uniformly failing to affect one's attitude toward white immigrants.

To illustrate this, consider Figure 8.4, which displays the effect of implicit attitude toward Latinos on one's explicit attitude toward Latino immigrants. There we see that among African Americans, going from the lowest to highest level of implicit bias generates a 22-point increase in negative feelings toward Latino immigrants. Among whites, the same shift in implicit bias produces an increase of 31 points in negative feelings toward the same immigrant group.

[3] The coding of these variables was discussed in Chapter 5. Recall that for each of these variables, higher values indicate greater levels of a given attitude (e.g., authoritarianism). Also, note that recent scholarship suggests the child-rearing scale of authoritarianism captures this trait more effectively among whites than non-whites (Pérez and Hetherington 2014). I deal with this challenge by interacting authoritarianism with race, which is meant to recover the stronger performance of the authoritarianism scale among whites.

[4] Specifically, I estimate: Explicit Attitude (Immigrant Group) = $\beta_0 + \beta_1$Implicit + β_2Authoritarianism + β_3Partisanship + β_4National ID + β_5Education + β_6Black + β_7Implicit × Black + β_8Authoritarianism × Black + β_9Partisanship × Black + β_{10}National ID × Black + β_{11}Education × Black.

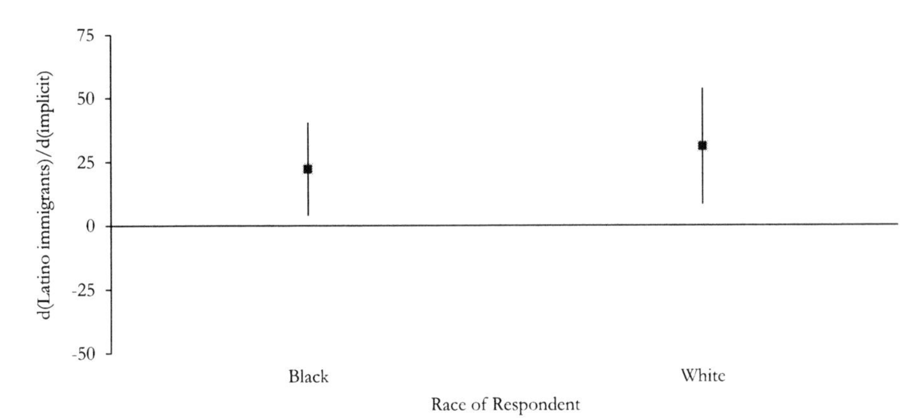

FIGURE 8.4. Marginal effect of implicit attitude on negative feelings toward Latino immigrants by race (90% confidence intervals).

These increases are numerically different, but they are statistically indistinguishable from each other, as evidenced by the overlap in the confidence intervals surrounding each estimate. This suggests the differences in this relationship are more likely due to chance rather than to race itself. And, we can be more confident about drawing this conclusion because we have filtered out the influence of other factors, besides implicit attitude, on one's self-reported attitude toward Latino immigrants.

Now consider Figure 8.5, which displays the relationship between implicit attitude toward Latino immigrants and explicit attitude toward white immigrants among African Americans and whites. Here we find that implicit attitude fails to affect black and white ratings of white immigrants. Among blacks, going from the lowest to highest level of implicit bias produces a 2-point decrease in

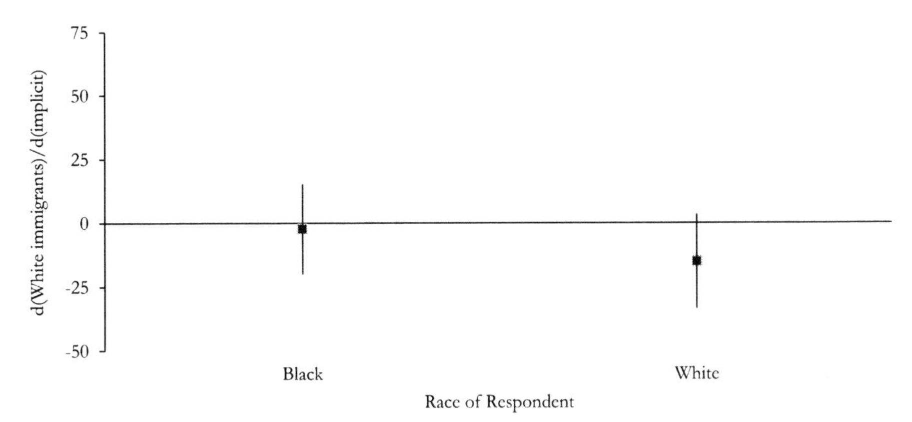

FIGURE 8.5. Marginal effect of implicit attitude on negative feelings toward white immigrants by race (90% confidence intervals).

negative feelings toward white immigrants. Among whites, the same change in implicit attitude produces a decrease of 15 points. Neither of these shifts, however, is statistically meaningful, as the confidence intervals for each estimate straddle the 0 value, which means we cannot reliably distinguish these effects from chance. Moreover, both decreases cannot even be distinguished from each other, given the overlap in the confidence intervals surrounding each estimate.

Viewed side by side, then, the findings displayed in Figures 8.4 and 8.5 affirm the important point that the IAT is capturing the same implicit attitude – to the same degree – across African Americans and whites. The racial differences in implicit attitude that we previously uncovered are therefore *not* artifacts of the tool we used to measure them. Hence, inasmuch as the IAT is concerned, blacks manifest less implicit bias against Latinos than whites do.

Does Less Implicit Attitude = Less Political Relevance for Blacks?

I have claimed that racial hierarchy – and one's position within it – affects the expression and influence of implicit attitudes in the political realm. Because a relatively higher position in this order entails more social power, members of more advantaged groups face greater incentives to develop and express negative attitudes toward outgroups as a way to preserve their privileged status. Hence, the expected (and observed) difference in levels of implicit attitude toward Latinos among African Americans and whites, with members of the former group expressing significantly weaker levels of this implicit bias.

This is a key result as far as the influence of hierarchy on the *manifestation* of implicit attitude is concerned. But what about the influence of this attitude on political judgments? After all, finding lower levels of implicit attitude among African Americans is not the same thing as finding that this attitude is a weak component of black opinion on immigration. Indeed, it might very well be the case that notwithstanding racial differences in levels of implicit bias, African Americans and whites use this attitude to the same degree to form their evaluations of immigration policy.

Yet that is not what my argument anticipates. Instead, I expect race to also weaken the connection between implicit attitude toward Latinos and opposition to immigration. Because minorities, by definition, do not enjoy as advantaged a position within the racial order, they face weaker incentives to "rehearse" these attitudes in the service of maintaining a privileged status. Less rehearsal should therefore make these implicit attitudes less automatic for members of a minority group, such as African Americans.

To assess this claim, I return to the Legal Immigration Experiment from the last chapter. Essentially, this experiment reduces to two key conditions: one focusing people's attention toward Latino immigrants, the second directing people's attention toward Chinese immigrants. With this design, we can ascertain whether and to what degree African Americans differ from whites in their joining of implicit attitude to immigration policy evaluations. And, to the extent that one's position within America's racial order matters for this linkage, we should find that relative to whites, the connection between implicit attitude and opposition to immigration should be significantly weaker among African Americans. In short, we should find racial differences in the *application* of implicit attitude to political judgments.

But in discovering a potential gap in the political use of implicit attitude, we must take special care to ensure that such a pattern is in fact due to race, and not to the myriad social and political differences that exist between blacks and whites. In particular, we should make certain that any emergent racial gap in the influence of implicit attitude is not due to differences in education and partisan allegiance, two dimensions along which black and white Americans differ significantly (e.g., Dawson 1994; Philpot 2007; see also US Census Bureau 2011). Hence, to meet these objectives, I estimate the following statistical equation:

$$\begin{aligned}&\text{Opposition (Immigration)}\\&= \beta_0 + \beta_1\text{Implicit} + \beta_2\text{Legal Chinese} + \beta_3\text{White} + \beta_4\text{Implicit}\\&\quad \times \text{Legal Chinese} + \beta_5\text{Implicit} \times \text{White} + \beta_6\text{Legal Chinese}\\&\quad \times \text{White} + \beta_7\text{Implicit} \times \text{Legal Chinese} \times \text{White} + \beta_8\text{Explicit}\\&\quad + \beta_9\text{Education} + \beta_{10}\text{Democrat} + \beta_{11}\text{Explicit} \times \text{White}\\&\quad + \beta_{12}\text{Education} \times \text{White} + \beta_{13}\text{Democrat} \times \text{White}.\end{aligned}$$

Here, β_1 through β_7 provide the key quantities of interest, with β_1 yielding the effect of implicit attitude among African Americans who are focused on Latino immigrants, and the remaining coefficients in this list providing the estimates necessary to calculate how this effect varies by people's racial group membership and the information they receive about immigrants. In turn, β_8 through β_{13} yield the effects of explicit attitude toward immigrants, education, and partisanship – plus any racial differences in these quantities.[5] In essence, the inclusion of these latter terms in this equation helps to increase confidence that any racial differences in the use of implicit attitude can really be attributed to race.

The full statistical results of this analysis are reported in Table A8.2 in the appendix at the end of the chapter. For our purposes, however, I visually display the effect of implicit attitude on opposition to immigration among blacks and whites under both experimental conditions.

Turning first to the results for black respondents, we see in Figure 8.6 that implicit bias registers a weak and statistically insignificant effect on black opposition to immigration when Latinos are directly cued. In other words, when

[5] Partisanship was originally measured via a conventional 7-point scale, with higher values indicating greater attachment to the Republican Party. Explicit attitude toward immigrants is the composite measure of feeling thermometer ratings analyzed earlier in the chapter, where higher values indicate greater negative attitude toward immigrants. Finally, education is the same item analyzed in previous chapters, with higher values indicating more education. For the purposes of this analysis, all variables are rescaled to have a 0–1 range.

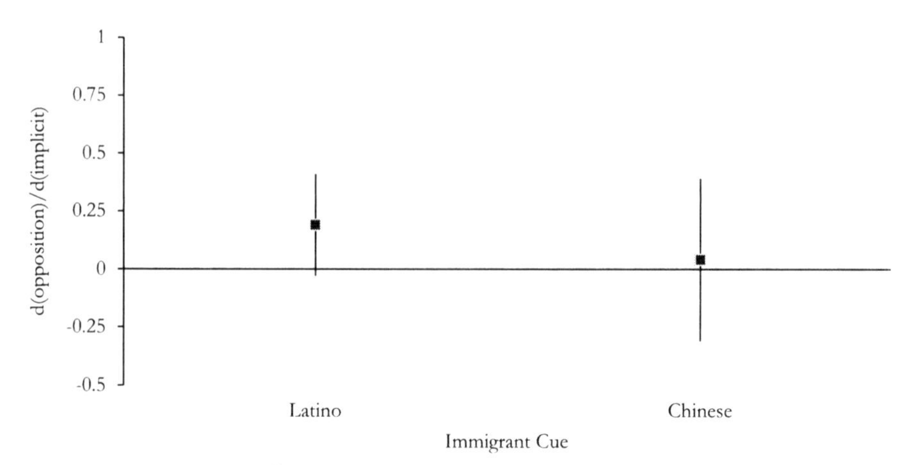

FIGURE 8.6. Marginal effect of black implicit attitude on opposition to immigration (90% confidence intervals).

there is a match between one's implicit attitude and the focus of one's immediate attention, the former has little bearing on black opposition to immigration. Indeed, going from the lowest to highest levels of implicit bias among African Americans increases their opposition by .19 unit, a shift that is statistically indistinguishable from zero. This basic pattern does not change much in substantive terms when the focus of African Americans' attention is Chinese immigrants. There we see that a change from the lowest to highest level of implicit attitude among blacks produces a shift of .04 unit, an effect that is also unreliably different from zero. Thus, even after filtering out the effects of explicit attitude toward immigrants, education, and partisan identification, implicit attitude continues to display a weak hold on black judgments of immigration.

For white Americans, however, the opposite is true (see Figure 8.7): implicit bias systematically increases individual opposition to immigration, irrespective of which immigrant group is cued. And this pattern, it is worth repeating, remains even after we account for racial differences in explicit attitude toward immigrants, education, and partisan identity. For instance, Figure 8.7 shows that when Latino immigrants are directly cued, implicit bias increases opposition to immigration by a hearty .38 unit – an effect that is reliably different from zero. In turn, when non-Latinos are cued (i.e., legal Chinese immigrants), the effect of implicit bias among Whites jumps to .49. The overlap in the confidence intervals around both estimates, however, suggests these effects are indistinguishable from each other. Hence, irrespective of whether Latinos are cued or not, implicit bias against Latinos heightens white opposition to immigration.[6]

[6] Having found that differences in explicit attitude toward immigrants, education, and partisanship leave intact racial differences in the influence of implicit bias, one may wonder if this pattern

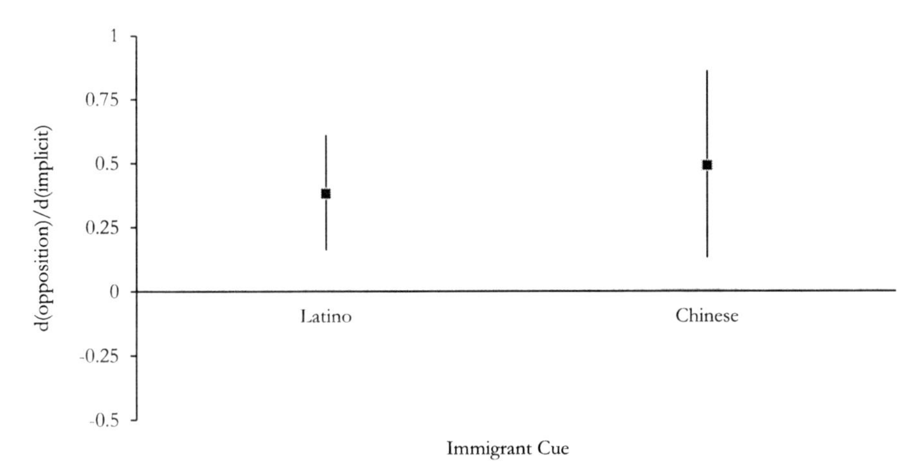

FIGURE 8.7. Marginal effect of white implicit attitude on opposition to immigration (90% confidence intervals).

This last pattern supports my claim that racial hierarchy affects, not only the expression of implicit attitudes, but also its relevance to political judgment. Given their relatively lower position within America's racial order (e.g., Dawson 2000; Kim 2000; Sears et al. 1999), African Americans face weaker incentives to develop implicit attitude toward Latino immigrants, as evidenced by their slower reaction times on the Implicit Association Test (IAT). These incentives, it appears, seep further below, into the psychology governing the use of implicit attitudes (e.g., Philpot and White 2010). Embedded in a lower tier within America's racial hierarchy, black Americans find themselves in a less powerful social station. Thus, they are less likely to rehearse such attitudes in the service of maintaining an advantageous position. The end result is that social structure – and one's location in it – modulates the manifestation and deployment of implicit attitude in political judgments.

Conclusions

We began this chapter with the observation that the study of implicit attitudes can easily be charged with being too psychological. By focusing exclusively on the innermost workings of the mind, the fact that individuals are situated within a larger social structure is often left on the sidelines of scholarly inquiry. Wary of this state of affairs, this chapter has investigated the influence of social structure on individual attitudes by coming to grips with the role of racial hierarchy in the United States (Dawson 2000; Masuoka and Junn 2013; see also Jost et al. 2004; Sidanius et al. 1997). My claim – dubbed the *social position* hypothesis – has

survives a more parsimonious statistical specification. It does. When I estimate the same interactive model for implicit bias but omit these covariates and their interactions with race, we arrive at essentially the same estimates as those displayed in Figures 8.6 and 8.7.

been that the position of individuals within America's racial order conditions both the manifestation and relevance of implicit attitude for political judgment. The reason for this is social power, with minority groups possessing less of it due to their relatively subordinate position within America's racial hierarchy (e.g., Dawson 2000; Kim 2000). Accordingly, the less social power one's racial group has, the weaker the incentives are to form and use implicit attitudes in the service of preserving the privileged position of one's group.

Our inquiry into this matter has turned up a consistent pattern of evidence: Race deeply affects the extent to which people make a connection between their implicit attitude toward Latinos and their opposition to immigration. The psychology behind implicit bias is deeply colored by race or, more precisely, by the position of one's racial group within America's racial hierarchy. These racial differences in implicit bias were found across several analyses, each showing a weaker tendency among blacks than whites to reach for implicit bias when making up their minds about immigration. And this racial difference, we learned, is really about race and not about differences in education or political affiliations between blacks and whites.

By illuminating the role that racial hierarchy plays in conditioning the influence of implicit attitudes, this chapter has identified a key set of conditions where implicit attitude exerts a weaker political force. This is an important insight to have. The main theoretical dynamic in this book has been the interplay between implicit attitude and political information, with the former coloring the interpretation and application of the latter. Several layers of evidence have affirmed the presence of this psychological process. Yet the results from this chapter suggest that although many Americans do, in fact, succumb to the political influence of "implicit expectations," plenty of Americans do not, at least not to the same degree. The psychology behind implicit attitudes does not uniformly apply to the mass public. And the reason for this is not a neurological or biological difference in people's brains, but rather the often ignored influence of social context on individuals' psyche.

TABLE A8.1. *Negative Feelings toward Immigrants by Implicit Attitude and Race (full results)*

	Latino Immigrants	White Immigrants	Asian Immigrants	Middle Eastern Immigrants
Implicit Attitude	30.92*	−15.10	13.03	18.11
	(13.83)	(11.16)	(11.46)	(12.79)
Authoritarianism	13.03*	8.51*	10.83*	15.48*
	(5.70)	(4.80)	(5.37)	(5.79)
Partisanship (Republican)	5.45	−2.78	−4.29	5.81
	(4.16)	(3.65)	(4.08)	(4.06)
American ID	−1.85	−.59	−.21	10.41*
	(6.68)	(5.41)	(6.40)	(6.05)
Education	−13.28*	−1.15	−10.64	−2.19
	(4.35)	(3.89)	(4.45)	(4.17)
Black	−7.85	−8.67	−1.30	6.37
	(12.20)	(11.45)	(11.08)	(12.15)
Implicit Bias × Black	−8.74	12.73	−8.67	−4.19
	(17.73)	(15.48)	(14.92)	(16.16)
Authoritarianism × Black	−8.18	−7.04	−12.51*	−17.71*
	(8.22)	(7.40)	(7.45)	(8.33)
Partisanship × Black	−14.36*	−1.30	−9.44	−16.52*
	(6.59)	(5.86)	(5.87)	(6.46)
American ID × Black	7.43	3.82	8.15	−.19
	(8.85)	(8.28)	(8.46)	(8.77)
Education × Black	12.65*	7.23	6.10	2.59
	(6.65)	(5.87)	(6.14)	(6.45)
Constant	29.62*	44.37*	37.41*	26.10*
	(9.26)	(7.99)	(8.22)	(8.94)
R^2	.10	.02	.05	.11

Notes: $N = 639$ for all equations. OLS coefficients with robust standard errors in parentheses. All predictors have a 0–1 interval. The dependent variable runs from 0 to 100 in one-point units.
* $p < .05$, one-tailed.

TABLE A8.2. *The Influence of Implicit Attitude Conditioned by Immigrant Cues and Race – Interactive Model*

	Opposition to Immigration
Implicit Attitude – Latinos	.19
	(.13)
Experimental Condition – Legal Chinese	.10
	(.15)
White	−.08
	(.14)
Implicit × Legal Chinese	−.15
	(.25)
Implicit × White	.20
	(.19)
Legal Chinese × White	−.15
	(.21)
Implicit × Legal Chinese × White	.25
	(.36)
Explicit Attitude – Immigrants	.60*
	(.07)
Education	−.02
	(.05)
Partisanship (Democrat)	.01
	(.01)
Explicit × White	.14
	(.10)
Education × White	−.14*
	(.07)
Partisanship × White	−.02*
	(.01)
Constant	.13
	(.10)
R^2	.29

Notes: $N = 639$. OLS coefficients with robust standard errors in parentheses. All variables have a 0–1 interval.
* $p < .05$, one-tailed.

9

Conclusion

Implicit Attitudes and Explicit Politics

We have arrived at the end of my investigative journey, as it were. But what is one to conclude from the various layers of results paraded across the previous chapters? The lessons are many. The objective behind this concluding chapter, therefore, is to bring order to this potentially unwieldy prospect by discussing the larger meaning of implicit attitudes for the study of immigration politics, specifically, and non-immigration politics, more generally. To effectively accomplish this task, I revisit – ever so briefly – the primary theoretical current running through this book, and the main tributaries of evidence on which it now draws. Against this backdrop, I discuss the implications of these findings for political scientists, especially those who study mass public opinion. This discussion forms the core of this chapter, and I organize it around five main points.

First, I consider what my results suggest about the nature of public opposition to illegal and legal immigration, given the indelible role played by implicit attitudes toward Latinos in contemporary times. Second, I clarify how and why the evidence in this book establishes the viability of implicit attitudes and their corresponding measures for political science research. Third, I discuss the connection between implicit attitudes and ongoing debates over the nature of public opinion. Fourth, I explain the relationship between implicit attitudes and the idealized democratic citizen. And fifth, I spell out the implications of implicit attitudes for the political prospects of immigration reforms. Let's begin this effort by first reviewing my claims and evidence.

Bottom Lines

I defined implicit attitudes as basic affective evaluations of political objects. As such, they reflect citizens' learned but unspoken judgments of political objects as *good* or *bad*, *favorable* or *unfavorable*, or *pleasant* or *unpleasant*. I explained that implicit attitudes are steeped in automaticity. They are spontaneously activated, hard to control, and can operate outside of immediate awareness.

Implicit attitudes, I pointed out, arise from people's mental capacity for associative reasoning. Even as part of our mind deliberates and reflects on political information, another part of our brain is engaged in identifying broad, but stable representations of what is *typical* in our environments. This part of our mind is geared toward uncovering, learning, and storing recurring patterns in information we encounter. And it is based on these patterns that we develop implicit attitudes toward political objects.

I weaved these insights into a theory of "implicit expectations." According to this framework, the broaching of the immigration issue spontaneously calls forth people's implicit attitudes toward Latinos, informing citizens about how they feel about policy proposals *before* they begin to actively consider relevant information about the topic at hand. In this way, many citizens often judge immigration policies in accordance with their implicit attitudes, even when these subjective thoughts are contradicted by the objective information before them. This occurs, I contend, because the interplay between implicit attitudes and explicit political reasoning is generally subconscious: that is, citizens are unaware of how their implicit attitudes shape the more explicit aspects of their decision making (Gawronski et al. 2006: 491).

This is a tall order of claims. And to corroborate them, I searched for and found evidence of implicit attitudes across news media content, a national opinion survey, and two lab experiments. From my view, the most critical threads running through this tapestry of evidence are as follows:

1. The American polity is flooded with political information that facilitates citizens' acquisition of implicit attitudes through associative reasoning. In the realm of immigration politics, news discourse facilitates this process. Through the twin mechanisms of priming and framing, news media across the last quarter century have systematically focused on Latino immigrants more than any other group of foreigners (i.e., priming), and this focus is often couched in negative terms (i.e., framing), as evidenced by a steady focus on illegal immigration. This stream of patterned information about Latino immigrants, I concluded, encourage many Americans to develop a strong and negative implicit attitude toward this group, consistent with the principles of associative reasoning.
2. Using the Implicit Association Test (IAT), I demonstrated that these implicit attitudes toward Latino immigrants can be measured. By timing how fast people sort stimuli using a set of classification pairs, we learned that people differ reliably and systematically from one another in terms of their implicit attitude toward this group. Moreover, the implicit attitude captured by the IAT displays an enveloping character, for it encompasses all Latinos – not just those who are foreign born. Most important of all, differences in people's IAT scores robustly explain their preferences for

illegal and legal immigration policy. In short, individuals with more negative implicit attitude toward Latinos are more supportive of exclusionary illegal and legal immigration policies.

3. With evidence that these implicit attitudes exist and can be reliably measured, I then used a series of survey experiments to reveal their subtle but powerful influence over citizens' decision making. I demonstrated that people often judge political issues according to the direction and intensity of their implicit attitudes, even when these attitudes are contradicted by the political information immediately before them. Specifically, we witnessed how in the realm of illegal and legal immigration, people's implicit attitude toward Latinos heightened their support for exclusionary policies, even when people's conscious attention was directed toward non-Latino groups and individuals. Citizens, in other words, really are unaware of how their implicit attitudes shape the more deliberative aspects of their political decisions.
4. After documenting the presence of "implicit expectations" in the realm of immigration politics, I then identified individuals and circumstances where the political influence of implicit attitudes becomes stronger – and, just as important, where it becomes weaker. In terms of the former, I used a survey experiment on legal immigration to show that levels of education and variations in immigrant cues modulate the joining of implicit attitude to explicit political judgments. In particular, we discovered that people with more years of education are in fact better able to fray the connection between their self-reported attitude toward Latinos and their judgments of immigration policy when their attention is directed away from this group. Yet these same people are unable to sever the link between their implicit attitude and their immigration policy evaluations, even when their focus is on non-Latinos. In fact, the influence of implicit attitude is relatively stronger among more educated Americans, a pattern that simultaneously highlights the lack of awareness over the possession of implicit attitude, and the acute ability of highly educated people to connect their predispositions to political judgments.
5. Finally, I used the lens of race to demonstrate where and why implicit attitude has weaker political effects. Drawing on an oversample of African American respondents from the National Study, I produced two interrelated patterns of evidence on this front. First, relative to white Americans, African Americans display significantly lower levels of implicit attitude toward Latinos. Second, African Americans, relative to white Americans, fail to join their implicit attitudes to their political judgments of immigration. Both patterns emerge, I argued, because of black Americans' minority status within America's larger racial order – a position that endows them with less social power, and thus, less incentive to manifest and use implicit attitude to preserve a privileged position.

The Indelible Imprint of Anti-Latino Attitudes

Each of the preceding layers of evidence reinforces the others, all with the purpose of corroborating my claims about "implicit expectations" in the world of immigration politics. Whether I have accomplished this successfully is, of course, up to my readers. But there is another goal behind this evidence: to illuminate the extent to which anti-Latino attitudes seep into immigration policy judgments. My results suggest that negative attitudes toward Latinos are more prevalent than most public opinion polls can reveal and incredibly hard to suppress when judging immigration policy proposals. Indeed, notwithstanding self-reported justifications for one's opposition to immigration (Lodge and Taber 2013), implicit attitudes toward Latinos are automatically evoked the moment the issue of immigration is broached and infused into people's decision making, thus shaping opposition to illegal and legal immigration. All of this suggests that despite people's best intentions, implicit attitudes are hard to avoid and strongly tied to immigration policy judgments.

This matters for how scholars characterize the nature of public opposition to immigration.

On May 25, 2006 the Senate passed S.2611, a bill that would have, perhaps most importantly, created a tiered legalization program for undocumented immigrants. Specifically, those unauthorized individuals who had been in the United States before April 5, 2001 could gain legal status after paying back taxes and undergoing extensive background checks, among other criteria. In the wake of this Senate bill (and a stricter parallel version passed by the House), many members of Congress participated in town hall meetings to assess public opposition to these proposed reforms. One of these meetings was nationally televised on CNN on October 29, during which Republican Congressman McCaul (R–Texas) asserted the following about public debate concerning these proposals for immigration reform: "Let me say, I think first we need to be very responsible in the rhetoric as we engage in this debate [about illegal immigration]. This is not about – it's not about race."

But it is about race, or so the empirical results in this book suggest.[1] Indeed, my findings reveal that negative attitude toward Latinos serves to increase opposition to illegal *and* legal immigration from the very moment these political topics are broached. What is more, my evidence suggests that many Americans hold an implicit attitude toward Latinos. This is not simply a mental quirk, but rather, the result of a strong congruence between public discourse on immigration, people's cognitive architecture, and one's social position. Acknowledging this last point helps us to appreciate more fully why implicit attitudes have strong effects on immigration policy judgments in some quarters of the mass public. It also implies possible solutions to those interested in

[1] More precisely, it is about ethnicity because Latinos are an ethnic, not a racial, group (Hattam 2007).

reforming our immigration system. For instance, although we cannot replace people's cognitive architecture – which is geared toward the development of implicit attitudes on patterns of information – we might be able to change the pool of information on which this cognitive apparatus is trained. Here, one possibility is to encourage reporters to pay more balanced attention to the many facets of immigration beyond unauthorized flows, including legal immigration.

Of course, it is only natural to wonder about the degree to which my theoretical framework can help us to understand political issues beyond immigration. To answer this, it is important to identify what is essential for this framework to "work." Recall that implicit attitudes are formed via associational reasoning, that part of the mind that draws inferences based on broad regularities in our information environment. In politics, this suggests that long-term regularities in discourse are critical to whether politically relevant implicit attitudes toward groups form. This is the idea of group-centrism (Converse 1964; Kinder 1998; Nelson and Kinder 1996). And it is critical for determining where else implicit attitudes might matter for political decision making. If one encounters group-centric discourse on a political issue, then one is likely to run up against implicit attitudes toward said group. To illustrate this, consider the following two possibilities.

In the wake of 9/11, antiterrorism has become a salient and contentious political issue (e.g., Davis 2007; Huddy et al. 2005). Although terrorists originate from and operate in various countries across the globe, some evidence suggests that news media regularly highlight Arabs relative to other groups in their reporting on this broad issue (e.g., Nacos and Torres-Reyna 2007). Moreover, within this news coverage, negative portrayals of Arabs outnumber positive portrayals. These depictions seem to matter. Saleem and Anderson (2013), for example, discover that negative portrayals boost implicit attitudes toward this group in lab studies with student subjects. Such prima facie evidence hints at the strong possibility that implicit attitudes toward Arabs may influence public support for antiterror policies, including those with an international scope (see also Sides and Gross 2013).

Implicit attitudes might also shape public support for anticrime policies, such as gun-control proposals. When it comes to crime news coverage, research suggests that mass media are inclined to present an imbalanced amount of stories focusing on violent crimes for which African Americans are responsible (Welch 2007). Consistent with this pattern, lab studies with student subjects have shown that priming subjects with black (vs. white) faces causes them to misidentify objects as guns (Payne et al. 2002). Moreover, other lab research finds that reports highlighting individual black crime suspects increases negative attitudes toward African Americans more generally (Akalis et al. 2008). Combined, these pieces of evidence underline the possibility that implicit attitudes toward African Americans might shape people's support for tougher crime policies.

A Seat at the Table of Public Opinion

In assembling a variety of empirical tests, I have also been trying to underscore the merit of grappling with implicit attitude and its *political* implications both for the immigration issue and beyond. For at least twenty years now, the concept of implicit attitude has transformed the way most social psychologists think of what is meant by thinking. I have drawn on some of these insights and adapted them to the specific study of immigration politics. But the fact that this book has endeavored to show that implicit attitude matters politically is, in a way, testament to another fact: that the study of implicit attitudes has barely made a dent in how most political scientists view public opinion. This is a mistake, in my view, and one that I hope this book has helped to further correct.

At the risk of belaboring this point, let me revisit two lasting criticisms about implicit attitudes and explain how my evidence further reduces these doubts. We encountered these skepticisms back in Chapter 2. Using established research from social psychology, I tried to explain why I thought these misgivings had less merit than they appear to have. Now we have evidence from the realm of immigration politics to further sustain my points. Thus, even if these criticisms are intuitive and resonant, they now stand on even less stable ground. Let us see how and why.

Are Implicit Attitudes Really Attitudes?

Some skeptics of implicit attitudes, we learned back in Chapter 2, have criticized this concept for not being an attitude at all (e.g., Arkes and Tetlock 2004; Karpinski and Hilton 2001). In their view, implicit attitudes reflect a cultural bias we all share, not an individual's personally endorsed evaluation of an object. Applied to the case at hand, this critique would suggest that implicit attitude toward Latinos is something that all Americans possess to some degree, but that ultimately, does not reflect how they personally feel about this group.

Scholars have demonstrated that the evidence in favor of this contention is either relatively weak or absent (e.g., Banaji 2001; Nosek and Hansen 2008). The findings in this book further dispel the notion that implicit attitude is nothing more than a cultural bias. Here is how.

Although it is true that many Americans do in fact possess a negative implicit attitude toward Latinos, the level of implicit attitude is not constant across the mass public, as implied by the "cultural consensus" argument. In fact, we uncovered very fine-grained distinctions in individuals' level of implicit attitude toward Latinos. Some individuals displayed higher levels of implicit attitude toward this group, others lower levels of this attitude, and still some in between. These individual-level differences, moreover, robustly predicted people's own personal preferences for immigration – in two domains, actually (i.e., illegal and legal immigration). And, we also saw that in some cases, some individuals were more likely to join their implicit attitude to their judgments of immigration.

In short, where the cultural consensus argument suggests a constant of sorts, I have uncovered rich variation in implicit attitudes as well as heterogeneity in the connection between these attitudes and people's political evaluations. And these patterns, I hasten to add, have emerged in the mass public – that is, outside the confines of experimental laboratories, in the rough and tumble world of immigration politics. By any other name, a concept attended by such evidence would merit, if not a hard-earned enthusiastic welcome, then at least the respect and curiosity any serious scientific endeavor commands.

Are Implicit Attitudes Really Different from Explicit Attitudes?

A second critique hurled at implicit attitudes is that this concept is really not distinct from their self-reported counterparts (see, e.g., Olson and Fazio 2009). Rather than representing a distinct evaluation, implicit attitudes reflect a person's judgment of an object in those split seconds before one's more deliberative capacities kick in.

Social psychologists have pushed back on this claim in two interrelated ways. First, they have demonstrated that many times, implicit and explicit attitudes are modestly correlated. And, when they are robustly correlated, the correspondence between both attitudes is not so high as to deem these attitudes conceptually identical (e.g., Cunningham et al. 2001; Nosek and Smyth 2007; Ranganath et al. 2008). Second, researchers have shown that implicit attitudes predict judgments and behavior independently of their self-reported analogs (e.g., Greenwald et al. 2009).

The evidence in this book reproduces and extends this pattern in several concrete ways. First, consistent with prior work, the correlation between implicit attitudes toward Latinos and relevant explicit attitudes has been modest at best. Second, implicit attitude toward Latinos robustly explains immigration policy judgments independently of, not only explicit attitude toward this group, but sundry explicit political and social predispositions, including partisanship, American identity, and education. Third, I demonstrated that although some individuals (i.e., highly educated) can censor their self-reported attitude toward this group when given the opportunity to do so, these same individuals cannot do the same with their implicit attitude when placed in the same circumstances. And once again, all of these patterns have been uncovered within the American mass public, which means these dynamics likely exist in the "real world" among adults, not just in controlled laboratory settings among student subjects (Sears 1986).

When added up, these layers of evidence cast further doubt on the view that implicit attitudes are conceptually identical to explicit attitudes. And, in the realm of politics, specifically, these patterns make it hard to ignore the relevance of implicit attitude to citizens' decision making. At minimum, the robust effects of implicit attitude on immigration policy judgments underlines the likely possibility that many public opinion models are grossly underspecified, given their strict emphasis on self-reported opinions. At the other end of the spectrum, the strong influence of implicit attitudes urges a collective reimagining of what qualifies as political thinking, one that takes us outside of the comfort zone provided by self-reported opinions. Both considerations deserve greater attention from political scientist if our discipline wishes to arrive at clearer understandings of public opinion that reflect how the mind actually operates.

Back to the Future: Implicit Attitudes and the Character of Public Opinion

The study of public opinion continues to be a thriving industry within political science. Yet across more than half a century of scholarship, one of the more enduring and influential insights is, ironically enough, that public opinion is not the structured, coherent, and informed phenomenon many initially assumed it was. In his seminal chapter on mass belief systems, Phillip Converse (1964) marshaled an impressive array of survey evidence to demonstrate that most Americans are actually *innocent* of political ideology (cf. Kinder 2006). Instead of finding that people threaded their opinions with an ideological needle, Converse found people's opinions to be untethered by even the most remote notions of liberal or conservative ideology. What is more, many people seemed to lack political attitudes that could be properly construed as opinions, as well as the necessary knowledge of politics to construct such evaluations. Ideological reasoning, if it existed, appeared to be an elite affair, with the bulk of the mass citizenry floating at a distance, unmoored from this esoteric reality.

Neither Converse's analysis nor his conclusions were taken lightly. A tidal wave of studies – still continuing today – rushed down on political scientists, all in an effort to (re)assess whether Converse's claims were, after all, correct or not. Yet if one were to judge this debate in terms of the total evidence up to now, the assessment would most certainly vindicate Converse: most Americans do, in fact, display little evidence of ideological reasoning, both then and now (e.g., for insightful overviews, see Kinder 1998, 2006).

But there is a catch to all this work – including the research produced by Converse's critics. By most accounts, the general absence of ideological reasoning within the mass public rests on self-reported evidence. The notion of implicit attitudes, however, suggests that ideology may exist on a wider scale, that its influence leaves a more systematic imprint on people's political thinking. By this view, the mass public appears ideologically innocent because most people find it difficult, if not impossible, to articulate this worldview. The implication is quite clear: most people possess a strong ideological orientation, we political scientists simply do not have the tools to tap into it.

To be fair, this notion is not an entirely new one. Some of Converse's earliest critics (e.g., Achen 1975) made it a point to show that by asking better questions, people displayed stronger evidence of ideological reasoning. Yet the implication I have identified here does not involve asking more refined questions, but rather, acknowledging that people might possess attitudes that they never express because they do not want to or because they cannot (Lodge et al. 1995). To paraphrase Donald Kinder (1998: 787), the possibility exists that "citizens know more – much more – than they can tell."

But if ideology is a complex phenomenon at the explicit level, how on earth could scholars assess this concept at an implicit level? There are no easy answers here, but any solution would likely seize on the fact that implicit attitudes revolve around attitude objects. Stripped down to basics like these, one can imagine assessing implicit ideology by, for example, having individuals complete an IAT that contrasts the objects "liberal" and "conservative."

In the end, implicit attitudes are not a panacea to ideological innocence. On their own, they cannot fully resolve this longstanding debate. But greater incorporation of implicit attitudes into studies of political cognition can enable scholars to formulate new hypotheses and recast established ones in ways that productively advance the frontiers of current public opinion research. These integrative efforts, in turn, should provide researchers new opportunities to further establish the theoretical importance of implicit attitudes to understandings of public opinion more generally. Yet this raises a crucial question. What standards *should* opinion researchers use as they furtherer evaluate the political importance of implicit attitudes?

By far, the most common yardstick has been to pit implicit attitudes against sundry explicit attitudes in prediction contests to assess whether the former's influence on judgments or behavior survives an onslaught of statistical controls (Chapter 5; see also Greenwald et al. 2009; Pasek et al. 2009; Pérez 2010). That is certainly one way to evaluate the importance of implicit attitudes. But it is a risky one, for such modeling strategies can inadvertently "control away" the influence of implicit attitudes, leading one to conclude that they do not matter (Chapter 5; see also Achen 2005). Of course, one can partially mitigate this possibility by first establishing a simple bivariate correlation between implicit attitudes and explicit opinions, thus showing that at a very basic level, implicit attitudes matter for people's political views. However, failure to find even such an elementary correlation would not warrant the conclusion that implicit attitudes are politically irrelevant to public opinion research. For under certain conditions and/or among some individuals, the same null association can become substantively and statistically significant (cf. Cameron et al. 2012; Greenwald et al. 2009; Nosek 2005). This is another way of saying that further corroborating the political importance of implicit attitudes demands from scholars greater theoretical imagination and more creative research designs to deepen our understanding of implicit attitudes' political role(s).

There are, though, additional criterions to use in assessing the political importance of implicit attitudes. One involves further evaluating the conceptual view of implicit attitudes as moderators (Chapter 6; see also Baron and Kenny 1986). In other words, to what extent do individual differences in implicit attitudes strengthen (weaken) the impact of other variables on public opinion? If, as much research suggests (e.g., Burdein et al. 2006; Erisen et al. 2014; Lodge and Taber 2013), implicit attitudes precede their explicit counterparts, then we should expect the former to modulate the influence of many "downstream" explicit attitudes. The key questions here are to identify and explain why specific explicit attitudes are moderated by their implicit counterparts, as well as ascertaining when and among whom these moderating relationships hold. Combined, such efforts can go a long way to bolster the claim that implicit attitudes are indeed politically influential.

A comparable set of opportunities lends itself in identifying and examining variables that mediate the influence of implicit attitudes on public opinion (Baron and Kenny 1986), thus further illuminating how implicit attitudes indirectly influence political judgments and behavior. As such, this approach can provide scholars with a clearer sense of the cognitive processes structuring the path(s) from implicit attitude to reported opinions and actual behavior (e.g., Brader et al. 2008). For example, given existing scholarship on emotion's role on political decision making, scholars might underscore the importance of implicit attitudes by mapping them onto their emotional substrates (Banks and Valentino 2012), thus allowing us to see if implicit attitudes affect public opinion by promoting certain emotional responses that have specific behavioral tendencies.

A final standard to further appraise the importance of implicit attitudes is to demonstrate that this construct operates in theoretically relevant ways across different types of populations. Most scholars who study implicit attitudes often examine them among majority racial groups (e.g., US whites). Up to a point, this is not hard to understand, as it is often easier and less expensive to recruit lab subjects or survey respondents from such groups. But this can provide scholars with an incomplete and distorted picture about the political influence of implicit attitudes. So what to do?

One approach is to investigate whether implicit attitudes can invigorate our understandings of key political concepts among multiple populations. For example, racial/ethnic minorities often self-report higher levels of group identity than whites, which implies that group identity is highly relevant for minorities but not majorities (e.g., Citrin and Sears 2014). Yet a focus on implicit identity might help us understand how much over-/underreporting goes on here and with what consequences. One possibility is that racial/ethnic minorities are less identified with their group than self-reports reveal, which is consistent with research on the effects of social stigmatization on some group members (e.g., Garcia Bedolla 2005). If true, then this might help to explain collective action problems among racial/ethnic groups, such as an inconsistent connection between group identity and political mobilization (cf. Junn 2006; Lee 2008). Among whites, a look at implicit racial identity might show that many within this group are more racially identified than self-reports indicate, which would be consistent with the view that social norms frown on the strong expression of racial identity among whites. Clarifying both of these possibilities would bolster the political importance of implicit attitudes by demonstrating their influence across populations.

Implicit Attitudes and the Idealized Democratic Citizen

In romanticized depictions of democracy, the individual citizen is one "who somehow had the time and resources to ... study ... the personas and problems that animated public life, and to think through all the policy proposals and philosophies swirling about the national debate" (Kinder 1998: 788).

If only it were so. Decades of systematic research into the mass citizenry reveals that the idealized citizen is just that – idealized (for a comprehensive overview, see Kinder 1998). Rather than being fully informed and politically engaged, most Americans know very little about politics, and dedicate little time and effort to learn more about them (e.g., Delli Carpini and Keeter 1996; Zaller 1992). In a democracy like the United States, where public preferences provide an important input to representation, these insights decrease faith in the health of our political system, for they suggest that most Americans may not really know what they want from their political system, or what best serves the general interests of the nation.

To counter the depressing implications of these findings, some scholars have conceded that many citizens do not, in fact, know much about politics. But that does not mean they cannot learn what they need to know (e.g., Lupia 1994; Lupia and McCubbins 2000; Popkin 1991; Sniderman et al. 1991). Under some conditions, for example, individuals can reason from fragments – rather than tomes – of information to arrive at sensible choices; what scholars refer to as heuristics. Of course, heuristics, too, are not a panacea for the apparent ignorance of the mass public. Yet their incorporation into political science research has allowed us to learn that the extent of public ignorance – and its consequences for political decision making – depends in large measure on how we assess this ignorance. By relaxing some assumptions about how people reason, political scientists' conceptual use of heuristics has opened up new and lasting perspectives on what people know and how they apply what they know to the political sphere.

And so it should be for implicit attitudes. Cast against the reported ignorance of the American public, the findings in this book collectively imply two things. First, as we saw before in our discussion of ideology, people may know much more than they care to admit, both to themselves and the researchers who inquire. Second, this repository of implicit knowledge and opinions, even if unexpressed, can anchor the very thoughts and attitudes one openly professes and applies to their political judgments. In this way, the presence of implicit attitudes suggests that individuals approach political issues and candidates with some of their mind already made up. Together, these implications suggest a further readjustment of the idealized portrait of democratic citizens. Whereas controlled and reflective thought is prioritized, if not championed, the existence of implicit attitudes suggests such deliberative efforts follow from thoughts and thought processes that have unfolded prior to one's alert engagement with political material (Lodge and Taber 2013).

But the fuller integration of implicit attitudes into political science involves more than a reorientation in our understanding of how citizens think. It also stands to breathe fresh life into established lines of inquiry. The possibilities are many, but in the interest of time, I focus on two I consider especially compelling. The first of these has to do with the connection between public opinion and representation. Research has demonstrated that elected representatives are keenly responsive to the preferences of the mass public (e.g., Erikson, MacKuen, and Stimson 2002; Stimson, MacKuen, and Erikson 1995; Wlezien 1995). This pattern, however, rests on representatives having their finger on the pulse of public opinion. So far as public opinion refers to self-reported evaluations, there is no problem. But, to the extent these preferences are implicit, complications arise. Without a record of people's implicit preferences, elected officials risk doing too much – or too little – when it comes to meeting the policy expectations of the mass public, potentially introducing more volatility into a generally stable democratic system.

The second area has to do with the connection between political communication and the persuasion of the mass citizenry. The bulk of this research has focused on short-term communications and their influence on self-reported opinions and evaluations (e.g., Brader 2006; Valentino et al. 2002; White 2007). The lesson from this book, however, is that as attentive as individual citizens might be, some of their attitudes are formed by long-term patterns in political information. What is more, these implicit attitudes might themselves be impervious to short-run communications. For individuals studying the connection between elites, political information, and the masses, this suggests that elites might actually have less leverage in persuading people to their corner of issues, positions, and philosophies. Or, to put it differently, the failure of political elites to mobilize public opinion might stem, in part, from the relative inertia of implicit attitudes.

Implicit Attitudes and Immigration Reform

Given my substantive focus on the link between implicit attitudes and public opposition to immigration, a natural question to ask is: what do implicit attitudes imply, if anything, for political prospects aimed at immigration reform? Many politicians, political observers, and pundits often decry America's immigration system as "broken." They also lament the halting, acrimonious, and often unsuccessful efforts to legislate solutions to this situation. A quick review of some recent political efforts to reform immigration policies illustrates this point. I then discuss some of the implications of implicit attitudes for these and other public debates about immigration reform.

- December 2005. The US House of Representatives passes H.R. 4437, also known as The Border Protection, Anti-Terrorism, and Illegal Immigration Control Act. Among other things, this bill makes unauthorized status a felony; establishes a mandatory employment verification process for all employers; and, funds 700 miles of new fencing along the US–Mexico border. At the time, polls reveal a public divided about decreasing immigration (Gallup 2005) and fractured over whether the US government should tackle illegal immigration by (1) allowing those living here and with a job to become legal US residents or (2) devising a plan to staunch the flow of illegal immigration (CNN 2005).
- Spring 2006. Millions of immigrants and their advocates protest across US cities, calling on Congress to reject H.R. 4437 and replace it with a bill setting a path to citizenship for illegal immigrants. The US Senate subsequently passes S.2611: The Comprehensive Immigration Reform Act (CIRA), which allows undocumented immigrants to earn US citizenship after working for six years, learning English, and paying a penalty and back taxes due. The bill also enhances border security and creates a guest worker program. Public opinion generally aligns with CIRA's thrust. For example, one national opinion poll at the time shows 63 percent of respondents preferring a policy where illegal immigrants who have lived in the United States for some time can apply for legal status and eventually become citizens (*ABC News* 2006). Neither bill is approved due to a political impasse between both Congressional chambers.
- April 2010. Arizona enacts S.B. 1070: the Support Our Law Enforcement and Safe Neighborhoods Act, which mandates that immigrants always carry their registration papers. The act also empowers local police to question individuals suspected of being undocumented. Opponents worry the law will cause Latinos to be racially profiled. Supporters argue it will stop illegal immigration into Arizona, with other states eventually passing related measures. A national poll at the time shows 54 percent of US adults believing the law will discriminate against Hispanics (CNN 2010a), with other polls showing an evenly divided public as to whether S.B. 1070 will actually reduce illegal immigration (CNN 2010b). In June 2012, the U.S. Supreme Court strikes down key provisions of S.B. 1070, but still allows police officers to investigate the immigration status of detained individuals.
- June 2012. With Congressional efforts at immigration reform stalled, President Barack Obama promulgates Deferred Action for Childhood Arrivals (DACA). This executive action instructs the Department of Homeland Security to suspend deportation proceedings for unauthorized immigrants who have arrived in the United States as children. DACA applicants must reside in the United States for at least five years; be a student, high school graduate, or veteran; and, have no criminal record. A national poll at the time finds 61 percent of adults supporting the president's action (Pew Research Center

2012). Critics denounce DACA as evidence of President Obama subverting the legislative process.
- June 2013. The US Senate approves a revised immigration bill proposing, inter alia, a long path to citizenship for many unauthorized immigrants; enhancing border security; and, mandating an employee verification system. In November, House Speaker Boehner says his chamber will not formally negotiate with the Senate to reconcile differences between House plans for immigration reform and the Senate bill passed in June. One national poll, however, shows 50 percent of adults feel it is "very" or "extremely" important that the president and Congress pass new immigration legislation that year (Pew Research Center 2013).
- Finally, in November 2014, President Obama again takes executive action toward unauthorized immigrants. This new effort suspends deportation proceedings for undocumented parents of US citizens and permanent residents, who have lived in the United States for at least five years. It also allows many of these individuals an opportunity to receive work permits. Further, this action expands DACA by extending eligibility to immigrants older than 30 and more recent arrivals. Some survey data show that at least 52 percent of US adults support this new DACA extension (*ABC News/Washington Post* 2014). Critics again denounce this executive action as also circumventing the legislative process.

Many of these cases reveal a disjuncture between legislative efforts and public opinion, thereby raising awkward questions about political representation. Though public opinion does not dictate legislation, lawmakers do consult it to inform their decisions (e.g., Erikson et al. 2002; Stimson 2004). Implicit attitudes complicate this process, as I alluded to earlier. If implicit attitudes are prevalent, as I find, then lawmakers' sense of what the public thinks about immigration is both distorted and incomplete. Consider that in a few of the preceding flash-points, sizeable portions of the American mass public seemed inclined toward some Congressional proposals and executive actions on illegal immigration. But this is self-reported opinion, remember, which means that lawmakers only know what people are willing or able to report. In particular, politicians do not have a clear sense about how unfavorably Latinos are viewed by many individuals.

This matters because implicit attitudes toward Latinos limit how far Americans will extend a welcome to all immigrants. When considering immigration policies, many people already have a specific immigrant group in mind, using how they feel about Latinos as a yardstick for their opposition to immigration, both illegal and legal. Such resistance is geared toward some of the most basic aspects of immigration policy, including which immigrants should be deported and which are worthy of citizenship – precisely the kind of considerations prominent in recent immigration debates. To be sure, some of these debates suggest nuance in the mass public's views about immigration. For example, many Americans have said they support deporting only those unauthorized immigrants who do not meet strict criteria, such as a clean criminal record and no back taxes due, which implies a clear distinction in people's minds between the "right" and "wrong" kind of unauthorized immigrants. But this might be reading too much into these self-reports, for my experimental analyses suggest that implicit attitudes toward Latinos shape how many people judge immigration policies, including deportation, even when the immigrants in question are non-Latino.

Perhaps a stickier question is how immigration reform can actually occur in light of implicit attitudes? One possibility here involves recognizing that implicit attitudes are a matter of degree. It is not the case that some people are implicitly biased and others are not. Individuals vary by how implicitly biased they are. Acknowledging these individual differences serves to remind us that although many individuals are very implicitly biased, others are much less so – to the point of having positive implicit attitudes toward Latino immigrants. These individuals are in the minority, to be sure. But even minorities, under certain circumstances, can be mobilized to support political objectives. The challenge is for politicians to devise effective strategies to galvanize this block, a feat that requires measuring implicit attitudes via public opinion polls.

Another possibility is to focus on mobilizing different constituencies toward immigration reform. Just like not all individuals possess negative implicit attitudes, not all groups in the United States necessarily rely on them for judging immigration. We saw evidence that African Americans fit this mold. This does not mean that blacks are not opposed to immigration. It simply suggests that their opinion on the issue is not as deeply colored by their implicit attitudes toward one group, which implies their opposition to immigration might not be as hard set. I leave it to subsequent researchers to identify where, in the American mass public, additional pockets like these exist.

An even trickier question, however, is whether implicit attitudes can be modified in order to introduce more flexibility into public evaluations of immigration policy proposals. I think they can be. Part of the answer, I believe, goes to the origins of implicit attitudes. We have learned that immigration news patterns help to promote and reinforce implicit attitudes toward Latinos. And by regular, I mean patterns that are clear in their focus on this group and widely and consistently disseminated. Volume and frequency, then, are the keys to understanding why implicit attitudes are so prominent and strong. They are also instrumental in figuring out how they might become less so.

The latter begins with systematic changes in immigration news patterns, changes that should come from news editors and the reporters they supervise. Writing about the media's role in promoting misperceptions about welfare recipients, Gilens (1999: 206) argues that "news organizations must become far more conscious of the process of selecting ... the specific ... people they will feature in their stories." In the realm of immigration, this entails more media attention to domains beyond illegal immigration, which currently receives an inordinate amount of coverage. Doing so should, in theory, reduce how negatively Latino immigrants are portrayed via their pairing with illegal immigration stories. Changing news patterns also calls for a brighter spotlight on non-Latino immigrants, as Latinos are regularly showcased in immigration reports, especially those on illegal immigration. True, most unauthorized immigrants are Latino. Yet most does not mean all, as nontrivial amounts arrive from Asian countries such as China and the Philippines (Hoefer et al. 2011).

Finally, amending immigration news patterns demands reports that more closely hew to empirical reality. For example, it is hard to imagine implicit attitudes toward Latinos still being as markedly negative if journalists more frequently highlighted the substantial portion of legal immigrants who are Latino, with Mexico as the nation producing the most legal permanent residents in the United States (Monger and Yankay 2014). Of course, I agree with Gilens (1999: 132) that expecting news media to depict a given topic in a "sociologically accurate" way might be too much to ask. But hoping for journalists to be more balanced and judicious in their coverage of Latinos and immigration strikes me as being less about producing accurate reports, and more about journalists simply being great journalists. Falling short of this standard, we can anticipate that implicit attitudes toward Latinos will remain as negative and consequential as we have seen them to be in this book.

Final Thought

Writing about the continued groundswell of implicit attitudes research within social psychology, Payne and Gawronski (2010:1) recently explained that "[w]ithin the space of two decades, virtually every intellectual question in social psychology ... has been shaped by the theories and methods of *implicit social cognition*." The same cannot be said of political science. In its vast sea of scholarship, the tides of implicit cognition have reached the shores of only a handful of scattered, but important, research isles. For example, there is the pioneering work of Milton Lodge, Charles Taber, and their associates on automaticity's key role in political thinking (Burdein et al. 2006; Erisen et al. 2014; Lodge and Taber 2005; Lodge and Taber 2013). There is also the ground-breaking work of Tali Mendelberg (2001) and others on the connection between implicit political communication and the activation of explicit racial attitudes (Valentino et al. 2002; see also White 2007; Winter 2008). Moreover, the work of George Marcus, Ted Brader, and their collaborators on the interplay between emotions and political evaluations has sensitized us to the fact that political cognition is underwritten, in no small part, by processes that are rapid, subtle, and subconscious (Brader 2006; Brader and Marcus 2013; Marcus et al. 2000). And, in an encouraging sign of interdisciplinary synergy, some social psychologists have begun studying expressly political topics, such as the role of implicit partisanship among self-reported independents (Hawkins and Nosek 2012) and the impact of implicit preferences on vote choice (cf. Arcuri et al. 2008; Friese et al. 2012; Galdi et al. 2008).

Seen from above, this might strike one as an impressive archipelago. Seen from the ground, however, one sees this is a research frontier in need of more intricate mapping, including further clarification about why, when, and among whom implicit political cognition matters (e.g., Albertson 2011; Iyengar and Westwood 2014; Ksiazkiewicz and Hedrick 2013; Mo 2014; Pérez 2010). Thus, at this critical juncture, political scientists have an important choice to make. We can actively promote the growth of this scientific venture or we can arrest its development, either through neglect or out of spite. Yet by choosing the latter, our discipline runs the risk of producing outmoded and woefully inadequate understandings of the mind and its deployment in individual political decision making.

Of course, it is true that intellectual fashions should not dictate the pace of science – and that very much includes political science. But from my perspective, two decades worth of psychological research into implicit cognition strikes me as less of a fad and more of a systematic reassessment of people's reasoning capabilities. Our discipline has vigorously engaged psychological developments like these before – and with appreciable gains in knowledge. We owe it to ourselves to dip ever more deeply into the connections between implicit attitudes and explicit politics.

Note on the Studies

The National Study

The National Study is an Internet survey of American adults eighteen years of age or older. Seven hundred ($N = 700$) individuals completed this fifteen-minute online study. With the exception of Chapter 8, the results in this book are mainly for non-Hispanic whites ($n = 350$) in this study.

All National Study participants were recruited from YouGovPolimetrix's (YGP) opt-in panel of survey respondents. YGP uses matching techniques to yield representative survey samples. For this study, YGP weighted the matched set of respondents to known distributions of age, gender, race, and education for the general US population from the 2006 American Community Survey. YGP administered this online study from July 16 through 26, 2008.

The National Study's protocol consisted of the following components:

Phase 0 – Pre-Study, fielded items measuring partisanship, education, and income. These data were collected prior to my study as part of respondents' enrollment in YGP's panel.

Phase 1, administered items tapping: (1) socioeconomic concerns (e.g., Do you think that the job prospects of Americans are getting worse?); (2) feeling thermometer ratings of political figures (e.g., Hillary Clinton) and immigrant groups (e.g., Latino immigrants); and (3) the Implicit Association Test (IAT). Items within batteries (1) and (2) were randomized.

Phase 2, included a three-item child-rearing battery to measure authoritarianism, as well as an item tapping national identity importance.

Phase 3 – Experiments, consisted of (1) the Deportation Experiment (manipulation: Juan Hernández vs. David Moore), immediately followed by assessment of support for deportation; and (2) the Legal Immigration Experiment (manipulation: control vs. legal Mexicans vs. legal Chinese), immediately followed by three items gauging support for legal immigration policies (e.g., increasing number of visas available to legal immigrants). These experiments were designed to be orthogonal to each other and their order was randomized.

Laboratory Study 1

Lab Study 1 was an experiment expressly designed to assess the performance of the Latino immigrant/white immigrant version of the Implicit Association Test (IAT), which had not existed before. The study was administered to 102 ($N = 102$) undergraduate student subjects at an elite Southern university during July 2007. Subjects were recruited to this study through advertisements placed throughout campus. Each subject received $5 for their participation. The results reported from this study are for non-Hispanic whites ($n = 44$).

The protocol for this study entailed the following components:

Phase 1, fielded feeling thermometer ratings (in randomized order) of political figures (e.g., George W. Bush) and immigrant groups (e.g., Latino immigrants, white immigrants).
Phase 2, administered the IAT contrasting Latino and white immigrants.
Phase 3, gauged opposition to illegal immigration (e.g., US immigration authorities should increase their efforts to curb the flow of illegal immigration?) and legal immigration (e.g., the United States should decrease the annual number of legal immigrants?).

Laboratory Study 2

The objective of Lab Study 2 was to compare the performance of the Latino/white and Latino immigrant/white immigrant versions of the Implicit Association Test (IAT). The experiment was administered, at the end of an omnibus study, to one hundred and twenty-two ($N = 122$) non-Hispanic white, undergraduate student subjects. The version of the IAT was randomly assigned to subjects. This study was conducted during March 2010 at a different elite Southern university than the one in Lab Study 1. All subjects received course credit for their participation in this study.

The protocol for this omnibus study entailed the following components:

Phase 1, collected demographic data (e.g., race, gender), assessed risk orientations, and administered a dictator game.
Phase 2, asked items assessing, inter alia, personality, trust in government, need for cognition, authoritarianism, dispositional emotions, and political knowledge.
Phase 3, administered an experiment on terror threat and politics.
Phase 4, randomly assigned individuals to the different IAT versions discussed in the preceding text.

References

ABC News. 2006. *ABC News/Washington Post* Poll, April 2006.

ABC News. 2014. *ABC News/Washington Post* News Poll, December 2014.

Achen, Christopher H. 1975. Mass Political Attitudes and the Survey Response. *American Political Science Review* 69(4): 1218–1231.

Achen, Christopher H. 2005. Let's Put Garbage-Can Regressions and Garbage-Can Probits Where They Belong. *Conflict Management and Peace Science* 22: 327–329.

Akalis, Scott A., Mahzarin R. Banaji, and Stephen M. Kosslyn. 2008. Crime Alert! How Thinking About a Single Suspect Automatically Shifts Stereotypes Toward an Entire Group. *DuBois Review* 5(2): 217–233.

Akrami, Nazar, and Bo Ekehammar. 2005. The Association between Implicit and Explicit Prejudice: The Moderating Role of Motivation to Control Prejudiced Reactions. *Scandinavian Journal of Psychology* 46(4): 361–366.

Albertson, Bethany. 2011. Religious Appeals and Implicit Attitudes. *Political Psychology* 32(1): 109–130.

Allport, Gordon W. 1935. Attitudes. In C. Murchison, ed., *Handbook of Social Psychology*, pp. 798–844. Worcester, MA: Clark University Press.

Althaus, Scott L. 1998. Information Effects in Collective Preferences. *American Political Science Review* 92(3): 545–558.

Althaus, Scott L., Nathaniel Swigger, Svitlana Chernykh, David J. Hendry, Sergio C. Wals, and Christopher Tiwald. 2011. Assumed Transmission in Political Science: A Call for Bringing Description Back In. *Journal of Politics* 73(4): 1065–1080.

Ames, Susan L., Jerry L. Grenard, Carolien Thush, Steve Sussman, Reinout W. Wiers, and Alan W. Stacy. Comparison of Indirect Assessments of Association as Predictors of Marijuana Use among At-Risk Adolescents. *Experimental and Clinical Psychopharmacology* 15(2): 204–218.

Amodio, David M., and Patricia G. Devine. 2006. Stereotyping and Evaluation in Implicit Race Bias: Evidence for Independent Constructs and Unique Effects on Behavior. *Journal of Personality and Social Psychology* 91(4): 652–661.

Arcuri, Luciano, Luigi Castelli, Silvia Galdi, Cristina Zogmaister, and Alessandro Amadori. 2008. Predicting the Vote: Implicit Attitudes as Predictors of the Future Behavior of Decided and Undecided Voters. *Political Psychology* 29(3): 369–387.

Arkes, Hal R., and Phillip E. Tetlock. 2004. Attributions of Implicit Prejudice, or "Would Jesse Jackson 'Fail' the Implicit Association Test? *Psychological Inquiry* 15(4): 257–278.

Asendorpf, Jens B., Rainer Banse, and Daniel Mücke. 2002. Double Dissociation between Implicit and Explicit Personality Self-Concept: The Case of Shy Behavior. *Journal of Personality and Social Psychology* 83(2): 380–393.

Ashburn-Nardo, Leslie, Megan L. Knowles, and Margo J. Monteith. 2003. Black Americans' Implicit Racial Associations and Their Implications for Intergroup Judgments. *Social Cognition* 21(3): 61–87.

Bachrach, Peter, and Morton S. Baratz. 1962. Two Faces of Power. *American Political Science Review* 56(4): 947–952.

Banaji, Mahzarin R. 2001. Implicit Attitudes Can Be Measured. In H. L. Roediger, I. N. Nairne, and A. M. Suprenant. *The Nature of Remembering: Essays in Honor of Robert G. Crowder*, pp. 117–149. Washington, DC: American Psychological Association.

Banaji, Mahzarin R., Irene V. Blair, and Norbert Schwarz. 1995. Implicit Memory and Survey Measurement. In N. Schwarz and S. Sudman, eds., *Answering Questions: Methodology for Determining Cognitive and Communicative Processes in Survey Research*, pp. 347–372. San Francisco: Jossey-Bass.

Banaji, Mahzarin R., Brian A. Nosek, and Anthony G. Greenwald. 2004. No Place for Nostalgia in Science: A Response to Arkes and Tetlock. *Psychological Inquiry* 15: 279–289.

Banks, Antoine J., and Nicholas A. Valentino. 2012. Emotional Substrates of White Racial Attitudes. *American Journal of Political Science* 56(2): 286–297.

Bargh, John A. 1994. The Four Horsemen of Automaticity: Awareness, Efficiency, Intention, and Control in Social Cognition. In Robert S. Wyer and Thomas K. Srull, eds., *Handbook of Social Cognition*, pp. 1–40. Tuxedo Park, NY: Lawrence Erlbaum.

Bargh, John A. 2007. *Social Psychology and the Unconscious: The Automaticity of Higher Mental Processes*. New York: Psychology Press.

Bargh, John A., and Paula Pietromonaco. 1982. Automatic Information Processing and Social Perception: The Influence of Trait Information Presented Outside of Conscious Awareness on Impression Formation. *Journal of Personality and Social Psychology* 43: 437–449.

Bargh, John A., Shelly Chaiken, Rajen Govender, and Felicia Pratto. 1992. The Generality of the Automatic Attitude Activation Effect. *Journal of Personality and Social Psychology* 62: 893–912.

Bargh, John A., Mark Chen, and Nalini Ambady. 1996. Automaticity of Social Behavior: Direct Effects of Trait Construct and Stereotype Activation on Action. *Journal of Personality and Social Psychology* 71(2): 230–244.

Baron, Reuben M., and David A. Kenny. 1986. The Moderator-Mediator Distinction in Social Psychological Research: Conceptual, Strategic, and Statistical Considerations. *Journal of Personality and Social Psychology* 51(6): 1173–1182.

Barreto, Matt, Sylvia Manzano, Ricardo Ramírez, and Kathy Rim. 2009. Immigrant Social Movement Participation: Understanding Involvement in the 2006 Immigration Protest Rallies. *Urban Affairs Review* 44(5): 736–764.

Bartels, Larry M. 1996. Uninformed Votes: Information Effects in Presidential Elections. *American Journal of Political Science* 40(1): 194–230.

Bartels, Larry. 2000. Partisanship and Voting Behavior, 1952–1996. *American Journal of Political Science* 44(1): 35–50.

Bernstein, Nina. 2006 (March 15). An Irish Face on the Cause of Citizenship. *The New York Times*.

Blanton, Hart, James Jaccard, Jonathan Klick, Barbara Mellers, Gregory Mitchell, and Philip Tetlock. 2009. Strong Claims and Weak Evidence: Reassessing the Predictive Validity of the IAT. *Journal of Applied Psychology* 94(3): 567–582.

Blumer, Herbert. 1958. Race Prejudice as a Sense of Group Position. *Pacific Sociological Review* 1(1): 3–7.

Bobo, Lawrence. 1983. Whites' Opposition to Busing: Symbolic Racism or Realistic Group Conflict? *Journal of Personality and Social Psychology* 45: 1195–1210.

Bobo, Lawrence, and Vincent L. Hutchings. 1996. Perceptions of Racial Group Competition: Extending Blumer's Theory of Group Position to a Multiracial Social Context. *American Sociological Review* 61(6): 951–972.

Bobo, Larry, and Frederick C. Licari. 1989. Education and Political Tolerance: Testing the Effects of Cognitive Sophistication and Target Group Affect. *Public Opinion Quarterly* 53: 285–308.

Bosson, Jennifer K.,William B. Swann, Jr., and James W. Pennebaker. 2000. Stalking the Perfect Measure of Implicit Self-Esteem: The Blind Men and the Elephant Revisited? *Journal of Personality and Social Psychology* 79(4): 631–643.

Brader, Ted. 2006. *Campaigning for Hearts and Minds: How Emotional Appeals in Political Ads Work*. Chicago: University of Chicago Press.

Brader, Ted, and George E. Marcus. 2013. Emotion and Political Psychology. In L. Huddy, D. Sears, and J. Levy, eds., *The Oxford Handbook of Political Psychology*, pp. 165–204. New York: Oxford University Press.

Brader, Ted, Nicholas A. Valentino, and Elizabeth Suhay. 2008. What Triggers Public Opposition to Immigration? Anxiety, Group Cues, and the Immigration Threat. *American Journal of Political Science* 52(4): 959–978.

Brady, Henry E., and Paul M. Sniderman. 1985. Attitude Attribution: A Group Basis for Political Reasoning. *American Political Science Review* 79: 1061–1078.

Branton, Regina P., and Johanna Dunaway. 2009. Slanted Newspaper Coverage of Immigration: The Importance of Economics and Geography. *The Policy Studies Journal* 37(2): 257–273.

Branton, Regina, Erin C. Cassese, Bradford S. Jones, and Chad Westerland. 2011. All Along the Watchtower: Acculturation Fear, Anti-Latino Affect, and Immigration. *The Journal of Politics* 73(3): 664–679.

Brehm, Jack W. 1993. Control, Its Loss, and Psychological Reactance. In G. Weary, F. H. Gleicher, and K. L. Marsh, eds., *Control and Motivation and Social Cognition*, pp. 3–30. New York: Springer-Verlag.

Brewer, Marilynn B. 1999. The Psychology of Prejudice: Ingroup Love or Outgroup Hate? *Journal of Social Issues* 55(3): 429–444.

Brown, Timothy A. 2006. *Confirmatory Factor Analysis for Applied Research*. New York: The Guilford Press.

Brown-Dean, Khalilah L. 2007. Permanent Outsiders: Felon Disenfranchisement and the Breakdown of Black Politics. *National Political Science Review* 11: 103–120.

Brunel, Frederic, Brian C. Tietje, and Anthony G. Greenwald. 2004. Is the Implicit Association Test a Valid and Valuable Measure of Implicit Consumer Social Cognition? *Journal of Consumer Psychology* 14(4): 385–404.

Burdein, Inna, Milton Lodge, and Charles Taber. 2006. Experiments on the Automaticity of Political Beliefs and Attitudes. *Political Psychology* 27(3): 359–371.

Burns, Peter, and James G. Gimpel. 2000. Economic Insecurity, Prejudicial Stereotypes, and Public Opinion on Immigration Policy. *Political Science Quarterly* 115: 201–225.

Cameron, C. Daryl, Jazmin L. Brown-Iannuzzi, and B. Keith Payne. 2012. Sequential Priming Measures of Implicit Social Cognition: A Meta-Analyses of Associations with Behavior and Explicit Attitudes. *Personality and Social Psychology Review* 16(4): 330–350.

Campbell, Angus, Phillip E. Converse, Warren E. Miller, and Donald E. Stokes. [1960]1980. *The American Voter*, unabridged ed. Chicago: Midway Reprint.

Cassino, Dan, and Milton Lodge. 2007. The Primacy of Affect in Political Evaluations. In W. R. Neuman, G. E. Marcus, M. MacKuen, and A. N. Crigler, eds., *The Affect Effect: Dynamics of Emotion in Political Thinking and Behavior*, pp. 101–123. Chicago: University of Chicago Press.

Chavez, Leo R. 2001. *Covering Immigration: Popular Images and the Politics of the Nation*. Berkeley: University of California Press.

Chavez, Leo R. 2008. *The Latino Threat: Constructing Immigrants, Citizens, and The Nation*. Palo Alto, CA: Stanford University Press.

Citrin, Jack, and David O. Sears. 2014. *American Identity and the Politics of Multiculturalism*. New York: Cambridge University Press.

Clawson, Rosalee A., and Rakuya Trice. 2000. Poverty as We Know It: Media Portrayals of the Poor. *Public Opinion Quarterly* 64(1): 53–64.

CNN. 2005. CNN Poll, June 2005.

CNN. 2010a. CNN/Opinion Research Corporation Poll, July 2010.

CNN. 2010b. CNN/Opinion Research Corporation Poll, July 2010.

Cohen, Jacob. 1988. *Statistical Power Analysis for the Behavioral Sciences*. Hillsdale, NJ: Lawrence Erlbaum.

Collins, Allan M., and Elizabeth F. Loftus. 1975. A Spreading-Activation Theory of Semantic Processing. *Psychological Review* 82(6): 407–428.

Conley, Dalton. 1999. *Being Black, Living in the Red: Race, Wealth, and Social Policy in America*. Berkeley: University of California Press.

Converse, Phillip E. 1964. The Nature of Belief Systems in Mass Publics. In David E. Apter, ed., *Ideology and Discontent*, pp. 206–261. New York: Free Press.

Correll, Joshua, Bernadette Park, Charles M. Judd, and Bernd Wittenbrink. 2002. The Police Officer's Dilemma: Using Ethnicity to Disambiguate Potentially Threatening Individuals. *Journal of Personality and Social Psychology* 83(6): 1314–1329.

Craemer, Thomas. 2008. Nonconscious Feelings of Closeness toward African Americans and Support for Pro-Black Policies. *Political Psychology* 29(3): 407–436.

Cunningham, William A., Kristopher J. Preacher, and Mahzarin R. Banaji. 2001. Implicit Attitude Measures: Consistency, Stability, and Convergent Validity. *Psychological Science* 12(2): 163–170.

Cunningham, William A., Carol L. Raye, and Marcia K. Johnson. 2004a. Implicit and Explicit Evaluation: fMRI Correlates of Valence, Emotional Intensity, and Control in the Processing of Attitudes. *Journal of Cognitive Neuroscience* 16(10): 1717–1729.

Cunningham, William A., Marcia K. Johnson, Carol L. Raye, J. Chris Gatenby, John C. Gore, and Mahzarin R. Banaji. 2004b. Separable Neural Components in the Processing of Black and White Faces. *Psychological Science* 15: 806–813.

Cunningham, William A., John B. Nezlek, and Mahzarin R. Banaji. 2004c. Implicit and Explicit Ethnocentrism: Revisiting Ideologies of Prejudice. *Personality and Social Psychology Bulletin* 30(10): 1332–1346.

Cvencek, Dario, Anthony G. Greenwald, Anthony S. Brown, Nicola S. Gray, and Robert J. Snowden. 2010. Faking of the Implicit Association Test Is Statistically Detectable and Partly Correctable. *Basic and Applied Social Psychology* 32: 302–314.

Dahl, Robert A. 1957. The Concept of Power. *Behavioral Science* 2(3): 201–215.

Dahl, Robert A. 1961. *Who Governs? Power and Democracy in an American City*. New Haven, CT: Yale University Press.

Dasgupta, Nilanjana. 2004. Implicit Ingroup Favoritism, Outgroup Favoritism, and Their Behavioral Manifestations. *Social Justice Research* 17: 143–169.

Dasgupta, Nilanjana, and Anthony G. Greenwald. 2001. On the Malleability of Automatic Attitudes: Combating Automatic Prejudice with Images of Admired and Disliked Individuals. *Journal of Personality and Social Psychology* 81(5): 800–814.

Dasgupta, Nilanjana, Anthony G. Greenwald, and Mahzarin R. Banaji. 2003. The First Ontological Challenge to the IAT: Attitude or Mere Familiarity? *Psychological Inquiry* 14: 238–243.

Davis, Darren W. 1997. The Direction of Race of Interviewer Effects among African Americans: Donning the Black Mask. *American Journal of Political Science* 41(1): 309–322.

Davis, Darren W. 2007. *Negative Liberty: Public Opinion and the Terrorist Attacks on America*. New York: Russell Sage Foundation.

Dawson, Michael C. 1994. *Behind the Mule: Race and Class in African American Politics*. Princeton, NJ: Princeton University Press.

Dawson, Michael C. 2000. Slowly Coming to Grips With the Effects of the American Racial Order on American Policy Preferences. In D. O. Sears, J. Sidanius, and L. Bobo, eds., *Racialized Politics: The Debate About Racism in America*, pp. 344–357. Chicago: University of Chicago Press.

de Figueiredo, Rui J. P., and Zachary Elkins. 2003. Are Patriots Bigots? An Inquiry into the Vices of In-Group Pride. *American Journal of Political Science* 47(1): 171–188.

De Houwer, Jan, Hilde Hendrickx, and Frank Baeyens. 1997. Evaluative Learning with "Subliminally" Presented Stimuli. *Consciousness and Cognition* 6(1): 87–107.

Delli Carpini, Michael X. and Scott Keeter. 1996. *What Americans Know about Politics and Why It Matters*. New Haven, CT: Yale University Press.

Deutsch, Roland and Fritz Strack. 2010. Building Blocks of Social Behavior: Reflective and Impulsive Processes. In B. Gawronski and B. K. Payne, eds., *Handbook of Implicit Social Cognition*, pp. 62–79. New York: Guilford Press.

Devine, Patricia G. 1989. Stereotypes and Prejudice: Their Automatic and Controlled Components. *Journal of Personality and Social Psychology* 56(1): 5–18.

Devos, Thierry, and Mahzarin R. Banaji. 2005. American = White? *Journal of Personality and Social Psychology* 88(3): 447–466.

Diamond, Jeff. 1998. African-American Attitudes towards United States Immigration Policy. *International Migration Review* 32(2): 451–470.

Dijksterhuis, A. 2004. I Like Myself But I Don't Know Why: Enhancing Implicit Self-Esteem by Subliminal Evaluative Conditioning. *Journal of Personality and Social Psychology* 86: 345–355.

Ditonto, Tessa, Richard R. Lau, and David O. Sears. 2013. AMPing Racial Attitudes: Comparing the Power of Explicit and Implicit Racism Measures in 2008. *Political Psychology* 34(4): 487–510.
Ditto, Peter H., and David F. Lopez. 1992. Motivated Skepticism: Use of Differential Decision Criteria for Preferred and Non-Preferred Conclusions. *Journal of Personality and Social Psychogy* 63(4): 568–584.
Doosje, Bertjan, Russell Spears, and Naomi Ellemers. 2002. Social Identity as Both Cause and Effect: The Development of Group Identification in Response to Anticipated and Actual Changes in the Intergroup Status Hierarchy. *British Journal of Social Psychology* 41(1): 57–76.
Dowley, Kathleen M., and Brian D. Silver. 2000. Subnational and National Loyalty: Cross-National Comparisons. *International Journal of Public Opinion Research* 12(4): 357–371.
Downs, Anthony. 1957. *An Economic Theory of Democracy*. New York: Harper.
Druckman, James N. 2001. The Implications of Framing Effects for Citizen Competence. *Political Behavior* 23: 225–256.
Dunton, Bridget C., and Russell H. Fazio. 1997. An Individual Difference Measure of Motivation to Control Prejudiced Reactions. *Personality and Social Psychology Bulletin* 23: 316–326.
Eagly, Alice H., and Shelly Chaiken. 1993. *The Psychology of Attitudes*. Fort Worth: Harcourt Brace Jovanovich.
Egloff, Boris, and Stefan C. Schmukle. 2002. Predictive Validity of an Implicit Association Test for Assessing Anxiety. *Journal of Personality and Social Psychology* 83(6): 1441–1455.
Entman, Robert M. 1994. Representation and Reality in the Portrayal of Blacks on Network Television News. *Journalism Quarterly* 71: 509–520.
Erikson, Robert S., Michael B. MacKuen, and James A. Stimsonn. 2002. *The Macro Polity*. Cambridge: Cambridge University Press.
Erisen, Cengiz, Milton Lodge, and Charles S. Taber. 2014. Affective Contagion in Effortful Political Thinking. *Political Psychology* 35(2): 187–206.
Fang, Carolyn Y., Jim Sidanius, and Felicia Pratto. 1998. Romance across the Social Status Continuum: Interracial Marriage and the Ideological Asymmetry Effect. *Journal of Cross-Cultural Psychbhology* 29(2): 290–305.
Fazio, Russell H. 1990. Multiple Processes by Which Attitudes Guide Behavior: The MODE Model as an Integrative Framework. In M. P. Zanna, ed., *Advances in Experimental Social Psychology*, pp. 75–109. San Diego: Academic Press.
Fazio, Russell H. 2007. Attitudes as Object-Evaluation Associations of Varying Strength. *Social Cognition* 25(5): 603–637.
Fazio, Russell H., and Bridget C. Dunton. 1997. Categorization by Race: The Impact of Automatic and Controlled Components of Racial Prejudice. *Journal of Experimental Social Psychology* 451–470.
Fazio, Russell H., and Michael A. Olson. 2003. Implicit Measures in Social Cognition Research: Their Meaning and Use. *Annual Review of Psychology* 54: 297–327.
Fazio, Russell H., and Tamara Towles-Schwen. 1999. The MODE Model of Attitude-Behavior Processes. In S. Chaiken and Y. Trope, eds., *Dual-Process Theories in Social Psychology*, pp. 97–116. New York: Guilford Press.
Fazio, Russell H., Jeaw-Mei Chen, Elizabeth C. McDonel, and Steven J. Sherman. 1982. Attitude Accessibility, Attitude-Behavior Consistency, and the Strength of the

Object-Evaluation Association. *Journal of Experimental Social Psychology* 18: 339–357.

Fazio, Russell H., David M. Sanbonmatsu, Martha C. Powell, and Frank R. Kardes. 1986. On the Automatic Activation of Attitudes. *Journal of Personality and Social Psychology* 50(2): 229–238.

Fazio, Russell H., Joni R. Jackson, Bridget C. Dunton, and Carol J. Williams. 1995. Variability in Automatic Activation as an Unobtrusive Measure of Racial Attitudes: A Bona Fide Pipeline? *Journal of Personality and Social Psychology* 69(6): 1013–1027.

Federico, Christopher. 2004. When Do Welfare Attitudes Become Racialized? The Paradoxical Effects of Education. *American Journal of Political Science* 48(2): 374–391.

Federico, Christopher, and James Sidanius. 2002. Sophistication and the Antecedents of Whites' Racial-Policy Attitudes: Racism, Ideology, and Affirmative Action in America. *Public Opinion Quarterly* 66: 145–176.

Fiedler, Klaus, and Matthias Bluemke. 2005. Faking the IAT: Aided and Unaided Response Control on the Implicit Association Test. *Basic and Applied Social Psychology* 27(4): 307–316.

Finnegan, William. 2013. The Deportation Machine: A Citizen Trapped in the System. *The New Yorker*

Fiske, Susan T. 1993. Controlling Other People: The Impact of Power on Stereotyping. *American Psychologist* 48(6): 621–628.

Forgas, Joseph P. and Hui Bing Tan. 2011. Affective Influences on the Perception, Management, and Resolution of Social Conflicts. In J. P. Forgas, A. W. Kruglanski, and K. D. Williams, eds., *The Psychology of Social Conflict and Aggression*, pp. 119–138. New York: Psychology Press.

Friese, Malte, Colin Tucker Smith, Thomas Plischke, Matthias Bluemke, and Brian A. Nosek. 2012. Do Implicit Attitudes Predict Actual Voting Behavior Particularly for Undecided Voters? *PLOS One.*

Gailliot, Matthew T., Roy F. Baumeister, C. Nathan DeWall, Jon K. Maner, E. Ashby Plant, Dianne M. Tice, Lauren E. Brewer, and Brandon J. Schmeichel. 2007. Self-Control Relies on Glucose as a Limited Energy Source: Willpower Is More Than a Metaphor. *Journal of Personality and Social Psychology* 92(2): 325–336.

Gaines, Brian J., James H. Kuklinski, and Paul J. Quirk. 2007. The Logic of the Survey Experiment Reexamined. *Political Analysis* 15: 1–20.

Galdi, Silvia, Luciano Arcuri, and Bertram Gawronski. 2008. Automatic Mental Associations Predict Future Choices of Undecided Decision-Makers. *Science* 321(5892): 1100–1102.

Gallup. 2005. Gallup Poll, June 2005.

Gamson, William A. 1992. *Talking Politics*. New York: Cambridge University Press.

Gamson, William A., and Andre Modigliani. 1987. The Changing Culture of Affirmative Action. *Research in Political Sociology* 3: 137–177.

Gamson, William A., and Andre Modigliani. 1989. Media Discourse and Public Opinion on Nuclear Power: A Constructionist Approach. *American Journal of Sociology* 95(1): 1–37.

Garcia Bedolla, Lisa. 2005. *Fluid Borders: Latino Power, Identity, and Politics in Los Angeles*. Berkeley: University of California Press.

Gawronski, Bertram. 2009. Ten Frequently Asked Questions About Implicit Measures and Their Frequently Supposed, But Not Entirely Correct Answers. *Canadian Psychology* 50(3): 141–150.

Gawronski, Bertram, and Galen V. Bodenhausen. 2006. Associative and Propositional Process in Evaluation: An Integrative Review of Implicit and Explicit Attitude Change. *Psychological Bulletin* 132(5): 692–731.

Gawronski, Bertram, and Galen V. Bodenhausen. 2011. The Associative-Propositional Model: Theory, Evidence, and Open Questions. *Advances in Experimental Social Psychology* 44: 59–127.

Gawronski, Bertram, and B. Keith Payne. 2010. *Handbook of Implicit Social Cognition*. New York: Guilford Press.

Gawronski, Bertram, Daniel Geschke, and Rainer Banse. 2003. Implicit Bias in Impression Formation: Associations Influence the Construal of Individuating Information. *European Journal of Social Psychology* 33: 573–589.

Gawronski, Bertram, Wilhelm Hofmann, and Christopher J. Wilbur. 2006. Are "Implicit" Attitudes Unconscious? *Consciousness and Cognition* 15: 485–499.

Gawronski, Bertram, Kurt R. Peters, Paula M. Brochu, and Fritz Strack. 2008. Understanding the Relations between Different Forms of Racial Prejudice: A Cognitive Consistency Perspective. *Personality and Social Psychology Bulletin* 34(5): 648–665.

Gawronski, Bertram, Robert J. Rydell, Bram Vervliet, and Jan De Houwer. 2010. Generalization versus Contextualization in Automatic Evaluation. *Journal of Experimental Psychology: General* 139(4): 683–701.

Gawronski, Bertram, Robert Balas, and Laura A. Creighton. 2014. Can the Formation of Conditioned Attitudes Be Intentionally Controlled? *Personality and Social Psychology Bulletin* 40(4): 419–432.

Gawronski, Bertram, Silvia Galdi, and Luciano Arcuri. 2015. What Can Political Psychology Learn From Implicit Measures? Empirical Evidence and New Directions. *Political Psychology* 36(1): 1–17.

Gay, Claudine. 2006. Seeing Difference: The Effect of Economic Disparity on Black Attitudes toward Latinos. *American Journal of Political Science* 50(4): 982–997.

Gerstle, Gary. 2001. *American Crucible: Race and Nation in the Twentieth Century*. Princeton, NJ: Princeton University Press.

Gilens, Martin. 1999. *Why Americans Hate Welfare: Race, Media, and the Politics of Antipoverty Policy*. Princeton, NJ: Princeton University Press.

Gilliam, Franklin D., and Shanto Iyengar. 2000. Prime Suspects: The Influence of Local Television New on the Viewing Public. *American Journal of Political Science* 44(3): 560–573.

Giner-Sorolla, Roger. 2012. *Judging Passions: Moral Emotions in Persons and Groups*. New York: Psychology Press.

Goodwin, Stephanie A., Alexandra Gubin, Susan T. Fiske, and Vincent Y. Yzerbyt. 2000. Power Can Bias Impression Processes: Stereotyping Subordinates by Default and by Design. *Group Processes and Intergroup Relations* 3(3): 227–256.

Green, Donald, Bradley Palmquist, and Eric Schickler. 2002. *Partisan Hearts and Minds: Political Parties and the Social Identities of Voters*. New Haven, CT: Yale University Press.

Greenwald, Anthony G., and Mahzarin R. Banaji. 1995. Implicit Social Cognition: Attitudes, Self-Esteem, and Stereotypes. *Psychological Review* 102(1): 4–27.

Greenwald, Anthony G., and Shelly D. Farnham. 2000. Using the Implicit Association Test to Measure Self-Esteem and Self-Concept. *Journal of Personality and Social Psychology* 79(6): 1022–1038.

Greenwald, Anthony G., and Brian A. Nosek. 2001. Health of the Implicit Association Test at Age 3. *Zeitschrift für Experimentelle Psychologie* 48(2): 85–93.
Greenwald, Anthony G., Debbie E. McGhee, and Jordan L. K. Schwartz. 1998. Measuring Individual Differences in Implicit Cognition: The Implicit Association Test. *Journal of Personality and Social Psychology* 74(6): 1464–1480.
Greenwald, Anthony G., Brian A. Nosek, and Mahzarin R. Banaji. 2003. Understanding and Using the Implicit Association Test: I. An Improved Scoring Algorithm. *Journal of Personality and Social Psychology* 85(2): 197–216.
Greenwald, Anthony G., T. Andrew Poehlman, Eric Luis Uhlmann, and Mahzarin R. Banaji. 2009. Understanding and Using the Implicit Association Test: III. Meta-Analysis of Predictive Validity. *Journal of Personality and Social Psychology*.
Gregg, Aiden P., Beate Seibt, and Mahzarin R. Banaji. 2006. Easier Done Than Undone: Asymmetry in the Malleability of Implicit Preferences. *Journal of Personality and Social Psychology* 90(1): 1–20.
Gruszcynski, Michael W., Amanda Balzer, Carly M. Jacobs, Kevin B. Smith, and John R. Hibbing. 2013. The Physiology of Political Participation. *Political Behavior* 35: 135–152.
Gutiérrez, David G. 1995. *Walls and Mirrors: Mexican Americans, Mexican Immigrants, and the Politics of Ethnicity*. Berkeley: University of California Press.
Hagendoorn, Louk. 1995. Intergroup Biases in Multiple Group Systems: The Perception of Ethnic Hierarchies. *European Review of Social Psychology* 6(1): 199–228.
Hagendoorn, Louk, Rian Drogendijk, Sergey Tumanov, and Joseph Hraba. 1998. Inter-Ethnic Preferences and Ethnic Hierarchies in the former Soviet Union. *International Journal of Intercultural Relations* 22(4): 483–503.
Hahn, Adam, and Bertram Gawronski. 2014. Do Implicit Evaluations Reflect Unconscious Attitudes? *Behavioral and Brain Sciences* 37: 28–29.
Haidt, Jonathan. 2012. *The Righteous Mind: Why Good People Are Divided by Politics and Religion*. New York: Pantheon.
Hainmueller, Jens, and Michael J. Hiscox. 2010. Attitudes toward Highly-Skilled and Low-Skilled Immigration: Evidence from a Survey Experiment. *American Political Science Review* 104(1): 61–84.
Hainmueller, Jens, and Daniel J. Hopkins. 2014a. Public Attitudes toward Immigration. *Annual Review of Political Science* 17: 225–249.
Hainmueller, Jens, and Daniel J. Hopkins. 2014b. The Hidden American Consensus: A Conjoint Analysis of Attitudes Toward Immigrants. *American Journal of Political Science* 97(1): 17–41.
Hamilton, James T. 2004. *All the News That's Fit to Sell: How the Market Transforms Information Into News*. Princeton, NJ: Princeton University Press.
Harris-Lacewell, Melissa. 2003. *Barbershops, Bibles, and BET: Everyday Talk and Black Political Thought*. Princeton, NJ: Princeton University Press.
Hartman, Todd K., Benjamin J. Newman, and C. Scott Bell. 2014. Decoding Prejudice toward Hispanics: Group Cues and Public Reactions to Threatening Immigrant Behavior. *Political Behavior* 36: 143–163.
Hassin, Ran R., Melissa J. Ferguson, Daniella Shidlovski, and Tamar Gross. 2007. Subliminal Exposure to National Flags Affects Political Thought and Behavior. *Proceedings of the National Academy of Sciences of the USA* 104(50): 19757–19761.

Hatchett, Shirley, and Howard Schuman. 1975–1976. White Respondents and Race-of-Interviewer Effects. *Public Opinion Quarterly* 39: 523–528.

Hattam, Victoria. 2007. *In the Shadow of Race: Jews, Latinos, and Immigrant Politics in the United States*. Chicago: University of Chicago Press.

Hawkins, Carlee Beth, and Brian A. Nosek. 2012. Motivated Independence? Implicit Party Identity Predicts Political Judgments among Self-Proclaimed Independents. *Personality and Social Psychology Bulletin* 38(11): 1437–1452.

Hendricks, Tyche. 2006. Irish Joining Battle over Illegal Immigration. *San Francisco Chronicle* March 15.

Henrich, Joseph, Steven J. Heine, and Ara Norenzayan. 2010. The Weirdest People in the World? *Behavioral and Brain Sciences* 33: 61–135.

Hetherington, Marc J., and Jonathan D. Weiler. 2009. *Authoritarianism and Polarization in American Politics*. Cambridge: Cambridge University Press.

Higham, John. 1981. *Strangers in the Land: Patterns of American Nativism, 1860–1925*. New York: Atheneum.

Ho, Arnold K., James Sidanius, Daniel T. Levin, and Mahzarin R. Banaji. 2011. Evidence for Hypodescent and Racial Hierarchy in the Categorization and Perception of Biracial Individuals. *Journal of Personality and Social Psychology* 100: 492–506.

Hoefer, Michael, Nancy Rytina, and Bryan C. Baker. 2011. Estimates of the Unauthorized Immigrant Population Residing in the United States: January 2010. Office of Immigration Statistics: Policy Directorate.

Hofmann, Wilhelm, and Timothy D. Wilson 2010. Consciousness, Introspection, and the Adaptive Unconscious. In B. Gawronski and B. K. Payne, eds., *Handbook of Implicit Social Cognition*, 197–215. New York: Guilford Press.

Hofmann, Wilhelm, Bertram Gawronski, Tobias Gshwendner, Huy Le, and Manfred Schmitt. 2005. A Meta-Analysis on the Correlation between the Implicit Association Test and Explicit Self-Report Measures. *Personality and Social Psychology Bulletin* 31(10): 1369–1385.

Horowitz, Donald L. 1985. *Ethnic Groups in Conflict*. Berkeley: University of California Press.

Huddy, Leonie. 2001. From Social to Political Identity: A Critical Examination of Social Identity Theory. *Political Psychology* 22(1): 127–156.

Huddy, Leonie. 2013. From Group Identity to Political Cohesion and Commitment. In L. Huddy, D. O. Sears, and J. S. Levy, eds., *Oxford Handbook of Political Psychology*, 737–773. New York: Oxford University Press.

Huddy, Leonie, and Stanley Feldman. 2009. On Assessing the Political Effects of Racial Prejudice. *Annual Review of Political Science* 12: 423–447.

Huddy, Leonie, and Nayda Terkildsen. 1993. Gender Stereotypes and the Perception of Male and Female Candidates. *American Journal of Political Science* 37(1): 119–147.

Huddy, Leonie, Stanley Feldman, Charles Taber, and Gallya Lahav. 2005. Threat, Anxiety, and Support for Antiterrorism Policies. *American Journal of Political Science* 49(3): 593–608.

Hugenberg, Kurt, and Galen V. Bodenhausen. 2003. Facing Prejudice: Implicit Prejudice and the Perception of Facial Threat. *Psychological Science* 14(6): 640–643.

Huntington, Samuel P. 2004. The Hispanic Challenge. *Foreign Policy* March/April: 30–45.

Ignatiev, Noel. 1995. *How the Irish Became White*. New York: Routledge.

Iyengar, Shanto. 1991. *Is Anyone Responsible? How Television Frames Political Issues*. Chicago: University of Chicago Press.

Iyengar, Shanto, and Donald R. Kinder. 1987. *News That Matters: Television and American Opinion*. Chicago: University of Chicago Press.

Iyengar, Shanto, and Sean J. Westwood. 2014. Fear and Loathing Across Party Lines: New Evidence on Group Polarization. *American Journal of Political Science* 59(3): 690–707.

Jacobson, Mathew Frye. 1998. *Whiteness of a Different Color: European Immigrants and the Alchemy of Race*. Cambridge, MA: Harvard University Press.

Jellison, William A., Allen R. McConnell, and Shira Gabriel. 2004. Implicit and Explicit Measures of Sexual Orientation Attitudes: Ingroup Preferences and Related Behaviors and Beliefs Among Gay and Straight Men. *Personality and Social Psychology Bulletin* 30(5): 629–642.

Jost, John T., Mahzarin R. Banaji, and Brian A. Nosek. 2004. A Decade of System Justification Theory: Accumulated Evidence of Conscious and Unconscious Bolstering of the Status Quo. *Political Psychology* 25: 881–919.

Junn, Jane. 2006. Mobilizing Group Consciousness: When Does Ethnicity Have Political Consequences? In T. Lee, S. K. Ramakrishnan, and R. Ramírez, eds., *Transforming Politics, Transforming America: The Political and Civic Incorporation of Immigrants in the United States*, pp. 32–50. Charlottesville: University of Virginia Press.

Kahn, Kimberly, Arnold K. Ho, Jim Sidanius, and Felicia Pratto. 2009. The Space between Us and Them: Perceptions of Status Differences. *Group Processes and Intergroup Relations* 12(5): 591–604.

Kahneman, Daniel. 2011. *Thinking, Fast and Slow*. New York: Farrar, Straus and Giroux.

Kalmoe, Nathan P., and Spencer Piston. 2013. Is Implicit Prejudice Against Blacks Politically Consequential? Evidence from the AMP. *Public Opinion Quarterly* 77(1): 305–322.

Kam, Cindy D. 2007. Implicit Attitudes, Explicit Choices: When Subliminal Priming Predicts Candidate Preference. *Political Behavior* 29(3): 343–367.

Kam, Cindy D., and Robert J. Franzese. 2007. *Modeling and Interpreting Interactive Hypotheses in Regression Analysis*. Ann Arbor: University of Michigan Press.

Karpinski, Andrew, and James L. Hilton. 2001. Attitudes and the Implicit Association Test. *Journal of Personality and Social Psychology* 81(5): 774–788.

Katz, Daniel. 1960. The Functional Approach to the Study of Attitudes. *Public Opinion Quarterly* 24: 163–204.

Kaufmann, Karen M. 2003. Black and Latino Voters in Denver: Responses to Each Other's Political Leadership. *Political Science Quarterly* 118(1): 107–126.

Kellstedt, Paul M. 2003. *The Mass Media and the Dynamics of American Racial Attitudes*. New York: Cambridge University Press.

Kim, Claire Jean. 2000. *Bitter Fruit: The Politics of Black-Korean Conflict in New York City*. New Haven, CT: Yale University Press.

Kim, Do-Yeong. 2003. Voluntary Controllability of the Implicit Association Test (IAT). *Social Psychology Quarterly* 66(1): 83–96.

Kinder, Donald R. 1998. Opinion and Action in the Realm of Politics. In D. T. Gilbert, S. T. Fiske, and G. Lindzey. *The Handbook of Social Psychology*, pp. 778–867. Boston: McGraw-Hill.

Kinder, Donald R. 2006. Belief Systems Today. *Critical Review* 18: 197–216.
Kinder, Donald R., and Cindy D. Kam. 2009. *Us Against Them: Ethnocentric Foundations of American Opinion*. Chicago: University of Chicago Press.
Kinder, Donald R., and Lynn M. Sanders. 1996. *Divided by Color: Racial Politics and Democratic Ideals*. Chicago: University of Chicago Press.
Kinder, Donald R., and David O. Sears. 1981. Prejudice and Politics: Symbolic Racism Versus Racial Threats to the Good Life. *Journal of Personality and Social Psychology* 40: 414–431.
King, Desmond. 2000. *Making Americans: Immigration, Race, and the Origins of the Diverse Democracy*. Cambridge, MA: Harvard University Press.
Knoll, Benjamin R., David P. Redlawsk, and Howard B. Sanborn. 2011. Framing Labels and Immigration Policy Attitudes in the Iowa Caucuses: "Trying to Out-Tancredo Tancredo." *Political Behavior* 33(3): 433–454.
Kramer, Roderick, Geoffrey Leonardelli, and Robert Livingston. 2011. *Social Cognition, Social Identity, and Intergroup Relations: A Festschrift in Honor of Marilynn B. Brewer.* New York: Psychology Press.
Krosnick, Jon A., and Donald R. Kinder. 1990. Altering the Foundations of Support for the President through Priming. *American Political Science Review* 84: 497–512.
Krueger, Joachim I. 2012. *Social Judgment and Decision-Making*. New York: Psychology Press.
Ksiazkiewicz, Aleksander, and James Hedrick. 2013. An Introduction to Implicit Attitudes in Political Science Research. *PS: Political Science & Politics* 46(3): 525–531.
Kuklinski, James H., Michael D. Cobb, and Martin Gilens. 1997. Racial Attitudes and the "New South." *The Journal of Politics* 59(2): 323–349.
Kunda, Ziva. 1990. The Case for Motivated Reasoning. *Psychological Bulletin* 108(3): 480–498.
Lane, Kristin A., Mahzarin R. Banaji, Brian A. Nosek, and Anthony G. Greenwald. 2007. Understanding and Using the Implicit Association Test: IV. What We Know (So Far) About the Method. In B. Wittenbrink and N. Schwarz, eds., *Implicit Measures of Attitudes*, pp. 59–102. New York: Guilford Press.
Leander, N. Pontus, and Tanya L. Chartrand. 2011. Nonconscious Battles of Will: Implicit Reactions Against the Goals and Motives of Others. In J. P. Forgas, A. W. Kruglanski, and K. D. Williams, eds., *The Psychology of Social Conflict and Aggression*, pp. 83–102. New York: Psychology Press.
Lee, Taeku. 2008. Race, Immigration, and the Identity-to-Politics Link. *Annual Review of Political Science* 11: 457–478.
Lippman, Walter. 1922. *Public Opinion*. New York: Macmillan.
Lipset, Seymour M. 1960. *Political Man*. New York: Doubleday.
Lodge, Milton, and Charles Taber. 2000. Three Steps Toward a Theory of Motivated Political Reasoning. In A. Lupia, M. D. McCubbins, and S. L. Popkin, eds., *Elements of Reason: Cognition, Choice, and the Bounds of Rationality*, pp. 183–213. New York: Cambridge University Press.
Lodge, Milton, and Charles Taber. 2005. The Automaticity of Affect for Political Leaders, Groups, and Issues: An Experimental Test of the Hot Cognition Hypothesis. *Political Psychology* 26(3): 455–482.
Lodge, Milton, and Charles Taber. 2013. *The Rationalizing Voter*: New York: Cambridge University Press.

Lodge, Milton, Kathleen M. McGraw, and Patrick Stroh. 1989. An Impression-Driven Model of Candidate Evaluation. *American Political Science Review* 83(2): 399–419.

Lodge, Milton, Marco R. Steenbergen, and Shawn Brau. 1995. The Responsive Voter: Campaign Information and the Dynamics of Candidate Evaluation. *American Political Science Review* 89(2): 309–326.

Lupia, Arthur. 1994. Shortcuts versus Encyclopedias: Information and Voting Behavior in California Insurance Reform Elections. *American Political Science Review* 88: 63–76.

Lupia, Arthur, and Mathew D. McCubbins. 2000. The Institutional Foundations of Political Competence: How Citizens Learn What They Need to Know. In A. Lupia, M. McCubbins, and S. L. Popkin, eds., *Elements of Reason: Cognition, Choice, and the Bounds of Rationality*, pp. 47–66. New York: Cambridge University Press.

Lupia, Arthur, Mathew D. McCubbins, and Samuel L. Popkin. 2000. *Elements of Reason: Cognition, Choice, and the Bounds of Rationality*. New York: Cambridge University Press.

Luskin, Robert C. 1987. Measuring Political Sophistication. *American Journal of Political Science* 31: 856–899.

Maison, Dominika, Anthony G. Greenwald, and Ralph H. Bruin. 2004. Predictive Validity of the Implicit Association Test in Studies of Brands, Consumer Attitudes, and Behavior. *Journal of Consumer Psychology* 14(4): 405–415.

Marcus, George E. 2003. The Psychology of Emotion and Politics. In D. O. Sears, L. Huddy, and R. Jervis, eds., *Oxford Handbook of Political Psychology*, pp. 182–221. New York: Oxford University Press.

Marcus, George E., W. Russell Neuman, and Michael MacKuen. 2000. *Affective Intelligence and Political Judgment*. Chicago: University of Chicago Press.

Martinez, Michael, and Holly Yan. 2014. Showdown: California Town Turns Away Buses of Detained Immigrants. *CNN.com*.

Marx, Anthony W. 1998. *Making Race and Nation: A Comparison of the United States, South Africa, and Brazil*. Cambridge: Cambridge University Press.

Massey, Douglas, Jorge Durand, and Nolan J. Malone. 2002. *Beyond Smoke and Mirrors: Mexican Immigration in an Era of Economic Integration*. New York: Russell Sage Foundation.

Masuoka, Natalie, and Jane Junn. 2013. *The Politics of Belonging: Race, Public Opinion, and Immigration*. Chicago: University of Chicago Press.

McClain, Paula D. 1993. The Changing Dynamics of Urban Politics: Black and Hispanic Municipal Employment – Is There Competition? *The Journal of Politics* 55: 399–414.

McClain, Paula D., and Albert K. Karnig. 1990. Black and Hispanic Socioeconomic and Political Competition. *American Political Science Review* 2: 535–545.

McClain, Paula D., and Joseph Stewart. 2005. *"Can We All Get Along?": Racial and Ethnic Minorities in American Politics*. Boulder, CO: Westview Press.

McClain, Paula D., Niambi M. Carter, Victoria M. DeFrancesco Soto, Monique L. Lyle, Jeffrey D. Grynaviski, Shayla C. Nunnally, Thomas J. Scotto, J. Alan Kendrick, Gerald F. Lackey, Kendra Davenport Cotton. 2006. Racial Distancing in a Southern City: Latino Immigrants' Views of Black Americans. *The Journal of Politics* 68(3): 571–584.

McClain, Paula D., Monique L. Lyle, Niambi M. Carter, Victoria M. DeFrancesco Soto, Gerald F. Lackey, Kendra Davenport Cotton, Shayla C. Nunnally, Thomas J. Scotto,

Jeffrey D. Grynaviski, and J. Alan Kendrick. 2007. Black Americans and Latino Immigrants in a Southern City: Friendly Neighbors or Economic Competitors? *The DuBois Review: Social Science Research on Race* 4(1): 97–117.

McClosky, Herbert, and John Zaller. 1984. *The American Ethos*. Cambridge, MA: Harvard University Press.

McConahay, John B., and J. C. Hough. 1976. Symbolic Racism. *Journal of Social Issues* 32: 23–46.

McConnell, Allen R., and Jill M. Leibold. 2001. Relations among the Implicit Association Test, Discriminatory Behavior, and Explicit Measures of Racial Attitudes. *Journal of Experimental Social Psychology* 37: 435–442.

McDermott. 2011. Internal and External Validity. In J. N. Druckman, D. P. Green, J. H. Kuklinski, and A. Lupia, eds., *Cambridge Handbook of Experimental Political Science*, pp. 27–40. New York: Cambridge University Press.

McGuire, William J. 1993. The Poly-Psy Relationship: Three Phases of a Long Affair. In S. Iyengar and W. J. McGuire, eds., *Explorations in Political Psychology*, pp. 9–35. Durham, NC: Duke University Press.

Meier, Kenneth J., Paula D. McClain, J. L. Polinard, and Robert D. Wrinkle. 2004. Divided or Together? Conflict and Cooperation between African Americans and Latinos. *Political Research Quarterly* 57: 399–409.

Mendelberg, Tali. 2001. *The Race Card: Campaign Strategy, Implicit Messages, and the Norm of Equality*. Princeton, NJ: Princeton University Press.

Merolla, Jennifer, S. Karthick Ramakrishnan, and Chris Haynes. 2013. "Illegal," "Undocumented," or "Unauthorized": Equivalency Frames, Issue Frames, and Public Opinion on Immigration. *Perspectives on Politics* 11(3): 789–807.

Miller, George A., 1957. The Magic Number Seven, Plus or Minus Two: Some Limits on Our Capacity for Processing Information. *Psychological Review* 63: 81–93.

Mo, Cecilia H. 2015. The Consequences of Explicit and Implicit Gender Attitudes and Candidate Quality in the Calculations of Voters. *Political Behavior* 37: 357–395.

Monger, Randall, and James Yankay. 2014. U.S. Lawful Permanent Residents: 2013. Annual Flow Report: U.S. Office of Immigration Statistics.

Morriss, Peter. 1972. Power in New Haven: A Reassessment of 'Who Governs?' *British Journal of Political Science* 2(4): 457–465.

Motel, Seth. 2012. Statistical Portrait of Hispanics in the United States, 2010. Pew Hispanic Center.

Murphy, Sheila T., and Robert B. Zajonc. 1993. Affect, Cognition, and Awareness: Affective Priming with Optimal and Suboptimal Stimulus Exposures. *Journal of Personality and Social Psychology* 64(5): 723–739.

Nacos, Brigitte L., and Oscar Torres-Reyna. 2007. *Fueling Our Fears: Stereotyping, Media Coverage, and Public Opinion of Muslim Americans*. Lanham, MD: Rowman & Littlefield.

Nelson, Thomas E., and Donald R. Kinder. 1996. Issue Frames and Group-Centrism in American Public Opinion. *The Journal of Politics* 58(4): 1055–1078.

Newman, Benjamin J., Todd K. Hartman, and Charles S. Taber. 2012. Foreign Language Exposure, Cultural Threat, and Opposition to Immigration. *Political Psychology* 33(5): 635–657.

Newman, Benjamin J., Todd K. Hartman, and Charles S. Taber. 2014. Social Dominance and the Cultural Politics of Immigration. *Political Psychology* 35(2): 165–186.

Ngai, Mae M. 2004. *Impossible Subjects: Illegal Aliens and the Making of Modern America*. Princeton, NJ: Princeton University Press.
Nisbett, Richard E., and Timothy DeCamp Wilson. 1977. Telling More Than We Can Know: Verbal Reports on Mental Processes. *Psychological Review* 84: 231–259.
Nosek, Brian A. 2005. Moderators of the Relationship between Implicit and Explicit Evaluation. *Journal of Experimental Psychology: General* 134: 656–584.
Nosek, Brian A., and Mahzarin R. Banaji. 2001. The Go/No-Go Association Task. *Social Cognition* 19(6): 161–176.
Nosek, Brian A., and Jeffrey J. Hansen. 2008. The Associations in Our Heads Belong to Us: Searching for Attitudes and Knowledge in Implicit Evaluation. *Cognition and Emotion* 22(4): 553–594.
Nosek, Brian A., and Frederick L. Smyth. 2007. A Multitrait-Multimethod Validation of the Implicit Association Test: Implicit and Explicit Attitudes Are Related but Distinct Constructs. *Experimental Psychology* 54(1): 14–29.
Nosek, Brian A., Mahzarin R. Banaji, and Anthony G. Greenwald. 2002. Harvesting Implicit Group Attitudes and Beliefs from a Demonstration Website. *Group Dynamics* 6: 101–115.
Nosek, Brian A., Jesse Graham, and Carlee Beth Hawkins. 2010. Implicit Political Cognition. In B. Gawronski and B. K. Payne, eds., *Handbook of Implicit Social Cognition*, pp. 548–564. New York: Guilford Press.
Nosek, Brian A., Anthony G. Greenwald, and Mahzarin R. Banaji. 2005. Understanding and Using the Implicit Association Test: II. Method Variables and Construct Validity. *Personality and Social Psychology Bulletin* 31(2): 166–180.
Nosek, Brian A., Anthony G. Greenwald, and Mahzarin R. Banaji. 2007a. The Implicit Association Test at the Age of 7: A Methodological and Conceptual Review. In J. A. Bargh, ed., *Automatic Processes in Social Thinking and Behavior*, pp. 265–292. New York: Psychology Press.
Nosek, Brian A., Frederick L. Smyth, Jeffrey Hansen, Thierry Devos, Nicole M. Lindner, Kate A. Ranganath, Colin Tucker, Kristina Olson, Dolly Chugh, Anthony G. Greenwald, and Mahzarin R. Banaji. 2007b. Pervasiveness and Correlates of Implicit Attitudes and Stereotypes. *European Review of Social Psychology* 18: 1–53.
Nunnally, Shayla C. 2010. Learning Race, Socializing Blackness: A Cross-Generational Analysis of Black Americans' Racial Socialization Experiences. *DuBois Review* 7(1): 185–217.
Olson, Michael A., and Russell H. Fazio. 2001. Implicit Attitude Formation through Classical Conditioning. *Psychological Science* 12: 413–417.
Olson, Michael A., and Russell H. Fazio. 2002. Implicit Acquisition and Manifestation of Classically Conditioned Attitudes. *Social Cognition* 20: 89–103.
Olson, Michael A., and Russell H. Fazio. 2003. Relations between Implicit Measures of Prejudice: What Are We Measuring? *Psychological Science* 14(6): 636–639.
Olson, Michael A., and Russell H. Fazio. 2004. Reducing the Influence of Extra-Personal Associations on the Implicit Association Test: Personalizing the IAT. *Journal of Personality and Social Psychology* 86: 653–667.
Olson, Michael A., and Russell H. Fazio. 2006. Reducing Automatically-Activated Racial Prejudice through Implicit Evaluative Conditioning. *Personality and Social Psychology Bulletin* 32: 421–433.
Olson, Michael. A., and Russell. H. Fazio, 2009. Implicit and Explicit Measures of Attitudes: The Perspective of the MODE Model. In Richard E. Petty, Russell H. Fazio, and

Pablo Briñol, eds., *Attitudes: Insights From the New Implicit Measures*, pp. 19–64. New York: Psychology Press.
Osgood, Charles E. 1962. Studies on the Generality of Affective Meaning Systems. *American Psychologist* 17(1): 10–28.
Ottati, Victor C. 1990. Determinant of Political Judgments: The Joint Influence of Normative and Heuristic Rules of Inference. *Political Behavior* 12: 159–179.
Ottaway, Scott A., Davis C. Hayden, and Mark A. Oakes. 2001. Implicit Attitudes and Racism: Effects of Word Familiarity and Frequency on the Implicit Association Test. *Social Cognition* 19(2): 97–144.
Pasek, Josh, Alexander Tahk, Yphatch Lelkes, Jon A. Krosnick, B. Keith Payne, Omair Akhtar, and Trevor Tompson. 2009. Determinants of Turnout and Candidate Choice in the 2008 U.S. Presidential Election: Illuminating the Impact of Racial Prejudice and Other Considerations. *Public Opinion Quarterly* 73(5): 943–994.
Passel, Jeffrey S., and D'Vera Cohn. 2008. Trends in Unauthorized Immigration: Undocumented Inflow Now Trails Legal Inflow. Pew Hispanic Center.
Passel, Jeffrey S., and D'Vera Cohn. 2012. U.S. Foreign-Born Population: How Much Change from 2009 to 2010? Pew Hispanic Center.
Passel, Jeffrey S., and Roberto Suro. 2005. Rise, Peak, and Decline: Trends in U.S. Immigration 1992–2004. Pew Hispanic Center.
Passel, Jeffrey, D'Vera Cohn, and Ana Gonzalez-Barrera. 2012. Net Migration from Mexico Falls to Zero – and Perhaps Less. Pew Hispanic Center.
Patterson, Thomas E. 1996. Bad News, Period. *PS: Political Science and Politics* 29(1): 17–20.
Payne, John W. 1982. Contingent Decision Behavior. *Psychology Bulletin* 92: 382–402.
Payne, B. Keith. 2006. Weapon Bias: Split-Second Decisions and Unintended Stereotyping. *Current Directions in Psychological Science* 15(6): 287–291.
Payne, B. Keith, Alan J. Lambert, and Larry L. Jacoby. 2002. Best Laid Plans: Effects of Goals on Accessibility Bias and Cognitive Control in Race-Based Misperceptions of Weapons. *Journal of Experimental Social Psychology* 38: 384–396.
Payne, B. Keith, Clara Michelle Cheng, Olseya Govorun, and Brandon D. Stewart. 2005. An Inkblot for Attitudes: Affect Misattribution as Implicit Measurement. *Journal of Personality and Social Psychology* 89(3): 277–293.
Payne, Keith B., Jon A. Krosnick, Josh Pasek, Yphtach Lelkes, Omair Akhtar, and Trevor Tompson. 2010. Implicit and Explicit Prejudice in the 2008 American Presidential Election. *Journal of Experimental Social Psychology* 46: 367–374.
Peña, Yesilernis, and James Sidanius. 2002. U.S. Patriotism and Ideologies of Group Dominance: A Tale of Asymmetry. *Journal of Social Psychology* 142(6): 782–790.
Pérez, Efrén O. 2010. Explicit Evidence on the Import of Implicit Attitudes: The IAT and Immigration Policy Judgments. *Political Behavior* 32(4): 517–545.
Pérez, Efrén O. 2013. Implicit Attitudes: Meaning, Measurement, and Synergy with Political Science. *Politics, Groups, and Identities* 1(2): 275–297.
Pérez, Efrén O., and Marc J. Hetherington. 2014. Authoritarianism in Black and White: Testing the Cross-Racial Validity of the Child Rearing Scale. *Political Analysis* 22(3): 398–412.
Petty, Richard E., Russell H. Fazio, and Pablo Briñol. 2009. *Attitudes: Insights from the New Implicit Measures*. New York: Psychology Press.

Pew Research Center. 2012. Pew Research Center for the People & the Press/Pew Forum on Religion & Public Life Religion & Politics Survey, June 2012.

Pew Research Center. 2013. Pew Research Center for the People & the Press Political Survey, June 2013.

Phelps, Elizabeth A., Kevin J. O'Connor, William A. Cunningham, Sumie Funayama, J. Christopher Gatenby, and John C. Gore, and Mahzarin R. Banaji. 2000. Performance on Indirect Measures of Race Evaluation Predicts Amygdala Activation. *Journal of Cognitive Neuroscience* 12(5): 729–238.

Philpot, Tasha S. 2007. *Race, Republicans, and the Return of the Party of Lincoln*. Ann Arbor: University of Michigan Press.

Philpot, Tasha S., and Ismail K. White. 2010. Introduction: Defining African American Political Psychology. In T. S. Philpot and I. K. White, eds., *African-American Political Psychology: Identity, Opinion, and Action in the Post-Civil Rights Era*, pp. 1–8. New York: Palgrave Macmillan.

Philpot, Tasha S., Ismail K. White, Kristin Wylie, and Ernest B. McGowen. 2010. Feeling Different: Racial Group-Based Emotional Response to Political Events. In T. S. Philpot and I. K. White, eds., *African-American Political Psychology: Identity, Opinion, and Action in the Post-Civil Rights Era*, pp. 55–70. New York: Palgrave Macmillan.

Pinter, Brad, and Anthony G. Greenwald. 2005. Clarifying the Role of the "Other" Category in the Self-Esteem IAT. *Experimental Psychology* 52(1): 74–79.

Polsby, Nelson W. 1960. How to Study Community Power: The Pluralist Alternative. *Journal of Politics* 22(3): 474–484.

Popkin, Samuel L. 1991. *The Reasoning Voter: Communication and Persuasion in Presidential Campaigns*. Chicago: University of Chicago Press.

Posner, Michael I., and C. R. R. Snyder. 1975. Attention and Cognitive Control. In R. L. Solso, ed., *Information Processing and Cognition: The Loyola Symposium*, pp. 55–85. Hillsdale, NJ: Lawrence Erlbaum.

Prior, Markus. 2009. The Immensely Inflated News Audience: Assessing Bias in Self-Reported News Exposure. *Public Opinion Quartelry* 73(1): 130–143.

Ranganath, Kate A., Colin Tucker Smith, and Brian A. Nosek. 2008. Distinguishing Automatic and Controlled Components of Attitudes from Direct and Indirect Measurement Methods. *Journal of Experimental Social Psychology* 44(2): 386–396.

Richeson, Jennifer A., and Nalini Ambady. 2003. Effects of Situational Power on Automatic Racial Prejudice. *Journal of Experimental Social Psychology* 39: 177–183.

Richeson, Jennifer A., and Maureen A. Craig. 2011. Intra-Minority Intergroup Relation in the Twenty-First Century. *Daedalus* 140(2): 166–175.

Riker, William H. 1964. Some Ambiguities in the Notion of Power. *American Political Science Review* 58(2): 341–349.

Rivers, Douglas. 2008. Understanding People: Sample Matching. Palo Alto: YouGov/Polimetrix.

Rodríguez-Bailón, Rosa, Miguel Moya, and Vincent Yzerbyt. 2000. Why Do Superiors Attend to Negative Stereotypic Information about Their Subordinates? Effects of Power Legitimacy on Social Perception. *European Journal of Social Psychology* 30: 651–671.

Roediger, David R. 2005. *Working toward Whiteness: How America's Immigrants Became White. The Strange Journey from Ellis Island to the Suburbs*. New York: Basic Books.

Roskos-Ewoldsen, David R., and Russell H. Fazio. 1992. On the Orienting Value of Attitudes: Attitude Accessibility as a Determinant of an Object's Attraction of Visual Attention. *Journal of Personality and Social Psychology* 63(2): 198–211.

Rothermund, Klaus, and Dirk Wentura. 2004. Underlying Processes in the Implicit Association Test: Dissociating Salience from Associations. *Journal of Experimental Psychology* 133(2): 139–165.

Rudman, Laurie A. 2004. Social Justice in Our Minds, Homes, and Society: The Nature, Causes, and Consequences of Implicit Bias. *Social Justice Research* 17(2): 129–142.

Rudman, Laurie A., Anthony G. Greenwald, Deborah S. Mellott, and Jordan L. K. Schwartz. 1999. Measuring the Automatic Components of Prejudice: Flexibility and Generality of the Implicit Association Test. *Social Cognition* 17(4): 437–465.

Rydell, Robert J., and Allen R. McConnell. 2006. Understanding Implicit and Explicit Attitude Change: A Systems of Reasoning Analysis. *Journal of Personality and Social Psychology* 91(6): 995–1008.

Rydell, Robert J., and Allen R. McConnell. 2010. Consistency and Inconsistency in Implicit Social Cognition: The Case of Implicit and Explicit Measures of Attitudes. In B. Gawronski and B. K. Payne, eds., *Handbook of Implicit Social Cognition* New York: Guilford Press.

Saleem, Muniba, and Craig A. Anderson. 2013. Arabs as Terrorists: Effects of Stereotypes within Violent Contexts on Attitudes, Perceptions, and Affect. *Psychology of Violence* 3(1): 84–99.

Santa Ana, Otto. 2002. *Brown Tide Rising: Metaphors of Latinos in Contemporary American Public Discourse*. Austin: University of Texas Press.

Santa Ana, Otto. 2013. *Juan in a Hundred: The Representation of Latinos on Network News*. Austin: University of Texas Press.

Sarnoff, Irving. 1960. Psychoanalytic Theory and Social Attitudes. *Public Opinion Quarterly* 24: 251–279.

Saxton, Alexander. 1972. *The Indispensable Enemy: Labor and the Anti-Chinese Movement in California*. Berkeley: University of California Press.

Schildkraut, Deborah J. 2013. Amnesty, Guest Workers, Fences! Oh My! Public Opinion About "Comprehensive Immigration Reform." In G. Freeman, R. Hansen, and D. Leal, eds., *Immigration and Public Opinion in Liberal Democracies*, pp. 207–231. New York: Routledge.

Schmukle, Stefan C., and Boris Egloff. 2004. Does the Implicit Association Test for Assessing Anxiety Measure Trait and State Variance? *European Journal of Personality* 18: 483–494.

Schuman, Howard, Charlotte Steeh, Lawrence Bobo, and Maria Krysan. 1997. *Racial Attitudes in America: Trends and Interpretations*. Cambridge, MA: Harvard University Press.

Schwarz, Norbert. 2007. Attitude Construction: Evaluation in Context. *Social Cognition* 25(5): 638–656.

Sears, David O. 1986. College Sophomores in the Laboratory: Influences of a Narrow Data Base on Social Psychology's View of Human Nature. *Journal of Personality and Social Psychology* 51(3): 515–530.

Sears, David O. 1988. Symbolic Racism. In P. Katz and D. A. Taylor, eds., *Eliminating Racism: Profiles in Controversy*, pp. 53–84. New York: Plenum.

Sears, David O. 2004. A Perspective on Implicit Prejudice from Survey Research. *Psychological Inquiry* 15: 293–297.

Sears, David O., Colette Van Laar, Mary Carrillo, and Rick Kosterman. 1997. Is It Really Racism? The Origins of White Americans' Opposition to Race-Targeted Policies. *Public Opinion Quarterly* 61: 16–53.

Sears, David O., Shana Levin, Joshua L. Rabinowitz, and Christopher Federico. 1999. Cultural Diversity and Multicultural Politics: Is Ethnic Balkanization Psychologically Inevitable? In D. A. Prentice, and D. T. Millers, eds., *Cultural Divides: Understanding and Overcoming Group Conflict*, pp. 35–79. New York: Russell Sage Foundation.

Shadish, William R., Thomas D. Cook, and Donald T. Campbell. 2002. *Experimental and Quasi-Experimental Designs for Generalized Causal Inference*. Boston: Houghton Mifflin Company.

Shankman, Arnold. 1982. *Ambivalent Friends: Afro-Americans View the Immigrant*. Westport, CT: Greenwood Press.

Shiffrin, Richard M., and Walter Schneider. 1977. Controlled and Automatic Human Information Processing: II. Perceptual Learning, Automatic Attending, and a General Theory. *Psychological Review* 84(2): 127–190.

Sidanius, Jim, and Felicia Pratto. 2001. *Social Dominance: An Intergroup Theory of Social Hierarchy and Oppression*. New York: Cambridge University Press.

Sidanius, Jim, and John R. Petrocik. 2001. Communal and National Identity in a Multiethnic State: A Comparison of Three Perspectives. In Richard D. Ashmore, Lee Jussim, and David Wilder, eds., *Social Identity, Intergroup Conflict, and Conflict Reduction*, pp. 101–132. Oxford: Oxford University Press.

Sidanius, Jim, Seymour Feshbach, Shana Levin, and Felicia Pratto. 1997. The Interface between Ethnic and National Attachment: Ethnic Pluralism or Ethnic Dominance? *Public Opinion Quarterly* 61(1): 102–133.

Sidanius, Jim, Pam Singh, John J. Hetts, and Chris Federico. 2000. Its Not Affirmative Action, It's the Blacks: The Continuing Relevance of Race in American Politics. In D. O. Sears, J. Sidanius, and B. Bobo, eds., *Racialized Politics: The Debate About Racism in America*, pp. 191–235. Chicago: University of Chicago Press.

Sides, John, and Jack Citrin. 2007. European Opinion about Immigration: The Role of Identities, Interests, and Information. *British Journal of Political Science* 37: 477–504.

Sides, John, and Kimberly Gross. 2013. Stereotypes of Muslims and Support for the War on Terror. *Journal of Politics* 75(3): 583–598.

Silver, Brian D., Barbara A. Anderson, and Paul R. Abramson. 1986. Who Overreports Voting? *American Political Science Review* 80(2): 613–624.

Simon, Herbert A. 1985. Human Nature in Politics: The Dialogue of Psychology with Political Science. *American Political Science Review* 79–293–304.

Simon, Rita J., and Susan H. Alexander. 1993. *The Ambivalent Welcome: Print Media, Public Opinion and Immigration*. Westport, CT: Praeger.

Sinclair, Stacey, Jim Sidanius, and Shana Levin. 1998. The Interface between Ethnic and Social System Attachment: The Differential Effects of Hierarchy-Enhancing and Hierarchy-Attenuating Environments. *Journal of Social Issues* 54(4): 741–757.

Sloman, Steven A. 1996. The Empirical Case for Two Systems of Reasoning. *Psychological Bulletin* 119(1): 3–22.

Smith, Rogers. 1997. *Civic Ideals: Conflicting Visions of Citizenship in U.S. History*. New Haven, CT: Yale University Press.

Smith, Eliot R., and Jamie DeCoster. 2000. Dual-Process Models in Social and Cognitive Psychology: Conceptual Integration and Links to Underlying Memory Systems. *Personality and Social Psychology Review* 4(2): 108–131.

Smith, Colin Tucker, and Brian A. Nosek. 2011. Affective Focus Increases the Concordance between Implicit and Explicit Attitudes. *Social Psychology* 42(4): 300–313.

Smith, Kevin B., Douglas Oxley, Matthew V. Hibbing, John R. Alford, and John R. Hibbing. 2011. Disgust Sensitivity and the Neurophysiology of Left-Right Political Orientations. *PLoS ONE* 6(10): 1–9.

Sniderman, Paul M., and Edward G. Carmines. 1997. *Reaching Beyond Race*. Cambridge, MA: Harvard University Press.

Sniderman, Paul M., and Louk Hagendoorn. 2007. *When Ways of Life Collide: Multiculturalism and Its Discontents in the Netherlands*. Princeton, NJ: Princeton University Press.

Sniderman, Paul M., and Thomas Piazza. 1993. *The Scar of Race*. Cambridge, MA: Harvard University Press.

Sniderman, Paul M., and Phillip E. Tetlock. 1986. Symbolic Racism: Problems of Motive Attribution in Political Analysis. *Journal of Social Issues* 42: 129–150.

Sniderman, Paul M., Louk Hagendoorn, and Markus Prior. 2004. Predisposing Factors and Situational Triggers: Exclusionary Reactions to Immigrant Minorities. *American Political Science Review* 98(1): 35–49.

Sniderman, Paul M., Richard A. Brody, and Phillip E. Tetlock. 1991. *Reasoning and Choice: Explorations in Political Psychology*. New York: Cambridge University Press.

Sniderman, Paul M., Pierangelo Peri, Rui J. De Figueiredo, Jr., and Thomas Piazza. 2000. *The Outsider: Prejudice and Politics in Italy*. Princeton, NJ: Princeton University Press.

Spence Alexa, and Ellen Townsend. 2008. Spontaneous Evaluations: Similarities and Differences Between the Affect Heuristic and Implicit Attitudes. *Cognition and Emotion* 22(1): 83–93.

Sritharan, Rajees, and Bertram Gawronski. 2010. Changing Implicit and Explicit Prejudice: Insights From the Associative-Propositional Evaluation Model. *Social Psychology* 41(3): 113–123.

Srull, Thomas K., and Robert S. Wyer. 1979. The Role of Category Accessibility in the Interpretation of Information About Persons: Some Determinants and Implications. *Journal of Personality and Social Psychology* 37: 1660–1672.

Staerklé, Christian, Jim Sidanius, Eva G. T. Green, and Ludwin E. Molina. 2010. Ethnic Minority-Majority Asymmetry in National Attitudes around the World: A Multilevel Analysis. *Political Psychology* 31(4): 491–519.

Steffens, Melanie C. 2004. Is the Implicit Association Test Immune to Faking? *Experimental Psychology* 51(3): 165–179.

Stenner, Karen. 2005. *The Authoritarian Dynamic*. Cambridge: Cambridge University Press.

Stevens, Jacqueline. 2009. Deporting American Citizens: ICE's Mexican-izing of Mark Lyttle. *Huffington Post*.

Stimson, James A. 1975. Belief Systems: Constraint, Complexity, and the 1972 Election. *American Journal of Political Science* 19: 393–417.

Stimson, James A. 1999. *Public Opinion in America: Moods, Cycles, and Swings*. Boulder, CO: Westview Press.

Stimson, James A. 2004. *Tides of Consent: How Public Opinion Shapes American Politics*. Cambridge: Cambridge University Press.

Stimson, James A., Michael B. MacKuen, and Robert S. Erikson. 1995. Dynamic Representation. *American Political Science Review* 89: 543–565.

Stoker, Laura. 1993. Judging Presidential Character: The Demise of Gary Hart. *Political Behavior* 15(2): 193–223.

Strack, Fritz, and Roland Deutsch. 2004. Reflective and Impulsive Determinant of Social Behavior. *Personality and Social Psychology Review* 8(3): 220–247.

Taber, Charles S. 2003. Information Processing and Public Opinion. In D. O. Sears, L. Huddy, and R. Jervis, eds., *Oxford Handbook of Political Psychology*, pp. 443–476. Oxford: Oxford University Press.

Taber, Charles, and Milton Lodge. 2006. Motivated Skepticism in Political Information Processing. *American Journal of Political Science* 50(3): 755–769.

Taber, Charles. and Everett Young. 2013. Political Information Processing. In L. Huddy, D. O. Sears, and J. S. Levy, eds., *Oxford Handbook of Political Psychology*, pp. 525–558. New York: Oxford University Press.

Tajfel, Henri, and John C. Turner. 1979. An Integrative Theory of Intergroup Conflict. In W. G. Austin and S. Worchel, eds., *The Social Psychology of Intergroup Relations*. Monterey: Brooks/Cole.

Takaki, Ronald. 1989. *Strangers from a Different Shore: A History of Asian Americans*. New York: Little, Brown and Company.

Tarman, Christopher, and David O. Sears. 2005. The Conceptualization and Measurement of Symbolic Racism. *The Journal of Politics* 67: 731–761.

Teige, Sarah, Konrad Schnabel, Rainer Banse, and Jens B. Asendorpf. 2004. Assessment of Multiple Implicit Self-Concept Dimensions Using the Extrinsic Affective Simon Task (EAST). *European Journal of Personality* 18: 495–520.

Tetlock, Phillip E. 1994. Political Psychology or Politicized Psychology: Is the Road to Scientific Hell Paved with Good Moral Intentions? *Political Psychology* 15: 509–530.

Tichenor, Daniel J. 2002. *Dividing Lines: The Politics of Immigration Control in America*. Princeton, NJ: Princeton University Press.

Tourangeau, Roger, Lance J. Rips, and Kenneth A. Rasinski. 2000. *The Psychology of Survey Response*. Cambridge: Cambridge University Press.

Transue, John E., Daniel J. Lee, and John H. Aldrich. 2007. Treatment Spillover Effects across Survey Experiments. *Political Analysis* 17(2): 143–161.

Valentino, Nicholas A., Ted Brader, and Ashley E. Jardina. 2013. Immigration Opposition among U.S. Whites: General Ethnocentrism or Media Priming of Attitudes About Latinos? *Political Psychology* 34(2): 149–166.

Valentino, Nicholas A., Vincent L. Hutchings, and Ismail K. White. 2002. Cues that Matter: How Political Ads Prime Racial Attitudes During Campaigns. *American Political Science Review* 96(1): 75–90.

Verba, Sidney, Kay Lehman Schlozman, and Henry E. Brady. 1995. *Voice and Inequality: Civic Voluntarism in American Politics*. Cambridge, MA: Harvard University Press.

Welch, Kelly. 2007. Black Criminal Stereotypes and Racial Profiling. *Journal of Contemporary Criminal Justice* 23(3): 276–288.

White, Ismail K. 2007. When Race Matters and When It Doesn't: Racial Group Differences in Response to Racial Cues. *American Political Science Review* 101(2): 339–354.

Wiers, Reinout W., Nieske van Woerden, Fren T. Y. Smulders, and Peter J. de Jong. 2002. Implicit and Explicit Alcohol-Related Cognitions in Heavy and Light Drinkers. *Journal of Abnormal Psychology* 111(4): 648–658.

Wilson, Timothy D., Samuel Lindsey, and Tonya Y. Schooler. 2000. A Model of Dual Attitudes. *Psychological Review* 107(1): 101–126.

Winter, Nicholas J. G. 2008. *Dangerous Frames: How Ideas about Race and Gender Shape Public Opinion*. Chicago: University of Chicago Press.

Winter, Nicholas, and Adam Berinsky. 1999. What's Your Temperature? Thermometer Ratings and Political Analysis. Paper Presented at the Annual Meeting of the American Political Science Association.

Wittenbrink, Bernd, and Norbert Schwarz. 2007. *Implicit Measures of Attitudes*. New York: Guilford Press.

Wittenbrink, Bernd, Charles M. Judd, and Bernadette Park. 2001. Spontaneous Prejudice in Context: Variability in Automatically Activated Attitudes. *Journal of Personality and Social Psychology* 81(5): 815–827.

Wlezien, Christopher. 1995. The Public as Thermostat: Dynamics of Preferences for Spending. *American Journal of Political Science* 39: 981–1000.

Wolfinger, Raymond E., and Steven J. Rosenstone. 1980. *Who Votes?* New Haven, CT: Yale University Press.

Wright, Matthew, Morris E. Levy, and Jack Citrin. 2014. Conflict and Consensus on American Public Opinion on Illegal Immigration. Working Paper. American University – School of Public Affairs.

Zajonc, Robert B. 1980. Feeling and Thinking: Preferences Need No Inferences. *American Psychologist* 35(2): 151–175.

Zajonc, Robert B. 1984. On the Primacy of Affect. *American Psychologist* 39(2): 117–123.

Zaller, John R. 1992. *The Nature and Origins of Mass Opinion*. New York: Cambridge University Press.

Zaller, John, and Stanley Feldman. 1992. A Simple Theory of the Survey Response: Answering Questions Versus Revealing Preferences. *American Journal of Political Science* 36(3): 579–616.

Index

affect contagion, 12, 34, 49, 50, 80, 107, 112, 113, 127. *See also John Q. Public*
affect transfer, 12, 34, 49, 79, 103, 105, 107. *See also John Q. Public*
affective gut reactions, 29–30. *See also* implicit attitudes
affective responses, 35, 36
African American, 5, 16, 37, 49, 133, 148, 171
  attitudes towards Latinos, 154–155
  explicit attitudes towards foreigners, 155–156
  explicit attitudes towards Latino immigrants, 156–157
  Implicit Association Test (IAT), 158, 159–162, 165, 171
  impact of implicit attitudes towards Latinos, 111, 150, 183
  implicit attitudes relative to whites, 150
  likelihood of manifestation of attitudes towards Latinos, 155–158, 162–165
  strength of implicit attitude towards Latinos, 22, 154–158, 159–162, 165, 166, 171
Althaus, Scott, 75
APE. *See* Associative Propositional-Evaluation model
Ambady, Nalini, 152
American identity (vs implicit attitudes towards Latino immigrants), 95, 96, 105, 106
Anderson, Craig A., 173
Arabs, 173
Asian, 16, 74. *See also* immigration, racial hierarchy
Associative Propositional-Evaluation (APE) model, 29–31, 33, 34, 50
associative reasoning, 30, 54, 59, 77, 170
authoritarian values, 95, 96, 105, 106

Bachrach, Peter, 151
Baratz, Morton S., 151
Bargh, John, 6, 27
Bodenhausen, Galen V., 29, 30
Boehner, John, 182
Border Protection, Anti-Terrorism, and Illegal Immigration Control Act (H. R. 4437), 181
Bracero Program, 60–61
Brader, Ted, 64, 184
Brown Tide Rising, 63

Chavez, Leo, 63
Chernobyl nuclear accident, 45
Chinese Exclusion Act (1882), 8
  Legal Immigration Experiment, 121–127
Chinese immigrants, 8, 87
  as group in Legal Immigration Experiment, 121–127, 143
  See also Asian
Citrin, Jack, 105
Cohn, D'Vera, 72
  The Comprehensive Immigration Reform Act (CIRA) (S.2611), 181
conceptual triggers, 46
Congress, U.S., 8–9, 66, 172, 181
consciously unappreciated events, 47
consciously unnoticed events, 47

Converse, Phillip, 52, 176
critics of, 176
Covering Immigration, 63
cultural learning, 37

DACA Deferred Action for Childhood Arrivals, 181–182
Dahl, Robert, 151
Dawson, Michael, 149
DeCoster, Jamie, 27
Deferred Action for Childhood Arrivals (DACA), 181–182
deliberation (political), 129, 135
democracy, 179–180
'Deportation Experiment', 113–120
explicit reactions, 115–116
implicit reactions, 116–120
Devine, Patricia, 131
dominant groups, 16
dueling effects hypothesis, 51, 130, 132, 136, 145
Dunton, Bridget C., 49
dyad ratios algorithm, 67

education levels, 131–134, 145, 171
explicit attitudes and immigration policy, 142, 143
implicit attitudes and immigration policy, 22, 138–141, 143–145
self-reporting, 100–101
elderly, 6
Entman, Robert, 54
ethnocentrism, 121
European immigrants, 9
explicit attitudes, 35
education, 135, 139–140, 142, 143
implicit attitudes, 107, 135, 177. *See also* explicit-implicit reasoning, explicit and implicit attitude reports
Latinos, 91–92
explicit cognition, 7, 26–27
physical effect of, 26
explicit immigration cues, 122–123
explicit-implicit reasoning, 29–32
explicit and implicit attitude reports
explicit and implicit attitude reports convergence/divergence, 39, 50
as differences in measurement, 39
as differences in substance, 39–40
See also self-reports

Fazio, Russell H., 28, 31, 39, 46, 49, 134, 153
feeling thermometer ratings, 91, 96
criticism and defense, 97
Fiske, Susan T., 152
framing, 45–46, 55, 65, 170
Federico, Christopher, 133

Gaillot, Mathew T., 26
Gawronski, Bertram, 29, 30, 48, 54–55, 79, 184
Gentlemen's Agreement (1907 regarding Japanese immigration), 8
German attitudes towards Turks, 49
Goodwin, Stephanie A., 152
Greenwald, Anthony G., 87
Gross, Tamar, 121
group centrism, 173
immigration, 172–173
group identities, 178–179

Hart-Celler Act (1965), 58–59
Hartman, Todd K., 11
heuristics, 179
Hernández, Juan (hypothetical Latino immigrant), 114–115, 117, 118–120
Hofmann, Wilhelm, 36
homo politicus, 3
hot cognition, 12, 33, 47, 112

'idealized democratic citizen'
implicit attitudes, 179–180
'illegal' as label and negative coverage, 56, 64–66
illegal immigration, 59, 113–120
empirical data on Latinos, 72–75
implicit attitudes towards Latinos and views on, 103, 171
media coverage, 55–56, 61–76, 170
immigration, 4, 8–9, 15, 49
African, 64
Asian, 8, 57, 62, 64, 74, 87, 121–127
cultural transaction costs, 11–12
dismantling U.S. quotas, 58–59
European, 56–58, 59, 62, 74, 87
illegal, 59, 113–120
Latino, 8–9, 19–20, 57–58, 59–61, 72–75
Mexican, 59–61
Muslim, 64
immigration legislation
H.R. 4437 (The Border Protection, Anti-Terrorism, and Illegal Immigration Control Act), 181

Proposition, 63, 127
S.2611 (The Comprehensive Immigration: Reform Act (CIRA)), 172, 181
S. B. 1070 (Support Our Law Enforcement and: Safe Neighborhoods Act), 181
immigration policy
and implicit attitudes, 8–11, 21, 47, 49, 103, 111, 140–141, 150, 172–173, 180–183, 184
Immigration and Customs Enforcement (ICE), 1–2
Implicit Association Test (IAT), 14, 38–39, 77–110, 119, 170, 177
African-American attitudes to Latinos, 158, 159–162, 165, 171
assumptions and method, 80–83
calculating individual scores, 83
description, 77–78
faking, 84
flower–insect hypothetical, 80–83
Latino immigrant=bad, results of experiment, 89–91
relevance to real world phenomenon, 78
reliability, 84–85
vs. self-reporting, 78–79, 83
validity, 36–39, 41, 78, 83–86, 100–101, 103
See also lab study 1, lab study 2, National Survey
implicit attitudes, 4, 5, 14–15, 25, 29–31, 169–170
African-Americans, 22, 154–158, 159–162, 165, 166, 171
as attitudes, 36–39, 41
automated, 153
caveats, 85–86, 174–176
character of public opinion, 176–179
changebility, 183–184
classic conditioning hypothesis as basis for implicit attitudes, 54–55, 75
criticisms, 38, 42
degree to which they are subconscious, 40–41
deportation, 113–120
education, 22, 131–134, 138–141, 143–145, 171
emotional roots, 35
environmental cues, 31
evaluating importance of, 177–179
explicit attitudes, 107, 135, 177. *See also* explicit-implicit reasoning, explicit and implicit attitude reports
explicit cues, 35, 118–120
explicit political choices, 80, 94–96, 101–102
formation of and public debate, 44–46
illegal immigration, 103, 172–173
immigration policy, 8–11, 21, 47, 49, 103, 111, 150, 172–173, 180–183, 184
individual differences, 52
individuals in democratic society, 179
legal immigration, 106–108, 120–126, 128, 134, 140–141, 172–173, 182–183
media, 15, 55–56, 61–69, 76, 170
as moderators, 177–178
political influence of, 47–51, 134
race, 153–155
relevancy across populations, 178–179
self-reporting, 78–79, 91–96
social foundations, 148, 171
testing predictive validity of, 102–108
towards Latinos, 89–93, 99, 121, 123–128, 134, 158, 170, 172, 182–183
See also Deportation Experiment, IAT, Legal Immigration Experiment
unawareness of, 40–41, 136, 138
valance of information surrounding an object, 54
versus self-reports, 39, 78–79, 91–96
implicit cognition, 2, 5, 7–8, 27–28
effort, 28
implicit expectations, 48, 112, 170, 171
subconscious nature of, 111–113, 134–135
as theoretical explanation, 44
intolerance, 94
Irish immigration, 114–115

Jardina, Ashley E., 64
John Q. Public (JQP), 11–12, 13, 15, 50, 52
affect, 12. *See also affect contagion* and *affect transfer*
Johnson administration, 58

Kam, Cindy D., 103
Kinder, Donald, 103, 177

lab study 1, 87, 90, 188
lab study 2, 89, 96–98, 188
Lane, Kristin A., 85
Latinos, 181
attitudes towards, 89–93, 99, 154–155, 170, 172
vs. Latino immigrants, 98–100

Latinos (*cont.*)
racial hierarchy, 16
racial profiling, 181
See also implicit attitudes, towards Latinos; Latino immigrants; Latino immigration; legal immigrants, Latino
Latino immigrants, 8–9, 44
vs. Asian immigrants, 121–127, 143
as a concept in long term memory, 47, 48
empirical data, 72–75
explicit attitudes towards, 49, 51, 96: amongst educated, 135–136
hypothetical vs. Irish immigrant, 113–120
implicit attitudes about, 56, 89–93, 99, 170
vs. Latino citizens, 98–100
immigration policy, 21, 49, 103, 150, 172–173, 181, 182–183. *See also* African Americans
news reports, 15, 19–20, 55–56, 61–76, 170
percentage of immigrants, 62
shift to legal immigration, 59–61
triggering of implicit attitudes towards, 49
See also IAT; Legal Immigrant Experiment; media
Latino immigration, 57–58, 72–75
news coverage, 19–20, 61–76
portrayal vs. numbers, 72–75
See also Latino immigrants
law, concern over, 114
legal immigrants, Latino
empirical data, 72–75
implicit attitudes, 106–108, 120–126, 141–145, 171
vs. Latino citizens, 98–100
Mexican, experiment, 121–127
news coverage, 64–66
'Legal Immigration Experiment', 120–126, 127, 131–132, 138–139, 145, 150, 162–165
legal immigration
implicit attitudes, 106–108, 120–126, 128, 134, 172–173, 182–183
opposition to across education levels, 142, 143
Lodge, Milton, 11, 13–14, 33, 46–47, 50, 52, 184
long-term memory (LTM), 12, 47–48, 49, 52
Los Angeles Times, 63, 65–66, 67–68
Lucas, William (hypothetical congressional candidate), 46
Lyttle, Mark D. (José Thomas), 1–2
Maison, Dominika, 85
Marcus, George, 35, 184
McCaul, Michael, 172
McConnell, Alan R., 26, 28, 46
media, 15, 19–20, 55–56, 61–76, 170
Mendelberg, Tali, 184
Mexican immigration to US, 59–61
Moore, David (hypothetical immigrant), 114–116, 117, 118–120
Morriss, Peter, 151
motivated skepticism, 133
Motivation and Opportunity as Determinants (MODE) model, 31–33, 50
political implications, 32
Murrieta, California, 9

National Origins Act (1924), 10
National Study (YouGov/Polimetrix), 89, 90–92, 96, 102, 112, 113, 116, 120, 155, 171, 187–188
neuroscience, 36
Neuse Correctional Institution, 1
Newman, Benjamin J., 11
Nosek, Brian A., 39, 85

Obama, Barrack H., 181–182
Olson, Michael A., 28
opportunity (clarity of political information), 135, 141–145
opposition to legal immigration
education levels, 139–141

partisanship (as variable in attitude towards immigration policy), 94–104, 105, 106
Passel, Jeffrey S., 62, 72
Payne, B. Keith, 184
Pérez, Efrén O., 38
Pinter, Brad, 87
police (automatic cognition), 5
political communication, 180
political decision making and explicit-implicit attitudes, 33
political discourse, 14, 19, 44
political ideology (in America), 176–177
political science
integration of implicit attitudes into area of study, 159–162, 184–185
notion of implicit attitudes, 17–18
power (social hierarchy), 149
criticism of concept, 150–151
-ful individuals, 151–152
individual attitudes, 150–152

prejudice, motivation to control, 32
priming condition, 45, 55, 76, 170
Proposition, 63, 127
propositional reasoning. *See* explicit reasoning
public debate
  formation of implicit attitudes, 44–46
public opinion, 3, 182
  importance of implicit attitude to study of, 174, 176–179
  studies on immigration, 101–102

race, 15–17, 148, 171, 172–173
  effect on implicit attitudes, 153–155
  manifestation of implicit attitudes, 155–158
racial attitudes, 115, 129–130, 133, 148–150
  educated, 136, 145
  experiment measuring response to changes in facial expression, 111
  (as variable), 106
racial hierarchy and strength of implicit attitudes, 15–17, 22–23, 41, 51, 149, 150, 154–155, 162, 165–166
racial minorities
  self-reporting on, 4
  status as impact on political attitudes. *See* racial hierarchy
  theory about explicit attitudes towards other minorities, 157
  See also African-Americans; Arabs; Asians; Latinos
racism, symbolic, 17–18
Ranganath, Kate A., 40
The Rationalizing Voter, 11
Richeson, Jennifer A., 152
Riker, William H., 151
Rydell, Robert J., 26, 28, 46

Saleem, Muniba, 173
Santa Ana, Otto, 63
scrambled sentence test, 6
self-reports, 4, 37–38, 39
  African American attitudes towards Latinos, 157
  education levels, 100–101
  group identities, 178–179
  IAT, 108
  implicit attitudes, 78–79, 91–96
  opposition to immigration, 138
Sidanius, Jim, 16
Sides, John, 105, 121
Sloman, Steven A., 26
Smith, Colin Tucker, 27
social psychology, 5, 151, 184
  political science, 17
social position, 15, 149–150, 154. *See also* racial hierarchy
socio-economic concerns, 95, 96, 105, 106
Stimson, James A., 67
Support Our Law Enforcement and Safe Neighborhoods Act (S. B. 1070), 181
Suro, Roberto, 62
symbolic racism, 17–18

Taber, Charles, 11, 33, 36–39, 41, 46–47, 50, 52, 184
television, 69–72
Thomas, José. *See* Lyttle, John D.
Turks, study of German attitudes towards, 49

U.S. Congress, 8, 66, 172, 181, 182

Valentino, Nicholas A., 64, 121–127

whites, 16, 22, 51, 152, 154, 159, 164, 178
  See also IAT; implicit attitudes; racial hierarchy
Wilson, Timothy D., 36
Wooley, Jason, 114
working memory (WM), 12, 27, 48, 49

Young, Everett, 36–39, 41

Zajonc, Robert B., 36

Books in the series

Asher Arian, *Security Threatened: Surveying Israeli Opinion on Peace and War*
James DeNardo, *The Amateur Strategist: Intuitive Deterrence Theories and the Politics of the Nuclear Arms Race*
Robert S. Erikson, Michael B. Mackeun, and James A. Stimson, *The Macro Polity*
James L. Gibson, *Overcoming Historical Injustices: Land Reconciliation in South Africa*
James L. Gibson and Amanda Gouws, *Overcoming Intolerance in South Africa: Experiments in Democratic Persuasion*
John R. Hibbing and Elizabeth Theiss-Morse, *Congress As Public Enemy: Public Attitudes Toward American Political Institutions*
John R. Hibbing and Elizabeth Theiss-Morse, *Stealth Democracy: Americans' Beliefs about How Government Should Work*
John R. Hibbing and Elizabeth Theiss-Morse, *What Is It about Government That Americans Dislike?*
Robert Huckfeldt and John Sprague, *Citizens, Politics, and Social Communication*
Robert Huckfeldt, Paul E. Johnson, and John Sprague, *Political Disagreement: The Survival of Diverse Opinions within Communication Networks*
James H. Kuklinski, *Thinking about Political Psychology*
James H. Kuklinski, *Citizens and Politics: Perspectives from Political Psychology*
Richard R. Lau and David P. Redlawsk, *How Voters Decide: Information Processing in Election Campaigns*
Milton Lodge and Charles S. Taber, *The Rationalizing Voter*
Arthur Lupia, Mathew McCubbins, and Samuel Popkin, *Elements of Reason: Cognition, Choice, and the Bounds of Rationality*
George E. Marcus, John L. Sullivan, Elizabeth Theiss-Morse, and Sandra L. Wood, *With Malice Toward Some: How People Make Civil Liberties Judgments*
Jeffery J. Mondak, *Personality and the Foundations of Political Behavior*
Diana C. Mutz, *Impersonal Influence: How Perceptions of Mass Collectives Affect Political Attitudes*
Hans Noel, *Political Ideologies and Political Parties in America*
Mark Peffley and Jon Hurwitz, *Justice in America: The Separate Realities of Blacks and Whites*
Markus Prior, *Post-Broadcast Democracy: How Media Choice Increases Inequality in Political Involvement and Polarizes Elections*
Paul M. Sniderman, Richard A. Brody, and Philip E. Tetlock, *Reasoning and Choice: Explorations in Political Psychology*
Karen Stenner, *The Authoritarian Dynamic*
Susan Welch, Timothy Bledsoe, Lee Sigelman, and Michael Combs, *Race and Place*
Cara J. Wong, *Boundaries of Obligation in American Politics: Geographic, National, and Racial Communities*
John Zaller, *The Nature and Origins of Mass Opinion*
Alan S. Zuckerman, Josip Dasovic, and Jennifer Fitzgerald, *Partisan Families: The Social Logic of Bounded Partisanship in Germany and Britain*

CPSIA information can be obtained
at www.ICGtesting.com
Printed in the USA
LVOW10s0224081117
555380LV00017B/210/P

9 781107 591219